▶FOCUS ON◀

Advanced English

C·A·E

SUE O'CONNELL

 LONGMAN

Acknowledgements

The author would like to thank the staff and students of the Abon Language School, Bristol for their cooperation at the piloting stage of this book. Special thanks are also due to David B Porter (Customer Relations Manager, Qantas Airways) and to Clare McDowell (Local Secretary Australia, UCLES) for their invaluable help with the recordings. She would also like to thank the following for their contributions to the book: Captain Les Hayward, Flight Service Director Bob Hills, both of Qantas Airways; Colin Anderson, Anthony Forrester, Charles Hatcher, Dr Jonathan King (Australian Rainforest Foundation), Brent Merrylees, Peter Montgomery, Roger Neal and Arthur Owens (NSW Fire Service) and Patricia Downey.

The author and publishers would especially like to thank Jennie Henderson for her comments at manuscript stage. Other valuable comments from Sue Inkster, Luke Prodromou, Mike Rogers and Giles Watson were most appreciated.

For my parents

The author and publishers are grateful to the following for permission to reproduce the copyright material on the pages indicated:

Extracts: Asia Magazine, Stress Test (28/29); Century Hutchinson, Embarrassing Situations from *Enquire Within Upon Modern Etiquette* by Moyra Bremner (172); Malcolm Brown, How boring can you really get? (169); Richard Burbidge Ltd. and the National Magazine Company, Work Bench, building a staircase (136); © The Daily Telegraph plc, Parents Who Copy Teenagers (79); Evening Standard Company Ltd, Today is Cancelled and extracts from In Brief (8), Where Snow Means Go (9); Express Newspapers plc, Pressure Points (34), The Big Day (203); Expression Magazine, the magazine for American Express Cardmembers, Conduct Becoming (174); Roy Flindall (Wings of Gold), Oh no! Not again (89); Health Education Authority, Look After Your Heart (115); ... And we also fight fires, (151), Crown Copyright, reproduced with permission of the Home Office; Philip Howard, Apostrophitis (65); The Innovations Report, The Amazing New Pocket Databank, (24); W. Jordan (Cereals) Ltd, Stamina (194); New Internationalist Publications Ltd, Trees - the Facts (128), Connect and Protect (135), Simply - nine ways to save the planet (138), Language - the Facts (55/56); © The Observer 1988, The Body Report (78), Candidate Column (165/166), etiquette extracts (170), Table Manners (181), Backs and Beyond (198), © The Observer 1986, Paradise Lost? (130); Orbis Publishing Ltd, The Day Chicago Died (141), EIU 1 (150); Private Eye, Wicker advertisement (69); Jack Seward (Wings of Gold), Gestures in Japan (191); William Rushton, Travelspeak (86); South China Morning Post, Killer Typhoon (13); The Sunday Times Magazine, FOL 1 (77); © The Sunday Times 1990, Mirror, Mirror on the Wall ... (186); Sydney Morning Herald, Packaging Gone Mad (6), Lucky Kids (116); © The Telegraph Sunday Magazine, The Air Traffic Controller (54), © The Telegraph Sunday Magazine 1987, Your True Colours (158-160); © Times Newspapers Ltd 1977, You are caught in a fire - then what? (143), © 1984, Broadcasting (167), © 1985, Secrets of the oldest man in the world (72, 74, 75), © 1986, What makes you blow your top? (33), Watch it, those mile-high shenanigans may be on film (48), Give us a break - from holidays (81), © 1987, How well do you travel? (83), Your mind, do you make the best use of it? (36), News in Brief (8), © 1988, Strategy for Success (41), © 1989, Hurry, catch that word (57); TMI, Are you too busy working to be successful? (23); Turkish Airlines Inc., Welcome on Board (53); Usborne Publishing Ltd, London, Weather Hazards (14), Cramp (200); Relax as you fly (195-6, 219), courtesy of Wings of Gold.

Illustrations: The Cartoon Gallery (8); Cathay Pacific (216; 214); Jeff Fisher/Redwood Publishing (175); Mark Hackett/Express Newspapers plc (34); Martin Honeysett/The Random Century Group Ltd (151); Michael Holt - Pan Pocket Puzzler (221); Gray Joliffe/Sunday Express Magazine (86); Gray Joliffe/The People (79); 'The Second Leunig' by Michael Leunig/Collins Angus & Robertson Publishers (167); 'The Penguin Leunig' by Michael Leunig/Penguin Books Australia Ltd (217); Linguaphone UK (62); New Internationalist (128); Geoffrey Norman (11); From an idea by Plexus Puzzles (209; 208; 218; 219); Gary Powell (78); Private Eye/Mike Turner (18); Private Eye Diary/Martin Honeysett (177); Private Eye (127); Punch (52; 80; 84); The Sunday Express/Des Lynch (202); The Sunday Express/Peter Till (201); © The Sunday Times 1986 (48; 33); Sunday Express Magazine/Joe Wright (172); © The Sunday Times 1987 (36); © The Sunday Times 1987/Michael Heath (169); © The Sunday Times 1989/Michael Heath (57); © The Sunday Times 1977/John Grimwade (143); Tim Hunkin (27; 164; 185); Time Manager International (23); TM/© 1991 King Features Syndicate Inc. (76); Steve Weston (128); You Magazine/Rick Brookes (205)

Photographs: Action Plus Photographic (30); Arcaid (136); Katalin Arkell/Network (128); Sue Baker (41); Barnaby's Picture Library (214); Bruce Coleman Ltd (130); Camera Press (55/56); Eye Ubiquitous (30); Feature-Pix Colour Library Ltd (83); Tim Graham (186); © Ken Griffiths/NHPA (139); Robert Harding Picture Library Ltd (71; 30); ICCE (130, 128); The Image Bank (71; 83; 30); Images Colour Library Ltd (71); Katz Pictures Ltd (54); The Kobal Collection Ltd (186); © Dean Lee/Oxford Scientific Films (139); Magnum Photos Ltd (125); Edward Parker/Still Pictures (131); Mary Evans Picture Library (186, 140); Melanie Friend/Format (55/56); The New Internationalist (55/56); NHPA (130, 131); NSP Group Ltd (24); Oxford Scientific Films Ltd (130); ; Panos Pictures (128); Pictures Colour Library Ltd (216); The Photographers' Library (71); Qantas Airlines (51); Rex Features Ltd (133); Richard Burbidge Ltd (136); Claude Sauvageot (55/56); Science Photo Library Ltd (186); Sporting Pictures (UK) Ltd (77); Tony Stone Worldwide Photolibrary (71); The South China Morning Post (13); © The Sunday Times 1985 (72); © Tony Tifford/Oxford Scientific Films (139); Times Books - The Times Atlas of the World Family Edition (10); © Babs & Bert Wells/Oxford Scientific Films (139); Wings of Gold (195, 219)

The publishers have made every effort to contact owners of copyright, but this was not possible in all cases. They apologise for any omissions, and if details are sent, will be glad to rectify these when the title is reprinted.

Additional artwork: Julie Anderson; Graham Bence; Peter Bull; Paul Catherall; Joan Corlass; John Crawford Fraser; Faranak; Colin Hadley; Illustrated Arts; Jonathan Inglis; Jonno; Nilesh Mistry; Graham Parker; Nancy Slonims; Emma Whiting.

Design: Gregor Arthur
Picture Research: Mandy Twells

All dictionary extracts in this book are taken from the *Collins COBUILD English Language Dictionary*. Information for the Phrasal Verb Checks and Reminders is taken from the *Collins COBUILD Dictionary of Phrasal Verbs*.

Addison Wesley Longman Limited
Edinburgh Gate, Harlow,
Essex CM20 2JE, England
and Associated Companies throughout the world.

First published by HarperCollins 1992
ISBN 0-003704246

© Sue O'Connell 1992

ISBN 0-17-556626-7
Fifth impression 1997

Contents

Map of Focus on Advanced English

Key: MC - Mini-check; SB - Study Box; CA - Communication Activity; ES - Exam Strategy; MM - Multiple Matching; MuC - Multiple Choice; GT - Gapped Text; PV - Phrasal Verb Check. Letters in brackets refer to a section of the relevant paper in the exam.

Unit/Topic	Grammar	Reading	Writing	English in Use	Listening/Speaking
Language Focus 1: Grammatical terms; Learning Focus 1: Reading strategies					
1 Severe Weather	Reduced relative clauses MC: Prepositions	1 Today is Cancelled 2 Where Snow Means Go	Formal letter	1 Cloze (A) 2 Editing skills (B)	1 Weather bulletin (A) 2 Personal account (B)
2 Time Eaters	1 Time clauses 2 Review of relative pronouns SB: *no matter*	Time Eaters	Personal Note	1 Cloze (A) 2 Editing skills (B)	1 Wasting time - extracts (D) 2 Board games (A) CA: Puzzles
Language Focus 2: Tenses/Dictionary abbreviations; Learning Focus 2: Listening strategies					
3 Stress	*-ing* forms SB: expressing cause and effect	Stress Test	Leaflet	1 Cloze (A) 2 Discourse cloze (C)	1 Stress - extracts (D) 2 Stress - interview (B)
4 Use Your Head	Review of conditionals 1 and 2 SB: *although/but; despite/in spite of* MC: the prefix *under-*	Your mind - do you make the most of it?	Report/review	1 Editing skills (B) 2 Guided writing (C)	CA: Learning - your expectations
Language Focus 3: Phrasal verbs; Learning Focus 3: Planning for writing					
5 Taking Off	1 Past simple/past continuous 2 Expressing the future PV 1	Watch it ...	1 Leaflet 2 Instructions	1 Cloze (A) 2 Guided writing (C)	1 Arriving at Sydney (B) 2 Customer complaints - interview (C) CA: Faulty maps
6 Language Matters	Comparisons 1 SB1: *no sooner ... than/ hardly/scarcely ...when* SB2: *like* v. *as; alike* PV 2	1 Language - the facts 2 Hurry, catch that word	Informal letter	1 Editing skills (B) 2 Editing skills (B)	1 Which language? - extracts (D) 2 Teach yourself Japanese (C) CA: Linguaphone advertisement
Language Focus 4: Vocabulary; Learning Focus 4: Developing editing skills					
7 Ages of Man	1 Comparisons 2 2 Present perfect SB: *would rather*	The World's Oldest Man	Article	1 Cloze (A) 2 Discourse cloze (C)	1 Age - extracts (D) 2 Life expectancy (B)
8 Wish You Were Here	1 Modal verbs 1 2 Review of reported speech MC: *-ing* or infinitive? PV 3	Taking a Break - from Holidays	Letter of complaint	1 Cloze (A) 2 Text completion (B)	CA1: What kind of traveller are you? - Quiz CA2: Travelspeak CA3: Roleplay

Grammar File

Writing File

Unit/Topic	Grammar	Reading	Writing	English in Use	Listening/Speaking

Exam Focus 1: Overview and Paper 1 - Reading

Unit/Topic	Grammar	Reading	Writing	English in Use	Listening/Speaking
9 Paradise Lost?	Relative clauses SB1: *each/every; either/neither* SB2: *hardly/scarcely* PV 4	1 Trees - the facts and quiz 2 Paradise Lost? (MM) ES: Paper 1	1 Formal letter (A) 2 Newspaper review (B)	1 Cloze 1 (A) 2 Editing (B)	Rainforest Foundation - interview (C) CA: describing and comparing ES: Paper 4
10 Fire	1 The past perfect 2 Conditional 3 and mixed conditionals PV 5	1 The Day Chicago Died - reordering and vocab skills 2 You are caught in a fire. (MuC) ES: Paper 1	Instructions (B)	1 Cloze 2 (A) 2 Editing skills (B)	1 Bush Fires (C) 2 How to survive a bush fire (A) ES: Paper 5 (Phase B) CA1: Problem solving CA2: Spot the difference

Exam Focus 2: Paper 2 Writing

Unit/Topic	Grammar	Reading	Writing	English in Use	Listening/Speaking
11 Personally Speaking	The passive MC: negative prefixes SB1: *the ... the* (comparatives) SB2: *make/cause* PV 6	1 Your True Colours 2 Test Your Personality (MM)	Informal letter and short personal ad (A) ES: Paper 2 (Section A)	1 Cloze 1 (A) 2 Discourse cloze (C)	Phone-in - discussion and description (C) CA1: Graphology CA2: Problem solving ES: Paper 5 (Phase C)
12 Mind Your Manners	Modal Verbs 2 MC1: dependent prepositions MC2: expressions with *make*	Conduct Becoming - GT and vocab skills ES: Paper 1/Paper 3	1 Letter of apology (A) 2 Short article (B) ES: Paper 2 (Section B)	1 Cloze 2 (A) 2 Guided Writing (C)	1 Etiquette - discussion (C) 2 Bad Manners - extracts (D) CA1: Embarrassing situations - discussion CA2: International Etiquette Quiz

Exam Focus 3: Paper 3 English in Use

Unit/Topic	Grammar	Reading	Writing	English in Use	Listening/Speaking
13 Head to Foot	Past tenses used to talk about hypothetical situations	1 Facedness (MM + MuC) 2 Gestures in Japan	Leaflet article (B)	1 Cloze 1 (A) 2 Stylistic cloze (B) ES: Paper 3 (Section B)	1 Sun Facts - talk (C) 2 Stamina exercise - talk (B) CA1: Relax as you fly - ordering CA2: Problem solving ES: Paper 5 (Phase D)
14 Testing Times	*-ing* v. infinitive	1 The Big Day (MM + MuC) 2 Beating Exam Nerves (GT)	Notes, Directions, Report (A)	1 Cloze 2 (A) 2 Editing skills (B) ES: Paper 3 (B)	1 Cambridge exams - talk (C) 2 Exam advice CA1: Discussion CA2: Describe and draw ES: paper 4 (Section B)

Exam Focus 4: Papers 4 and 5 - Listening and Speaking

Language Focus 1: Grammatical terms

1 What kind of word is it?

List A contains some basic grammatical terms used in dictionaries and grammar reference books. Choose a term to fit each definition in List B and then match the definition with examples chosen from List C.

List A

Preposition

Article

Adjective

Adverb

Pronoun

Verb

Noun

Conjunction

List B

a . . . . a word which is used to refer to a person, a thing or an abstract idea such as a feeling or a quality. e.g. . . .

b . . . . a word that is used to replace a noun that has already been mentioned or that will be mentioned later. e.g. . . .

c . . . . a word which gives more information about a noun or pronoun. e.g. . . .

d . . . . a word which is concerned with what people and things do, and what happens to them. e.g. . . .

e . . . . a word which adds information about a verb, or about an adjective or adverb. e.g. . . .

f . . . . a word or group of words often placed before a noun or pronoun to indicate place, direction, source, method etc. e.g. . . .

g . . . . a word or group of words that join together words, groups of words or clauses. e.g. . . .

h . . . . a word with no meaning on its own which is used in front of a noun or noun phrase e.g. . . .

List C

1 *I, you, him, it*

2 *and, although, if*

3 *run, make, behave*

4 *a, an, the*

5 *Tim, clock, strength*

6 *long, heavy, difficult*

7 *in, from, by*

8 *easily, fast, extremely*

2 Other terms

a **Match each term on the left with an explanation on the right.**

Base Form	An auxiliary verb which is used with a main verb to show a particular attitude such as possibility, obligation or prediction.
Auxiliary Verb	A form of the verb that can be used in compound tenses of the verb or as an adjective. There are two types: the past, usually ending in -*ed* ; and the present, ending in -*ing*.
Modal	A noun formed from a verb and ending in -*ing*. Also called a gerund.
Participle	The form of the verb which has no letters added to it. Also called the infinitive.
-*ing Noun	A verb which is used with a main verb to form tenses, negatives, questions etc.

b Find examples for each of the terms above from the letter.

Base Form   e.g. ....

Auxiliary   e.g. ....

Modal   e.g. ....

Participle   e.g. ....

-ing Noun   e.g. ....

Packaging gone mad

SIR: Take a bottle of typewriter correcting fluid. It is quite small and very strong. In all my years of letter-writing, I've never seen one broken. A smart hammer blow on a hard surface might do the trick, but I don't keep a hammer beside the typewriter.

It's exactly the sort of small object that would be found miraculously unharmed in the ruins of a heavy bombardment.

Now, stick it to a piece of stout cardboard, swaddle it in shrink-wrapped plastic and put it on a supermarket shelf.

There you have it: the ultimate in wasteful packaging.

Are marketing consultants really so stupid and irresponsible that they can't think of a better way of drawing the shopper's eye to their products?

They cut down trees for this. And that's not all. We pay for this pointless rubbish in the price of the product, too.

Geoff Dawson,
July 24   Carstensz Street,
Griffith (ACT).

Learning Focus 1: Reading strategies

1 Think about how you would read the following pieces of written language, then discuss the questions below with another student.

1 a A list of results for an exam you've taken. (3 pages)
   b A letter from a friend who's studying in Australia. (3 pages)

2 a Detailed instructions for reaching a friend's house. (half a page)
   b A review of a film you were thinking of going to see. (half a page)

3 a A newspaper in your own language. (16 pages)
   b A newspaper in English. (16 pages)

1 Would you read all six pieces in the same way? If not, why not?

2 Would each pair take the same amount of time to read? Why/Why not?

3 Would you be likely to read any of the pieces above a second time and in a different way? If so, which ones and why?

4 What kinds of things affect the way we read?

2 Read the descriptions below of two basic strategies for reading:

Skimming.
If you skim a newspaper or other piece of writing, you read through quickly to understand the main points without bothering about the details. e.g. *Just skimming through the papers, I saw a headline about the Pope's visit.*

Scanning.
When you scan something, you look at it or through it to find some particular information.
e.g. *The lifeguards scanned the sea for shark fins. I only scanned his letter for news of my sister.*

3 Which of the examples in exercise 1 above:

1 would you only skim?
2 would you only scan?
3 would you skim first and read in more detail later?
4 would you scan first and read in more detail later?
5 would you read in detail immediately?

Work with a partner and think of other examples of reading where you would a) skim and b) scan.

Severe Weather

Lead-in

1
From the list of 20 words below, underline the 10 words which describe weather conditions.

typhoid	*draught*	*hail*	*gale*
breeze	*tornado*	*blockade*	*fluid*
harpoon	*flood*	*turnip*	*blizzard*
bungalow	*sleet*	*typhoon*	*slump*
hurricane	*hazard*	*cholera*	*drought*

When you have finished, compare your answers with another student's.

2
With your partner, divide the words you've underlined into three groups, those connected with *wind*, those connected with *water*, and those connected with *neither wind nor water*.

3
Now say which of the words concern *severe* weather. Which of these severe weather conditions have you experienced? Tell your partner when and how.

Text 1

1 Skimming

Read through the main newspaper article, from the London *Evening Standard*, to find out what the chief effects of the severe weather were.
When you've finished reading, see how much you can recall. Work with a partner.

2 Scanning

Now scan the 'In Brief' section in order to find answers to the following questions as quickly as possible.

a Where did rescuers have to be rescued?
b Where were winter sports events cancelled, and why?
c Where did winter conditions give someone's game away?
d Where was the temperature especially news-worthy?
e Where was there a warm welcome for the elderly?
f Where was warm water a life-saver, and why?
g Where was hot water potentially dangerous, and why?
h Who or what might have benefited from some frozen water?
i Who found two legs better than four wheels?

3 Find words or phrases in the two reports which mean the same as:

Main article

First two paras
    a people who travel to and from work regularly
    b urgent request

Left-hand column
    c depressing
    d piles of snow blown up by the wind
    e a very slow speed

Right-hand column   f surrender (*noun*)

g unable to get away

h have no false beliefs

In Brief

a in a desperate situation (*adjective*)

b keep away/delay

c hiding place

Forget it, says BR, the weather has beaten us

And don't try by car, it's a nightmare

TODAY IS CANCELLED!

by Colin Adamson and Patrick McGowan

BLINDING BLIZZARDS brought London to a virtual standstill today and British Rail told 700,000 commuters: "Forget it. There's no way we can get you to work.'

As Arctic conditions spread eastwards from snowbound Essex and Kent into Sussex and Surrey, rail chiefs extended their "stay at home" plea to the whole of the Southern and Eastern regions.

The chilling admission of defeat was the greatest threat so far to commerce and industry in the capital. Weather men warned there could be worse to come.

The nightmare was no better on the roads. Millions of commuters forced to take to their cars faced the worst conditions since the big freeze began.

Heavy overnight snowfalls, driven into huge drifts by fierce winds, brought chaos to every major route into London and reduced traffic to a crawl.

Even in the heart of London where snow rarely settles the heavy falls gave roads the appearance of isolated country lanes.

South of the Thames, only one bus in ten was running on some routes. Others had no more than a one-in-five service.

North of the river, only half the usual number of buses were running. They were caught up in huge traffic jams in many areas.

The Jubilee and Victoria Underground lines were the only ones with anything like a normal service. All the others ran into trouble as soon as lines came up onto the surface.

The rail capitulation reached its lowest point at 6 am with the total closure of Waterloo Station, caused by major drifts

As thousands of freezing commuters were left stranded on empty platforms and trapped in dozens of London-bound trains, British Rail said: "That's it. We can no longer guarantee any sort of service. The weather has beaten us."

Only a tiny number of trains were still attempting to move across the Eastern and Southern Regions.

An Eastern Region spokesman said: " If people have any sense at all they will stay indoors and forget trying to make it to work.

Those who do make the effort should be under no illusions that they will get there. Even if by some miracle they do, it will be a rotten journey. The service everywhere is awful."

In brief

MOTORISTS stranded in snow and traffic yesterday were overtaken by a man on a pair of skis on the A12 in Essex.

HOVE's swimming pool complex, which is kept at a steamy 80 degrees F, is to open its doors free to pensioners today so they can keep warm.

A FIRE crew was called in to help dig out five ambulances snowed in at Chelmsford Ambulance Station in Essex overnight.

A POLICEMAN who went to pull a stricken schoolboy from a frozen lake in Dagenham had to be rescued himself . . . when he fell in.

In Lincolnshire, an outdoor skating championship at Baston Fen, near Spalding, was cancelled because there was too much snow on the ice.

At London Zoo, lion keepers kept the animals indoors to prevent them escaping when the moats surrounding their enclosures froze. Elephants were given warm baths to stave off hypothermia.

In Blyth, Northumberland, the snow trapped burglars who had raided a supermarket. Their footprints led police to their hideout.

In Switzerland, the village of La Brevine recorded a record low temperature for the country of -41.8°C. The village lies on an exposed plain known as the Siberia of Switzerland, more than 3,000 ft above sea level near the French border.

Parts of Norway were colder than the North Pole yesterday. The Norwegian ice skating championships at Hamar were cancelled because officials considered temperatures of -30°C too dangerous to the contestants. Doctors there warned people against taking hot drinks immediately after coming in from the extreme cold, to avoid cracking tooth enamel.

Text 2

Read the article from another newspaper about how the Swiss deal with problems of severe weather, and note the differences!

Reproduced by permission of the Evening Standard Company Ltd.

How Swiss skate over the problems of a big freeze-up

Where snow means go

from John Marshall in Berne

AS SNOW and ice bring chaos to Britain, life in Switzerland — experiencing a record minus 41·8° C — runs as smoothly as an expert skier.

"The latest any train has been this week was 20 minutes," said a railway spokesman.

At the slightest hint of snow, engines fitted with ploughs and blowers are out clearing the tracks.

Where there is a train hold-

● Trains: longest delay only 20 minutes

up due to freezing points or failure of the electrical contact points, teams of repair men on stand-by quickly move into action.

In fact the use of trains goes up by 10 per cent as drivers switch from road to rail.

The unemployed are kept busy clearing minor roads and sweeping the snow off open-air railway platforms.

To obtain unemployment benefit, a claimant must show that he or she has applied for

● Roads: jobless sweep up the snow

at least 10 jobs in the past month.

Work done for the state, such as clearing snow, counts as a job application.

Most roads and all motorways are cleared of snow by 7 a.m. and regularly during snowfalls throughout the day.

Custom posts warn foreign drivers they should drive with snow tyres or carry chains.

Chains are obligatory in almost all of the ski resorts. Anyone trying to drive with-

● Pavements: residents must keep them clear

out them will be stopped by the police.

Keeping the pavement outside a house or business clear is the legal responsibility of the owner.

Hospitals report a slight increase in the number of accidents involving aged people falling on icy pathways, but say it is only slight.

Farmers in the mountain regions are well stocked up. Food for cattle is flown in, as many towns have communal helicopters.

Discuss with a partner the main differences in the Swiss and British response to winter conditions. The following CONTRAST LINKS will be useful:

| ..., *while* ... |
| ..., *whereas* ..., |
| ..., *yet* ... |
| *In fact,* ... |

e.g. Tim is idealistic *while*/ *whereas* Jane is more practical.

e.g. He knows the problem *yet* he does nothing about it.

e.g. You would expect him to be upset. *In fact,* he doesn't care at all.

Mini-check: prepositions

Look at these phrases from the texts. Complete them with the missing prepositions.

Text 1

1 An *admission* .... defeat
2 buses running ..... *some routes*
3 People should be .... *no illusions* that
4 Doctors *warned* people ..... tak*ing* hot drinks

Text 2

5 engines *fitted* .... ploughs
6 men ..... *stand-by*
7 teams of men *move* ..... *action*
8 work which *counts* .... a job application
9 motorways are *cleared* .... snow
10 an *increase* .... accidents

Check your answers by looking at the texts, or ask your teacher.

Focus on Writing: Formal letters

Task	Using the information in the two articles (and your own ideas), write a letter to the Editor of the London *Evening Standard* expressing your annoyance at the recent chaos on the roads and railways, and suggesting what could be done to avoid a repetition of this situation in the future. Write about 180 words (excluding the addresses) and sign yourself 'Exasperated Commuter'.

Planning

How much do you know about writing formal letters in English? Discuss the following questions with another student.

1 Where do you write your own address and where do you put the address of the person you are writing to?
2 Where do you put the date, and how should you write it?
3 When do you use *Yours faithfully* and when do you use *Yours sincerely?*
4 Where do you write the first line of your letter?
5 What should you include in the first paragraph of a formal letter?

Now check your answers by turning to the notes on the layout and organisation of formal letters in the Writing File, page 111.

6 How should you begin and end this letter?
7 How many paragraphs are you likely to need and what will they contain?
8 What could you say in the final paragraph?

Before you begin, look at Useful Language on page 112.

Focus on Listening 1

You are going to hear a short weather bulletin from a Sydney radio station. Fill in the information missing from the table below.

General situation

1 The announcer mentions warnings of one kind of severe weather. What is it? . . . .

Temperature ranges

2	City and Liverpool	
	Richmond	10 - 14
3	Blue Mountains	

Further outlook

4	Friday	clearing
	Weekend	

Current situation

5	Temperature	
6	Humidity	
7	Winds	from the east. at . . . . an hour.

Focus on Listening 2

You are going to hear a speaker describing an experience of severe weather which he had in New Zealand. Write short answers to the questions below.

1 What's unusual about Wellington? ....

2 How old was the speaker at the time? ....

3 What time of year was it? ....

4 What did his father ask about when he rang? ....

5 What did his father tell him? ....

6 How fast were the winds travelling? ....

7 What disaster had occurred? ....

Focus on Grammar: Reduced relative clauses

1 Look at the sentence below:

Trees *blown over in the storm* were blocking the road in several places.

The part in italics is a reduced relative clause. It follows directly after the noun (*trees*) and shows how the noun has been affected by an action (*blown over*). It therefore has a passive meaning and could be expanded into a full relative clause:

Trees *which had been blown over in the storm* were blocking the road ...

2 Complete the examples from the texts in this unit with a suitable past participle. The missing verbs (base form) are:

snow   do   drive   fit   strand   force

a Millions of commuters .... to take to their cars faced the worst conditions since the big freeze began.

b Heavy overnight snowfalls .... into huge drifts by fierce winds brought chaos to every major route into London

c Motorists .... in snow and traffic yesterday were overtaken by a man on a pair of skis.

d A fire crew was called in to dig out five ambulances .... in at Chelmsford Ambulance Station.

e Engines .... with snow ploughs and blowers are out clearing the tracks.

f Work .... for the state such as clearing snow counts as a job application.

3 Complete the following sentences with a suitable past participle (+ preposition if necessary) or reduced relative clause. Remember, there should be a passive meaning.

a Letters .... in Paris on Monday usually get to us by Friday.

b Examination answers .... pencil will not be marked.

c They chose the hotel .... the travel agent.

d We had a delicious meal of fish ....

e Cars .... will be towed away.

f A man .... is to receive compensation of £10,000.

For more information on relative clauses, see the Grammar File, page 103.

Check: Spelling

1 Look at these extracts from the two articles, and say what the three verbs in italics have in common.

Today is *Cancelled*!   ... only one bus in ten was *running*...
... the snow *trapped* burglars ...

They illustrate one spelling change which can occur when participles are formed by adding *-ing* or *-ed* to the verb stem. There are also a few other possible changes. Try the exercise below to see how accurate you are in this area of spelling.

2 Not all the verbs on the next page are spelt correctly. Underline and correct those which are wrongly spelt. (Ignore the reference numbers in brackets for the moment.)

beating(1:1) raiding (1:1) panicked (2:5)
blinded (1:1) clearing (1:1) admitted (1:2)
aging (2:1*) controling (1:3) signalled (1:3)
benefiting (1:2) refering (1:2) happenning (1:2)
occurring (1:2) fitted (1:1) fulfiled (1:3)
travelled (1:3) swimming (1:1) forgeting (1:2)
enterring (1:2) dying (2:4) sweeping (1:1)
developping (1:2) enjoied (2:3) kidnapped (1:2*)

Check your answers with another student and then with the teacher.

There are spelling rules which may be helpful if you have problems with this area of spelling. The reference numbers in brackets refer to the rules and exceptions (*) which you can find in the Grammar File on page 105.

Check: Irregular verbs

1 The texts in this unit contain many examples of irregular verb forms. One is *brought* (base form *bring*). Say what the base forms of the following are.

The weather has *beaten* us . . . . *driven* into huge drifts . . . .
their enclosures *froze* . . . . Arctic conditions *spread* . . . .
caught up in huge traffic jams . . . . Food for cattle is *flown* in . . . .
The taxi *shook* . . . . trees *swung* dangerously . . . .

2 Complete the table of irregular verb forms below.

Base Form	Past Form	Past Participle	Base Form	Past Form	Past Participle
bear	. . . .	. . . .	grind	. . . .	. . . .
bend	. . . .	. . . .	lay	. . . .	. . . .
. . . .	. . . .	bet	. . . .	. . . .	shone
. . . .	bit	. . . .	. . . .	. . . .	shrunk
. . . .	bred	. . . .	slide	. . . .	. . . .
burst	. . . .	. . . .	spin	. . . .	. . . .
. . . .	. . . .	clung	. . . .	struck	. . . .
. . . .	crept	. . . .	. . . .	. . . .	sworn
deal	. . . .	. . . .	. . . .	tore	. . . .
. . . .	drew	. . . .	. . . .	trod	. . . .
fling	. . . .	. . . .	. . . .	. . . .	wound
. . . .	. . . .	forbidden	wring	. . . .	. . . .

Compare your answers with another student and then check the list in the Grammar File, page 107.

English in Use 1: Cloze

Complete the following article from *The South China Morning Post* by writing the missing words in the spaces provided. Use *only one word* in each space. All the missing words are of one grammatical type. Can you say what this is?

The article is about a violent typhoon called 'Peggy' and it was written by reporter Louis Liu who followed Peggy's path into China.

TYPHOON Peggy and a freak tornado have claimed 53 lives (1) . . . . the last 48 hours.

TEN DIED at Shantou when two-thirds of the city was flooded (2). . . . . torrential rain and high tides.

IN HONG KONG 228.8 mm of rain fell (3) . . . . Wednesday and 10 pm last night as the typhoon hit the Guandong coastline.

Travelling in the wake of the killer typhoon

Typhoon No 7, the name (4) . . . . which Typhoon Peggy was known (5) . . . . China, crossed the coast 50 kilometres east (6) . . . . Shanwei, a fishing port of 100,000 people in Guandong province.

Our instructions were to get to Shanwei before the typhoon came (7) . . . . at 3.30 pm on Friday. Taxi driver Ah Lam took a little convincing that we really wanted to chase a typhoon but, (8) . . . . some negotiations about the fare, we were (9) . . . . our way.

(10) . . . . the last two hours of the journey, we battled through driving rain and roaring winds. The taxi shook and swayed, and all too often the trees (11) . . . . the roadside swung dangerously (12) . . . . our path. Visibility was down to less than five metres.

We took the officials at the typhoon prevention centre in Shanwei (13) . . . . surprise. They hadn't had any reporters from Hong Kong drop in during a typhoon before. The town, they told us, had been attacked (14) . . . . . grade 12 winds - the strongest (15) . . . . the Chinese scale.

Shanwei came back to life quickly after the storm. (16) . . . . . early yesterday morning, children were going to school and factories were back (17) . . . . production. But traffic was (18) . . . . chaos for several hours (19) . . . . . . the closure of the main highway (20) . . . . to heavy flooding.

Reproduced by permission of the South China Morning Post

English in Use 2: Editing skills

There is one spelling mistake in each line in the following text. Read the text and underline every word which is wrongly spelt. Then write the correct spelling in the space provided at the end of the line. The first mistake has been corrected as an example.

Weather Hazards

High Winds

In strong winds, never walk on narrow <u>mountian</u> ledges or
peaks: you could get blown off by a guest. If it suddenly
becomes windy, tuck your clothes into your trowsers; a
flaping coat or jacket can catch the wind and throw you
of balance. If the wind is very strong, lie flat on the
ground.

1. *mountain*
2. ....
3. ....
4. ....
5. ....

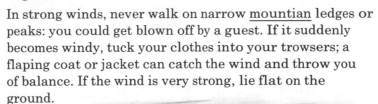

Floods

Try to avoid camping close to a river. There is a posibility
of heavy rain occuring up-river and flood water could come
rashing down when you are asleep or away from the tent. If
their is a flood warning, take food, drinking water and
spare cloths, and make for high ground. If you are swept
away by flood water, try to grab hold of a floatting object
such as a log or a peace of wood. If it is big enough,
clime on top and use it as a raft. Paddle to safety using
your hands.

6. ....
7. ....
8. ....
9. ....
10. ....
11. ....
12. ....
13. ....

Avalanches

Avalanches are extremly dangerous and can happen very
suddenly; they are especialy likely to occur during a
thaw and after a new full of snow. Listen to the weather
forcasts for your area and if there are any warnings of
avalanches, don't go out walking or sking.

14. ....
15. ....
16. ....
17. ....
18. ....

Time Eaters

Lead-in

Look at the pictures below. What connection with the title of this unit do you think they might have?

Work with a partner. Do any of the pictures show things that *you* spend time on? If so, tell your partner about them. How much time do you spend on them (and do you ever try to cut down on this)? What is their appeal? What other 'time eaters' in people's lives can you think of?

Focus on Listening 1

You are going to hear five people talking about ways of wasting time. You will hear the recording twice.

Question 1 lists the different ways of wasting time which they mention. Put them in the order in which they are mentioned by completing the boxes with the numbers 1 - 5. Two boxes will remain empty.

1

A cutting the grass

B not being able to make up one's mind

C making typing mistakes

D doing puzzles

E putting things in order

F working slowly and inefficiently

G reading books

Question 2 lists features mentioned in the five extracts. Put them in order by completing the boxes with the numbers 1 - 5. Two boxes will remain empty.

2 Which extract is about somebody who:

A wastes most time thinking about small things?

B is criticised by other people for wasting time?

C is afraid of what other people will think?

D says they'd like to have a secretary?

E is poorer than they used to be?

F has lost their old habit?

G tries to limit the time they waste every day?

Text

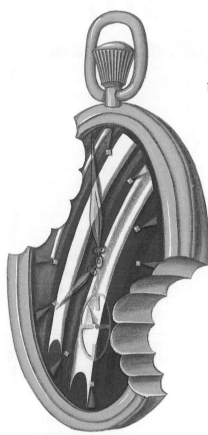

1 Skimming

a Skim the article to find out who it was written for. Was it mainly:

1 students planning their studies?
2 people in business?
3 parents of children taking exams?
4 people working at home?

Which words did you notice which helped you to answer the question?

b In general, the advice given is to:

1 disconnect the telephone.
2 experiment with relaxation techniques.
3 study the principles of Business Management.
4 identify the problems and make changes to overcome them.

2 Scanning

The writer suggests a number of ways we can work more efficiently. Scan the article to find where the points below are mentioned. Match each suggestion to one of the three sections of the article. Write one of the letters A, B or C after each one.

Interrupting Yourself	Drop-in Visitors	Telephone Interruptions
A	B	C

a Making a list of the interruptions you have during the day.   . . . .
b Making sure you have everything you need before you start work. . . . .
c Putting a sign on your office door.   . . . .
d Asking someone to answer the phone on your behalf.   . . . .
e Working on a group of similar tasks together.   . . . .
f Finding out what causes most interruptions.   . . . .
g Giving yourself some private time each day.   . . . .

3 Reading for detail

First scan the text to find the information you need to answer the following questions and then read that section more carefully.

Interrupting Yourself
a What are the two principles relating to time?
b What are some of the ways we interrupt ourselves when we are working?
c How does the writer suggest we can improve the way we work?

Drop-in Visitors
a What are the two ways you can solve this problem?
b Explain what a 'Quiet Hour' is.
c What are the advantages of a 'Quiet Hour'?

Telephone Interruptions
a What is the problem about telephone interruptions?
b How can they be avoided?
c What telephone calls should not be avoided?
d What does the writer recommend in the case of serious problems with telephone interruptions?

TIME-EATERS AND WHAT YOU CAN DO ABOUT THEM

The refrigerator door opened. I turned the TV down so I could listen. Bottles rattled. The fridge door closed - Heather came back upstairs to her homework.

5 My daughter had just fallen victim to the third most prevalent time-eater.

Interrupting yourself

In business or in homework, your time gets wasted because you think of
10 something that had slipped your mind, so you drop everything and are off to complete it before you forget it again. Or you use any excuse to break from a less than favorite task, and go off to the
15 washroom, coffee room, copier room or refrigerator.

What's the solution? There are several things you can do to reduce the amount of time stolen from you by yourself.
20 Firstly, remember two principles governing time. The Principle of Consolidation states that you get more done if you group like activities and execute them all in one time frame. The reason
25 behind this logic is that the preparation time period occurs once for all the tasks, and your mind gets set once for all the tasks. When you intersperse activities, you are winding up and winding down,
30 reducing your concentration and not functioning at peak mental effectiveness. And so it takes longer to complete each task.

The other law that affects your time is
35 one you've heard for years. 'A stitch in time saves nine'. In other words, if you spend some time in preparation before actually beginning to work on a job, you will be able to work right through and
40 complete it. The total time for the getting ready and the doing will be less than the time you would spend if you just started right in performing the task. If you clear your work area, before
45 beginning an activity, you won't be distracted by some paperwork your eyes fall on as you're on your priority task. So if you want a drink while you work or need to get some supplies or reference
50 material, do so before you actually begin working. Once you do start, use conscious self-discipline to stick to it

until it's finished. Don't have your time stolen by interrupting yourself.
55 The second major time-eater occurs when others visit your work area:

Drop-in visitors

You know the person. Every organization has one or two or three, or maybe
60 you're it. You have just sat down to your desk to tackle your daily tasks and knock, knock "How's it going?" or they arrive with a fast business question then stay to visit long after.
65 The solution can be two-pronged - you can discourage the visitors altogether or reduce the length of their stay when they do drop in. To discourage visitors, adopt a closed door policy for at least 1 hour a
70 day. A Quiet Hour. Pick an hour during the day when you feel at your best, or sharpest. It might be from 10.00 a.m. to 11.00 a.m. or it may be in the afternoon. Some companies decide this for their
75 employees. They don't open the switchboard and ban all visitors and inter-office telephone calls for the first half-hour of the work day. The procedure is straightforward, just tell your fellow
80 employees and those with whom you deal outside the company that you are not available for that specific hour unless it is an emergency.

Then, close your door. Maybe you want
85 to make a sign like they have in hotels to hang over the door knob - Do Not Disturb Until 11 a.m. - If you don't have a door, pin a notice on the divider or stand it on the corner of your desk -
90 Gone Fishing Until 4 p.m.

This quiet hour will take a few days or even a week to begin to pay off for you. Once people who work with you get the idea, they will plan to see you before
95 your quiet hour begins or be content to wait until it is over. You will be more and more enthusiastic as well when you realize the amount of work that you will accomplish during this hour.
100 We now arrive at the most time-consuming interruption faced by most people in business. It is also Heather's favorite interruption while she is doing her homework:

Telephone interruptions

105 No matter what we are doing or what project we are working on, we usually allow the almighty telephone to butt in. Telephone company literature even
110 exhorts us to answer before the third ring. This practice drastically reduces our concentration. How do we control this intruder? Have someone else screen your calls during your quiet hour. If you
115 do not have a secretary or assistant, ask the switchboard operator to take messages for you or make an arrangement with a peer to take messages for you during your quiet hour if you take their
120 messages during their quiet hour. A polite "I'm sorry, s(he) is busy right now. May I have him/her return your call after 11?" Screening the calls properly should not annoy anyone. If it
125 is an emergency, by your definition of an emergency, of course the call should be allowed to interrupt you.

If you suspect that interruptions are a major time-eater, you should keep an
130 'interruptions log' from time to time. On a separate piece of paper, jot down the time and date, the type of interruption and who it is that is interrupting. After a week or so, analyze the listing to
135 isolate the cause of the interruption that is wasting the greatest percentage of the total time. It may be your insecure boss, the lack of an assistant, or an untrained staff member. Or it could be you.
140 Perhaps you think you are the only person who can answer questions, handle telephone calls, etc. The big step is to isolate the cause, the next step is to deal with it.
145 I urge you to recognize the importance of the interruptions to your time management programme and the power of interruptions to eat away at your time. By minimizing the effect of interrup-
150 tions, you could save up to 2 hours a day. Just think of all those things you will be able to find time for in an extra 2 hours a day. Heather could even finish her homework.

Reprinted with the permission of the Drake Business Review, a publication of Drake International

Vocabulary

1 What kind of word?

Look at the way the following words are used in the text and then circle the correct part of speech. The first one is done for you.

a *excuse* (line 13)	(noun)	verb	adjective
b *group* (line 23)	noun	verb	adjective
c *like* (line 23)	verb	adjective	preposition
d *execute* (line 23)	noun	verb	adjective
e *frame* (line 24)	noun	verb	adjective
f *peak* (line 31)	noun	verb	adjective
g *drastically* (line 111)	verb	adjective	adverb
h *screen* (line 113)	noun	verb	adverb
i *peer* (line 118)	noun	verb	adverb
j *log* (line 130)	noun	verb	adverb

2 Which meaning?

Many words have more than one meaning or can be used in more than one way, so it's important to check their dictionary entries carefully. Choose the correct meanings for the following words as used in the text.

1 group (line 23)
a a number of people or things that are found in one place (*noun*)
b to bring things or people together (*verb*)
c a number of musicians who perform together (*noun*)

2 like (line 23)
a similar to (*preposition*) e.g. *They looked like twins.*
b similar (*adjective*) e.g. *He's interested in chemistry and like subjects.*
c to enjoy or prefer (*verb*) e.g. *There's nothing I like about town life.*

3 execute (line 23)
a to kill someone as a punishment for a serious crime (*verb*)
b to do something in the way it has been planned or agreed (*verb*)
c to create something such as a work of art (*verb*)

4 frame (line 24)
a a hollow structure which you can fit round something like a window, door or picture (*noun*)
b the general context or setting of something (*noun*)
c to put something like a picture or a photograph in a frame (*verb*)

5 peak (line 31)
a the peak level of something is the level when it is strongest or highest (*adjective*)
b the pointed top of a mountain (*noun*)
c the front part of a cap that sticks out above the eyes (*noun*)

6 screen (line 113)
a a flat, vertical surface on which a picture is shown (*noun*)
b to show in the cinema or broadcast on television (*verb*)
c to check people or things and select only those which are acceptable (*verb*)

7 peer (line 118)
a to look carefully at something, especially when it's difficult to see (*verb*)
b a person who is a member of the aristocracy such as a lord (*noun*)
c a person who is the same as you in age, status, profession etc. (*noun*)

8 log (line 130)
a a piece of a thick branch or of the trunk of a tree (*noun*)
b an official written account which describes important events which happen each day (*noun*)
c to record events or facts officially (*verb*)

3 Which meaning?

Here are some other words from the text which you may not know. Match them with a meaning from the list (1 - 10) below.

a *prevalent* (line 6)
b *consolidation* (line 21/22)
c *intersperse* (line 28)
d *tackle* (line 61)
e *ban* (line 76)
f *pay off* (line 92)
g *butt in* (line 108)
h *drastically* (line 111)
i *intruder* (line 113)
j *isolate* (line 135)

1 greatly, significantly (*adverb*)
2 be successful (*verb*)
3 someone who enters without invitation (*noun*)
4 rudely interrupt (*verb*)
5 identify something in order to deal with it (*verb*)
6 very common (*adjective*)
7 deal with a task in a determined way (*verb*)
8 strengthening, making more effective (*noun*)
9 put things in, here and there (*verb*)
10 state officially that something must not be done (*verb*)

MIKE TURNER.

> ┌─────────────┐
> │ STUDY   │
> │ **BOX** ▶   │
> └─────────────┘
> *no matter...*
> **Look at these examples. The first is from the text.**
>
> *No matter what* we are doing or *what project* we are working on, we usually allow the almighty telephone to butt in.
> I'll certainly meet you, *no matter when* you arrive.
>
> **The phrase *no matter* is followed by *what/who/where/when/which/how* and *whose* + a clause. It means that something is true in all circumstances.**
>
> **Note that the present tense can be used with future meaning after *no matter* as in the second example.**

Focus on Grammar 1: Time clauses

1 **Look at these examples from the text:**

You will be more and more enthusiastic *when* you realise the amount of work that you will accomplish during this time.

Once people who work with you get the idea, they will plan to see you before your quiet hour begins.

Notice that after the conjunctions of time *once* and *when* the present tense is used although the meaning is future. The present perfect tense is used to make it clear that an action or event will be completed *before* the action in the main clause. For example:

The Committee will make its decision when it has considered all the evidence.

Other conjunctions of time which are followed by a present tense with future meaning are: *before, after, until, while* and *as soon as.*

2 **Make sentences by matching clauses from columns A and B at the bottom of the page and joining them with a suitable conjunction of time. Each complete sentence refers to a piece of equipment. Can you say what the six items are?**

3 **Complete the following sentences with suitable time clauses.**

a You'd better clear up this mess before . . . .
b He won't pass his driving test until . . . .
c Once . . . ., I'll be happier.
d The 'No Smoking' sign will be switched on . . . .
e She'll be exhausted . . . .
f . . . ., you'll be amazed!

4 **Write three true sentences about yourself or someone you know using time clauses.**

A

a It won't work
b You'll find it easier than writing by hand
c A red light will come on
d Please leave your message
e You'll have to take the lens cap off
f I'll put it back in the cupboard

as soon as
before
while
after
when
until
once

B

1 you take any pictures.
2 it's recording a programme.
3 you wind it up.
4 it has cooled down.
5 you get used to the keys.
6 you hear the tone.

Sayings

1 **Match the two halves of the well-known British sayings below.**

1 A stitch in time	a is worth two in the bush.
2 A bird in the hand	b is a dangerous thing.
3 Every cloud	c waits.
4 One man's meat	d catches the worm.
5 Everything comes to him who	e has a silver lining.
6 A little learning	f is another man's poison.
7 The early bird	g saves nine.

2 **Now match each saying with a situation below.**

a The plane was delayed but at least I got my last few postcards written and posted.

b He said he'd done a course on home electrics but when he tried to mend my table lamp, he fused all the lights!

c My brother just loves adventurous holidays in exotic places. Me, I'm more of an armchair traveller.

d I'd take the job while you've got the chance. It may not be all that exciting but you could hold out for something better and not get it.

e There's no point in hoping for a bargain unless you're near the head of the queue when the sale starts.

f Remember to check your oil, water and tyres before you set off.

g I hear he's finally managed to talk her into marrying him!

Focus on Writing: Personal notes

Task

You were planning to spend a relaxing afternoon* with an English friend of yours* soon* but as you've got a lot of work to do* you think you ought to get on with that instead. Write a note to your friend explaining the situation and suggesting an alternative arrangement*. Write about 120 words.

Planning

A task like this will be more realistic and more successful if you decide on some concrete details before you start. If you can use true facts, it's very easy, but if you can't, invent some interesting and believable ones!

1 **On your own:**

Look at the details marked with a * and decide on answers to the questions below.

*   **Your friend:**
    Male/female? Age? Where do they live? How long have you known them? How did you meet? How well do you know them? How often do you see each other? What do you usually do together?

*   **The afternoon:**
    What were you planning to do? Where? When? How long ago did you make the arrangement? How much is your friend likely to mind this change of plan?

*   **Your work:**
    What have you got to do and why is it important? Why can't you take an afternoon off?

*   **An alternative:**
    When will you have some free time? How much time will you be able to spare? What could you do together?

2 With a partner:

a Ask your partner about their friend, the arrangement and the problem. Ask for more information if necessary. Explain the details of your situation to your partner.

b Discuss:

1 What is the difference between a letter and a note?
2 What would be a suitable way to begin this note?
3 What would be a suitable way to end the note?

Before you begin, look at the information about personal notes and messages and Useful Language in the Writing File on pages 113 and 114.

Focus on Grammar 2: Review of relative pronouns

1 In the following sentence, the relative pronoun *which* is used. What other word could be used in its place? Relative pronouns can be the subjects or objects of verbs. In this case, *which* is the subject of the verb *arrived*.

Have you seen the letter which arrived this morning?

2

a Underline the relative pronouns in the following sentences. The first five are extracts from the text.

a The other law that affects your time is one you've heard for years.
b Pick an hour of the day when you feel your best.
c Just tell . . . those with whom you deal outside the company that you are not available for that specific hour . . .
d Once people who work with you get the idea they will plan to see you before your quiet hour begins.
e You will be more and more enthusiastic . . . when you realise the amount of work that you will accomplish during this hour.
f I must've left my keys in the shop where we bought the bread.
g She's the only person that knows how to operate the computer.
h Don't look now! That's the man whose car I backed into.
i He's the funniest comedian that I've ever seen.
j Give me one good reason why I should trust you.

b Say whether each relative pronoun is a subject or an object.

3 Complete the following table, using information from the sentences in exercise 2.

4 Relative pronouns have been omitted in the following examples. Say *where* they have been omitted and *when* relative pronouns can be omitted.

a There are several things you can do to reduce the amount of time stolen from you by yourself.
b The other law . . . is one you've heard for years.
c Just think of those things you will be able to find time for in an extra two hours a day.

To check your answers to exercises 3 and 4, and find more information about relative clauses, look at the Grammar File on page 103.

5 Complete the following sentences with a suitable relative clause.

a Alexander Fleming was the man . . . . penicillin.
b 'Candy' is the word . . . . when the British would say 'sweet'.
c Bats are the only mammals . . . .
d Burkino Faso is a country . . . . Upper Volta.
e Pablo Picasso was the painter . . . . were dominated by the colour blue.
f Santa Maria was the name of the ship . . . . in 1492.
g The FIFA World Cup is a tournament . . . . four years.
h Nobody knows the reason . . . . died out 65 million years ago.
i *David Copperfield* is one of the best-known books . . . . wrote.
j 1953 . . . . Mount Everest.

	People	Thing			
Subject		which/that	Place	Time	Reason
Object					
Possessive					

Focus on Listening 2: Board games

1 Discuss these questions:

a Can you think of a game which is played with 32 pieces on a board?
b What board games did you play as a child, or do you play now?
c Describe how to play a board game you know.

2 You are going to hear descriptions of some other board games.

Before you listen: look carefully at the table below, which summarises the information. The pictures below illustrate the games. One of these is not correct.

As you listen: fill in the missing information for Questions 1 - 10. You can hear the recording a second time if necessary.

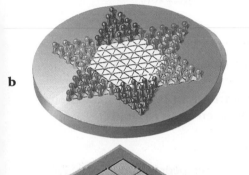

a

b

c

GAME	PLAYERS	PICTURE	EQUIPMENT		DIFFICULTY
Fox and Geese	2	1	Board + 13 pieces		2
Chinese Chequers	3	4	Board + 90 pieces		* * *
5	2	a	Board +·361 pieces		6
Solitaire	7	f	8	Board +	* *
9	2	c	10	Board +	*

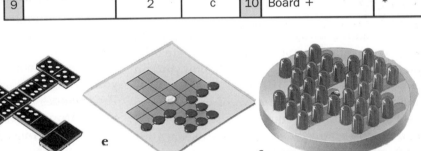

d   e   f

Communication Activity

Here are some typical time-eating activities which will at least practise your English! Work with a partner to solve the three puzzles.

1 Mini crossword

There are only five clues to this little crossword because the answers read the same across as down. Check your answers on page 218.

Clues

1 Used in another time-eating activity! (*N Pl*)
2 Separated (*Adj*)
3 Relationship between two measurements (*N*)
4 With less moisture (*Adj*)
5 Place where things are kept (*N*)

K	L	I	R	A	D	I	R	I	M	D
M	R	G	R	L	R	O	F	A	E	S
R	N	E	N	O	P	R	L	U	C	L
O	I	E	L	I	A	E	T	L	F	L
U	D	P	R	N	L	S	S	L	A	E
B	C	U	C	T	C	L	N	E	E	R
L	L	R	F	H	S	I	I	R	T	L
E	B	B	M	D	R	A	C	H	M	A
L	I	A	U	O	T	P	I	U	C	D
S	R	U	L	O	D	U	C	S	E	S
K	G	F	S	O	R	S	U	F	R	D

2 Word square

The square contains the names of 10 different currencies. They are printed in straight lines but the lines can run in any direction.
Here are the names of the countries to help you:

Germany   USA   Greece   Portugal   France

Spain   Italy/Turkey   Russia   India   Austria

Check your answers on page 218.

3 Spot the difference

Look at the two drawings of Inspector Clueless on page 221. There are 14 differences between them. Find them as quickly as possible and be prepared to say exactly what they are. Check your answers on page 218.

English in Use 1: Cloze

Read the advertisement below and circle the letter next to the word which best fits each space. The first answer has been given as an example.

Are you too busy working to be successful?

Here you are, digging away at your professional life, (1)... your private life disappears slowly but steadily from view. It's hardly fulfilling, is it? Well, now you can get (2)... into proportion and still be a success.

You can start by (3)... just two days of your time to follow the TMI Time Management programme. You'll be (4)... to a unique system devoted to increasing your personal effectiveness and building on your management (5)... . You'll learn a new (6)... towards getting results. (7)... , you'll have a superb tool - the Time Management system - to put it all into (8)...

So far, over half a million people have (9)... Time Management courses. (10)... they've all found is that the best training can be more than educational - it can (11)... be fun. You can reserve a place on the programme (12)... £405 per person. (Let us know if you need accommodation. We'll be pleased to (13)... you arrange it.)

Programmes are (14)... throughout the year in major towns around the UK and Ireland. So there's (15)... to be one near you.

Simply use the coupon to (16)... full information and a programme schedule.

Adapted and reprinted wib the permission of TMI from an advertisement in Intercity Magazine

1	A and	B because	Ⓒwhile	D since
2	A everything	B all	C it	D those
3	A making	B saving	C putting	D investing
4	A welcomed	B invited	C taught	D introduced
5	A art	B skills	C intelligence	D information
6	A attitude	B idea	C method	D style
7	A Next	B Following	C After	D Afterwards
8	A practice	B work	C employment	D service
9	A assisted	B attended	C taken part	D taken place
10	A This	B That	C What	D Which
11	A essentially	B ideally	C finally	D actually
12	A with	B for	C by	D from
13	A assist	B let	C help	D offer
14	A directed	B made	C held	D produced
15	A bound	B definite	C certainly	D surely
16	A collect	B send	C require	D obtain

English in Use 2: Editing skills

In this exercise you need to transfer information from one text to another which has a different style and purpose. This means expressing the same meaning but using vocabulary and structure which suits the new context.

You work in an advertising agency. Read the following informal note about a new product which you have received from a colleague. Use the information to complete the more formal advertisement below by writing the missing words in the spaces provided on the right. The first answer has been given as an example. Use *not more than two words* in each space.

MEMO

I've been trying out one of the new products and it's really helping me to organise my life. (I know that's hard to believe but it's true!) It's a wonderful gadget called a databank and it's really an all-in-one calculator, diary and address book. It's got a huge amount of memory - the others you can buy only have half as much, in fact - but it's only about the size of a small diary. You can keep all sorts of important information in it so I find it really useful not only in the office but also at home. You can set it to remind you about things like meetings and birthdays for up to a year (so I'll have no excuse if I miss yours!). Oh, one last thing there's a secret code number which lets you keep your information strictly to yourself. So, even though I haven't got much time, I do feel I'm a bit better organised at last! Highly recommended! J

The amazing new pocket databank

The new folding Databank has a memory with (1)... the capacity of others on (2)... yet it (3)... only 6 cm x 9 cm when closed. The memory allows you to get totally organised (4)... or at home, and to keep a whole (5)... of facts and figures at your fingertips. Its special features (6)... a clock, a diary, an alarm and appointments reminder which can be set a year (7)..., address and phone number storage and a calculator. A secret code number (8)... your information to be kept strictly (9)... . An invaluable aid for anyone who likes to be organised but has (10)... time to spare.

1. *twice* . . . .
2. . . . .
3. . . . .
4. . . . .
5. . . . .
6. . . . .
7. . . . .
8. . . . .
9. . . . .
10 . . . .

Language Focus 2: Tenses / Abbreviations

What tense is it?

1 Match the tenses listed on the left with the forms (for *regular* verbs) listed on the right. The first one is done for you. Check your answers with a partner and fill in an example for each one.

Present   *had+* past participle   e.g. ....

Present perfect   *will+* base form   e.g. ....

Past   base form/base form *+ -s*   e.g. *walk/walks*

Past perfect   *will have+* past participle   e.g. ....

Future   *have/has+* past participle   e.g. ....

Future perfect   base form *+ -ed*   e.g. ....

These are simple tenses. Continuous tenses (sometimes also called progressive tenses) are formed with the verb *to be* and the present participle e.g. *is studying / were running*.

2 Look at the verb forms in italics in these sentences. Each one represents a different tense. Write the name of the tense on the right hand side. There is a complete list of tenses below.

a   The restaurant *was* just *closing* when we got there.   ....

b   I *'ve been looking* everywhere for you!   ....

c   I *'ll leave* it for you at the reception desk.   ....

d   As he *had missed* the last bus, he walked home.   ....

e   She *'s* thoroughly *enjoying* the course.   ....

f   Tim *will have left* the office by now.   ....

g   When *did* you last *go* to the cinema?   ....

h   *Have* you already *had* something to eat?   ....

i   They *'ll be announcing* the winner at 6pm.   ....

j   What *do* you *do*?   ....

k   We *'ll have been travelling* for 24 hours by then.   ....

l   I *'d been hoping* to see you.   ....

present simple	present perfect simple	future simple
present continuous	present perfect continuous	future continuous
past simple	past perfect simple	future perfect simple
past continuous	past perfect continuous	future perfect continuous

Dictionary Abbreviations

What do the following common abbreviations in dictionaries refer to?

ADJ	....	N	....	PREP	....
ADV	....	NEG	....	PRON	....
COMPAR	....	O or OBJ	....	S or SUBJ	....
CONJ	....	PASS	....	SUPERL	....
INF	....	POSS	....	V or VB	....

Learning Focus 2: Listening strategies

As with reading, we listen in different ways according to the kind of thing we're listening to and the reason we are listening.

1 What would you be listening to if you heard the following?

a 'Loveliness' is a totally new concept in skin care. Try it and see a new stunning you.

b In a moment I'll give out the papers. Please do not turn the paper over until I tell you to begin.

c "Laura, I love you. I've loved you since the very first moment we met." "Oh, Ashley, don't be such an ass."

d So, a fairly murky day to begin with, but brightening up by the afternoon with the possibility of sunshine in the south east.

e When you get to the roundabout, turn right into Sheep Street - you can't go far because it's a dead end - and we're the fifth house on the left.

f Reports are coming in of a major earth tremor in southern Iran. There's been a military coup in the tiny state of Oxiana. The army is now in control of ...

g Expect lengthy delays on the A28 near Oxton. A lorry has shed its load of wallpaper paste so a rather sticky situation there! Sorry! An area to avoid anyway. Better news on the M19, I'm glad to say ...

Compare your answers with another student and then read the following description of two basic strategies for listening.

Extensive:
We listen extensively when we are interested in the general meaning or *gist*: the main points in a long conversation for example.

Intensive:
We listen intensively when we are interested in *specific* information: the exact details of an airport announcement, for example.

2 Discuss with a partner which of the extracts above you would listen to:

A extensively throughout?
B intensively throughout?
C intensively in parts?

3 Think of other examples of things you would listen to for each of the three categories.

Guessing unknown words

1 The words below appeared in the listening extracts from the previous section. Can you explain any of them *without* looking back at the texts?

stunning Adj (a)	*ass N (c)*	*murky Adj (d)*
dead end N (e)	*tremor N (f)*	*coup N (f)*
shed V (g)	*sticky Adj (g)*	

2 Look back at the words in their contexts and then discuss their likely or possible meanings with another student. See how much help you can get from the general situation and from other words around.
For example, is *stunning* likely to be a positive or a negative word? What result might skin care be expected to have?
Decide on a suitable word or expression which would make sense if used instead of each of the words above.

3 Choose the correct meanings for the words above from the list below.

a an attempt to get rid of the president or government of a country
b a small earthquake
c 1. covered with a substance that can stick to other things; 2. very difficult, awkward or embarrassing
d to drop accidentally
e dark and rather unpleasant
f extremely beautiful or impressive
g someone who says or does silly things
h a street with no way out at one end

How many meanings did you guess correctly or nearly correctly?

4 Discuss with a partner why it's important to train yourself to make intelligent guesses about the meanings of new words you hear (or read).

Stress

Lead-in

1 Work with another student to discuss the following questions.

a What *is* stress?

b What situations cause stress?

c What harmful effects can stress have on the body?

Check your answers by *scanning* the information below fairly quickly.

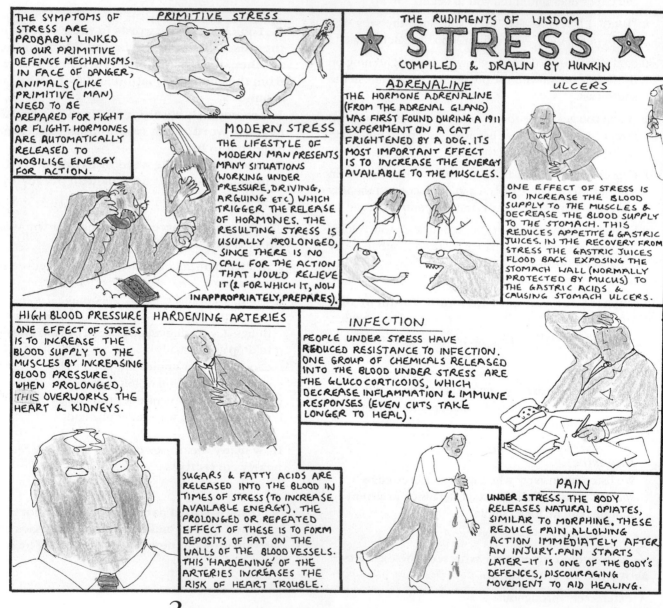

2 Discuss these questions.

a What level of stress would you consider there to be in *your* life - high, medium or low?

b What situations cause *you* stress?

c Suggest some ways in which we can help to reduce stress.

Text

1 **Read the first section of the text (lines 1 - 25).**

A certain degree of stress is unavoidable in life. But the pressures of modern, urbanised societies can push stress to
5 dangerously high levels. While we can't completely eliminate stress, we can learn to modify our behaviour in ways that lessen its harmful effects on our minds and bodies. Experts have
10 identified a number of indicators that affect our vulnerability[1] to stress. Some of them have to do with physical factors, some are related to mental and emotional behaviours,
15 and some have to do with nutrition.

The following questionnaire was developed by psychologist researchers at the Boston University Medical Centre, to evaluate vulnerability to
20 stress, and to highlight those areas in which improvement can be made.

To answer the questionnaire, rate each item according to how often it is true of you. Answer all the items, even
25 if they seem not to apply.

1 *vulnerability* - our ability to be affected or harmed by something

Stress Test

1	I eat at least one hot, balanced meal a day.	( )
2	I get 7- 8 hours of sleep at least four nights a week.	( )
3	I regularly give and receive affection.	( )
4	I have at least one relative within 50 miles on whom I can rely.	( )
5	I exercise to the point of perspiration at least twice a week.	( )
6	I smoke less than half a pack of cigarettes a day.	( )
7	I take fewer than five alcoholic drinks a week.	( )
8	I am at the appropriate weight for my height.	( )
9	I have an income to meet my basic expenses.	( )
10	I get strength from my religious beliefs.	( )
11	I regularly attend club or social activities.	( )
12	I have a network of friends and acquaintances.	( )
13	I have one or more friends to confide in.	( )
14	I am in good health.	( )
15	I am able to speak openly about my feelings when I am angry or worried.	( )
16	I have regular conversations with the people I live with about domestic problems.	( )
17	I do something for fun at least once a week.	( )
18	I am able to organise my time effectively.	( )
19	I drink fewer than three cups of caffeine-rich drinks (coffee, tea, soft drinks) a day.	( )
20	I take some quiet time for myself during the day.	( )

(1) Almost always (2) Frequently (3) Occasionally (4) Almost never (5) Never

2 Guessing unknown words

Discuss with another student what you think the following words might mean.

a *urbanised* (line 3/4)
b *eliminate* (line 6)
c *modify* (line 7)
d *indicators* (line 10)
e *nutrition* (line 15)
f *evaluate* (line 19)
g *highlight* (line 20)

Ask yourself:
- What parts of speech are they?
- Is there a part of the word you recognise which might be a clue to meaning?
  (e.g. *evaluate* - *value*)
- What meaning does the *context* suggest?

3 Communication Activity

a Work with a partner to discuss the points in the Stress Test. Fill in the scores *for your partner.*

b Read the first paragraph on the next page (lines 1 - 10) in order to check each other's results.

Add up the figures of your answers and subtract 20. If you have scored below 10, you have an excellent resistance to stress. If your score was over 30 you are vulnerable to stress in your life; a score of over 50 indicates you are seriously vulnerable to stress, and you should begin making some changes in your life.

Take a look at the items on which you scored '3' or higher, and begin trying to modify your behaviour. For instance, if you scored '4' on Number 19, you can cut your consumption of caffeine-rich beverages, and reduce your vulnerability to stress. Tackle the easy-to-change items, before the more difficult ones.

Work is a major source of stress for many people. Again, while normal work pressures can stimulate performance, a stress overload at work can lead to serious health problems. In the UK a recent stress study found that many factors influence stress ratings. A job can rate low stress on autonomy [2], high on physical danger, financial insecurity, time constraints or legal accountability [3]. One job that was omitted from the study was that of housewife/mother. Other studies have shown that housewives experience significant stress, something that will be no surprise to those who fall into that category.

Fighting stress in the workplace requires the cooperation of employee and employer. Far-sighted companies are providing sports and exercise facilities for employees, day-care or nurseries for working mothers, drug and alcoholism counselling. Job design is changing, too, in this age of dual-career families. More and more firms allow 'job-sharing', or work at home.

Employees can protect themselves from the effects of stress in simple ways. Taking a walk at lunchtime can help, as can simply getting up from the desk occasionally. Winston Churchill was wont to retire for a nap every afternoon, declaring that it enabled him to 'press a day-and-a-half's work into one'. John F Kennedy was another famous afternoon napper who calmed his mind and boosted energy with an afternoon snooze. Not all of us are able to take siestas, but there is sound evidence that a 10 minute to one hour nap will do much to renew energy and relieve daily stress. The best time for a stress-busting nap? Mid-afternoon.

Mary Trevelyan Hodder

2 *autonomy* - freedom to make one's own decisions
3 *accountability* - responsibility

Reproduced by kind courtesy of Asia Magazine

4 Finally, finish reading the text and then answer the questions below.

a What advice is given about changing our behaviour to reduce stress?

b What factors in a work situation can lead to stress?

c Who is unlikely to be surprised to hear that housewives can suffer from stress? What phrase gives you the answer?

d What can employers do to help their employees avoid stress? Why are such employers described as 'far-sighted' (line 41)?

e What is meant by 'dual-career families' (line 47), and what new patterns of work are there to help them?

f What did Winston Churchill and John F Kennedy have in common?

Focus on Writing: Leaflet

Task

The company you work for has recently spent a considerable sum of money on providing sports and exercise facilities for its employees. The intention was to help fight stress and so improve employees' health and performance.

So far, however, the response has been rather disappointing, and the company feels that more people need to be made aware of the opportunities which are available.

There are a large number of English-speaking employees in the company, and you have been asked to prepare the text for a leaflet aimed at them. You are to:

1 explain the background to the new development

2 encourage people to make full use of the new facilities

3 give general advice on ways of avoiding stress in daily life

Using the information you have read so far, and your own ideas, write about 250 words.

Planning

1 **Work in pairs or groups to do the following.**

a Draw up a list of possible sports and exercise facilities.

b Discuss guidelines for the use of the different facilities e.g. suggestions for sensible activities for the not-so-fit to begin with, and how to increase fitness *gradually*.

c Discuss the possible points to include in the 'general advice' section.

2 **Look at the notes on the *layout*, *organisation* and *style* of leaflets in the Writing File on page 114. Then make your personal decisions about these features.**

a What headings should there be?

b How can the text be divided up to be easy and attractive to read?

c How can you catch the reader's attention and keep him or her reading?

Focus on Listening 1

You are going to hear six people talking about stress in their lives. You will hear the tape twice. As you listen the first time, answer question 1. As you listen the second time, answer question 2. Read through each question before you listen.

Question 1 lists the main ways of dealing with stress which they mention. Put them in the order in which you hear them by completing the boxes with the numbers 1 - 6. One box will remain empty.

1

A being careful about their diet

B having a drink with friends

C painting pictures

D taking part in a sport

E collecting things as a hobby

F doing some home decorating

G watching a film

Question 2 lists other points which are mentioned by the six speakers. Put them in order by completing the boxes with the numbers 1 - 6. One box will remain empty.

2 **Which speaker mentions:**

A a part of their work which causes stress?

B being happy in their work?

C some of the physical signs of stress?

D stress being a warning to be kinder to themselves?

E getting away from the cause of the stress?

F sleeping for a long time?

G liking things which contrast with their work?

Focus on Listening 2

You are going to hear Peter talking about the stress in his life. As you listen, fill each space in the sentences below with 1 - 4 words. You do not have to use the exact words on the tape. You will hear the piece twice.

1 Peter says the two main sources of stress in his life are . . . . and . . . .

2 He works as a . . . .

3 In his work, he dictates tapes which last . . . .

4 Recently he spent . . . . dictating documents.

5 What caused him stress was that he had to do . . . . in the afternoon.

6 Another cause of stress in his work is . . . . of time.

7 He also finds it stressful dealing with work which is . . . . to an individual client.

8 His clients are usually at . . . . point in their lives.

9 He finds his work . . . . , however.

10 At home it's stressful when his children are . . . . or . . . .

11 The previous week, when it was his turn to look after his daughter, she was sick . . . . throughout the night.

12 As a result, he . . . . and felt under stress at work the next day.

STUDY BOX ▶

expressing cause and effect

Nouns:

| Work is a major | source cause | of stress.   (Text 1) |

One   effect   of stress is to increase the blood supply . . .   (Lead-in)

Verbs:

| (A sleepless night) can and does | cause lead to result in | stress.   (Listening 2) |

| Stress can | result from | sleepless nights. |

Links:

| High blood pressure can be | caused by due to the result of | stress. |

| Stress has increased | as a result of because of | our modern lifestyle. |

Check: Language

The sentences below contain points of language which are covered in the Focus on Grammar section (FG) in this unit (page 32), the Study Box (SB) (page 31), or in the Grammar File (GF) (pages 95/96).

To see how much you know already, study the sentences and find the *six* which contain mistakes. Compare your answers with another student and discuss *why* the sentences are incorrect.

a My hair badly needs cutting. (FG3)
b The signing the treaty took place the following month. (GF)
c Don't worry, I'm used to look after children. (FG2)
d I look forward to hearing from you. (FG2)
e It's no use to argue with him. (FG3)
f There are long delays on the motorway caused from road works. (SB)
g I'm afraid there'll be many hammerings while I build the bookcase. (FG1c)
h Please read the small print before filling in the booking form. (FG2)
i I hope you won't mind my interrupting you. (GF)
j I'd given up hope to ever see you again. (FG2)

Focus on Grammar: - *ing* forms

-*ing* forms include:

present participles which are used to form verb tenses (e.g. I was *cutting* the grass) and as adjectives in some cases (e.g That was a very *cutting* remark).
-ing nouns which function as nouns (e.g. *Cutting* the grass is not my job).

They look the same and it's usually not important to distinguish between the two.

1 -*ing* nouns

a In the first part of the Focus on Listening section in Unit 2, seven ways of wasting time were listed. One was *cutting* the grass - how many others can you remember?

b Here are some other ways of spending time. Find a partner for each -*ing* noun.

A		B	
playing	parties	tap	painting
doing	camping	train	skating
exchanging	money	bird	building
taking	guests	autograph	dancing
going	pictures	figure	watching
throwing	cards	long-distance	hunting
making	gossip	portrait	spotting
entertaining	jigsaws	body-	running

The examples under A show how -*ing* nouns can also take objects. The examples under B show how they can be used in compound nouns.

For general information about -*ing* nouns, see Grammar File page 94.

c -*ing* nouns usually refer to activites in a general way, so they are usually uncountable (they cannot be used with numbers or with words like *each/every/few/many* etc.).

A few -*ing* nouns can be countable, however. These often refer to the result of an activity, eg. *a building, a painting* but some have a meaning which is more particular than the general meaning of

the verb. The word *living* in the expression *to earn a living* , for example, refers to the money needed to buy the basic things of life.

d Look at the examples of countable -*ing* nouns in the sentences below and explain the particular meaning of each one.

1 The Accident Investigation Committee's *findings* were published today.
2 There are two *showings* of 'Godfather 3', one at 6.30 and one at 9.00.
3 There's an English *saying*: 'Many hands make light work'.
4 Take the second *turning* on the left.
5 Would you prefer the early or the late *sitting* for dinner?
6 The hotel was in a wonderful *setting*, surrounded by mountains.
7 I collect newspaper *cuttings* about my brother's career.

2 -*ing* forms after prepositions

Look at these examples from an earlier text.

Before actually beginning ... *By* minimising the effect ...

Verbs used after prepositions are always in the -*ing* form. Note that *to* is a preposition rather than a part of the infinitive in the expressions *look forward to, be/get used to, object to*.

Complete the following sentences by adding the correct preposition and the -*ing* form of a suitable verb.

a Doctors warned people .... hot drinks immediately after coming in from the extreme cold. (See Unit 1, Mini-check, page 9.)
b Why do you always insist .... an argument?
c He's never apologised .... so rude to my friends.
d She didn't try and prevent him .... a fool of himself.
e I'm interested .... for the post of Personal Assistant.
f I congratulated them .... engaged.
g You can save time .... a short cut through the park.
h Several patients complained .... dizzy all the time.

i .... the aircraft, make sure you have all your hand baggage with you.

j The union saw little hope .... agreement with the management on the issue.

3 -*ing* forms after verbs and other expressions

Some verbs can only be followed by an -*ing* form: e.g. *mind, enjoy.*

I don't mind helping.
Do you enjoy watching sport on TV?

There is a list of verbs which are followed by -*ing* forms in the Grammar File, page 105. Other verbs can be followed by both -*ing* forms and infinitives and these are listed on page 105.

An -*ing* form after the verb *need* has a passive meaning.

The carpet needs cleaning. (= needs to be cleaned)

-*ing* forms are also used after certain expressions like *can't bear* and *no use*. These are listed in the Grammar File on page 105.

Complete the following sentences. Be careful, not all the verbs are followed by -*ing* forms.

1 It's not worth .... him to the party. He hates ....
2 I couldn't resist .... a joke on him.
3 He told them that if they didn't stop .... the drums that instant, he wouldn't hesitate .... the police.
4 If you don't keep up your mortgage payments, you risk .... your home.
5 I can't help .... that he does so little work that he deserves .... the exam.
6 You may consider .... a holiday in the Alps, but no one should attempt .... mountain climbing without the proper equipment.
7 He denied .... anything to do with the robbery at first, but then agreed .... guilty.
8 I can't cut anything with this knife. It needs ....
9 The guidebook suggests .... the Sydney Tower where you can spend some time .... the view over the city.
10 You can choose .... a stand-by ticket if you don't mind not .... if you can travel until the last minute.

Check your answers by looking at the Reference List in the Grammar File, page 105.

English in Use 1: Cloze

Read the article below and circle the letter next to the word which best fits each space. The first answer has been given as an example.

What makes you lose your temper?

You think it is (1) ... time your neighbour put a new gate up between your two gardens. Do you a) (2) ... the matter with him in a friendly way? b) (3) ... him over the disputed fence? Or c) Kick the old one down?

This is not a new board game, (4) ... a question from researchers at the University of Birmingham, trying to find out why people lose their tempers. Their research shows that there are some very angry people (5) ... One man who had been rung up at random had no (6) ... in answering (c). He was one of 50 people picked from the phone book and asked (7) ... sort of things really (8) ... them mad. The team found that, despite our calm (9) ..., Britons get upset about the strangest things - (10) ... men wearing polyester ties or putting creases in their denim jeans, to people who (11) ... their food in tomato sauce or bus drivers who drive badly and bounce their passengers down the stairs.

The question the researchers are now asking is: Why? And what do we do to (12) ... that anger? The work is being (13) ... by two clinical psychologists and (14) ... from being a light-hearted study, it has a serious (15) ... They are hoping it will provide a (16) ... to more effective treatment of violent criminals.

© *Times Newspapers Ltd.*

1	A just	B about	C over	D the
2	A talk	B deal	C explain	D discuss
3	A Argue	B Face	C Meet	D Propose
4	A nor	B though	C but	D however
5	A about	B outside	C nearby	D round
6	A reason	B doubt	C hesitation	D choice
7	A the	B any	C that	D what
8	A set	B made	C put	D had
9	A image	B character	C name	D face
10	A like	B as	C from	D even
11	A spread	B eat	C spoil	D cover
12	A refuse	B revise	C control	D cope
13	A followed	B done	C practised	D made
14	A different	B far	C instead	D away
15	A project	B cause	C promise	D purpose
16	A key	B result	C method	D help

(1 B is circled as the example.)

English in Use 2: Discourse cloze

The article below gives advice on how to cope in eight stressful situations. Read through the article and think about what situation each section refers to.

Pressure POINTS

We also suggest how to keep stress at bay in everyday situations. By Susanna Goodden

HOW TO COPE

What to do about everyday stress in some common situations

1_____

Ease tension by taking . your clenched hands off the steering wheel, and feet off the pedals. Give your arms a shake, stretch your 5 hands, circle wrists and shoulders. Wriggle your toes and circle ankles. Breathe away tension by sighing—breathe in normally then exhale in long slow sighs.

2_____

10 Stuck in the supermarket or bank ? Regain your balance by doing something positive. Use the time to write a list or check your diary. Accept the situation and focus on 15 something enjoyable.

3_____

Stroke your child and whisper in its ear to relax you and the child. Take a break, a short walk if possible. Hit the pillow, not the child.

4_____

20 Win through it by thinking positively from the beginning. Be prepared, which means no pills and no swotting the night before. Do something physical on the eve of 25 the exam like swimming or going for a run. When you're actually doing the exam sit properly. If you sit all curled up you will only produce more tension. Breathe slowly.

5_____

30 Lie down in bed and learn to relax. Starting with your toes, tense and curl them up then relax, move up to your calves, then thighs, then grip your hands and relax. Tense 35 and relax every part, finishing with your face. Fix your eyes on something in the room. Stare at it then close your eyes and try to visualise it again—this calms the mind.

6_____

40 Arguments need defusing. If you can anticipate a combative situation, change your posture so you look and feel more open. Lower your shoulders, stick your elbows out a 45 bit, try and smile and breathe slowly. Listen rather than concentrating on what you are going to retort, and answer in a way that shows understanding for the other side's 50 point of view. If you lose your temper you lose the argument.

7_____

Weigh up the pros and cons; write them out in two columns. Don't be rushed; some decisions need pro- 55 fessional advice and time to evaluate. Beware of hiding from decisions by leaving problems in your in-tray or in filing cabinets.

8_____

When someone else is putting on 60 the pressure for you to work faster, learn to say no. Try asking for 15 minutes rather than being told to complete an impossible task in 10. Aim to take control of the situation. 65 Don't let it take control of you.

Reproduced by permission of Express Newspapers plc.

1 Discuss your ideas with another student, and then make a list of short headings for each section. For example, one of the original headings was 'Screaming Kids'. Which section did that heading refer to?

2 Now choose the eight original headings from the list of ten possible headings below. Write one letter (A - J) in each of the numbered spaces.

A Making Up Your Mind   F Sleeplessness
B Exam Time   G Relaxing
C Queues   H Screaming Kids
D Exercise   I Traffic Jam
E Faster, faster!   J Cross Words

3 The advice above mentions several parts of the body. See how many you can find and mark them with a cross (X) on the picture. Compare your result with another student's.

Use Your Head

Lead-in

1 **Work with one or two other students and discuss the following questions.**

a Think of something you have learnt to do successfully (e.g. driving, playing the piano, using a computer). Why do you think you were successful? How did you succeed?

b Think of something you had less success in learning (maybe at school). Why do you think you were less successful? What went wrong?

2 **Discuss whether you think the following statements are *true* or *false*.**

a Most people have better memories than they think.
b Drinking black coffee can help people to remember information.
c We learn better at certain times of the day than at others.
d When you're studying, it's best not to take many breaks.
e Our memories are bound to get worse as we get older.
f We learn best when we are relaxed.
g It's possible to learn while you sleep.
h When studying a book, it's best to remember information in the author's own words.

Now read the text to find out if your answers were correct.

Text

1 Skimming

a **The text deals with several different aspects of memory and learning. The main topics are listed below in the order they appear in the text.**

Skim through the text fairly quickly and write the numbers of the paragraphs which deal with each topic in the second column. Include all the paragraphs. Leave the last column empty for the moment.

Topic	Paragraph(s)	Tip
Memory		
Learning Rhythms		
Effects of Ageing on Intelligence		
Learning: Psychological Factors		
Learning Strategies		

b **Now look at these tips which correspond to what the writer says. Match them to the topics above by writing the correct letter in the third column.**

A Make your own notes.
B Find out what your best time for learning is.
C If you want to remember something, try to reproduce the conditions you were in when you were learning it.
D Keep mentally active.

c **One of the topics has no specific tip. Work with another student and write your own tip for that topic.**

YOUR MIND
DO YOU MAKE THE MOST OF IT?

● Lifeplan psychology adviser **JOHN NICHOLSON** explains how to reveal the hidden potential of your mind, and how to improve your mental efficiency

1 PSYCHOLOGICAL research shows we consistently underestimate our mental powers. If you think this does not apply to you, then here is a simple test to show you are wrong.

2 Write down the names of all the American states you can remember. Put the list away and then set yourself the same task a week later. Provided you have not cheated by consulting an atlas, you will notice something rather surprising. The two lists will contain roughly the same number of states, but they will not be identical. Some names will have slipped away, but others will have replaced them. This suggests that somewhere in your mind you may well have a record of virtually every state. So it is not really your *memory* letting you down; just your ability to retrieve information from it.

3 We would remember a lot more if we had more confidence in our memories and knew how to use them properly. One useful tip is that things are more likely to be remembered if you are in exactly the same state and place as you were when you learned them.

4 So if you are a student who always revises on black coffee, perhaps it would be sensible to prime yourself with a cup before going into the exam. If possible, you should also try to learn information in the room where it is going to be tested.

5 *When* you learn is also important. Lots of people swear they can absorb new information more efficiently at some times of day than at others. Research shows this is not just imagination. There is a biological rhythm for learning, though it affects different people in different ways. For most of us, the best plan is to take in new information in the morning and then try to consolidate it into memory during the afternoon.

© *Times Newspapers Ltd.*

6 But this does not apply to everyone, so it is essential to establish your own rhythm. You can do this by learning a set number of lines of poetry at different times of the day and seeing when most lines stick. When you have done this, try to organise your life so that the time set aside for learning coincides with the time when your memory is at its best.

▲ Other people can provide you with information, but only *you* can learn it ▼

7 Avoid learning marathons – they do not make the best use of your mind. Take plenty of breaks, because they offer a double bonus: the time off gives your mind a chance to do some preliminary consolidation and it also gives a memory boost to the learning which occurs on either side of it.

8 Popular fears about the effects of ageing on intelligence are based on a misconception. Research shows that although we *do* slow down mentally as we approach the end of life, becoming stupid or losing your grip in the world

is not an inevitable consequence of the ageing process. On some measures – vocabulary, for example – we actually improve in the second half of life. In old age, intellectual functioning is closely related to physical health. But there also seems to be a lot of truth in the old adage: If you do not want to lose it, use it.

9 Learning goes well when people feel challenged and badly when they feel threatened. Whenever a learning task becomes threatening, both adults and children feel anxious. Anxiety interferes with the process of learning because it is distracting. In order to learn effectively you have to be attending closely to the task. An anxious person is likely to be worrying about what will happen if he fails, to the detriment of his attempts to succeed. If his mind is full of thoughts such as "I'm sure I'm going to fail this test", or "What are my parents going to say?", he will not do as well as he should.

10 Learning is an active process. Despite claims to the contrary, you cannot learn when you are asleep. "Sleep learning" (accomplished by having a tape recorder under the pillow, playing soothing but improving messages while you are recharging your tissues) is unfortunately a myth. Any learning that seems to have occurred in this situation will actually have been done after you woke up but were still drowsy.

11 Other people can provide you with information, but only *you* can learn it. It also has to be "chewed over" before it can be integrated into your body of knowledge. That is why just reading a book is no way to acquire information unless you happen to possess a photographic memory. Parroting the author's words is not much better. You have to make your own notes because this obliges you to apply an extra stage of processing to the information before committing it to memory. Effective revision always involves reworking material, making notes on notes, and perhaps re-ordering information in the light of newly-observed connections.

12 As a general rule, the greater your brain's investment in a body of information, the better its chances of reproducing it accurately and effectively when you need it.

2 Reading for Detail

Work in pairs. Read through the questions below and see if you can answer them without looking back at the text. If you need to check, *scan* through the text till you find the information you need, then read more carefully.

1 If you try the memory test suggested, how much time should pass between the first and second test?
2 What two conditions should be the same if we want to help our memories to recall something that has been learned?
3 How can learning poetry help us understand how we learn best?
4 What are the advantages of taking breaks during study?
5 What aspect of intelligence gets better as we get older?
6 Why can't we learn effectively if we are anxious?
7 Why doesn't 'sleep learning' work? If you try it, when will learning actually take place?
8 You can only learn by just reading if you have a very special quality. What is it?

Vocabulary

Find words or phrases in the text to match the dictionary definitions below.

1 *V: to deceive; used showing disapproval.* If you . . . . , you behave dishonestly in order to get what you want. (para. 2)

2 *V + Obj: a fairly formal word.* If you . . . . something, you succeed in getting it back from a place where you have hidden it or where it should not be. (para. 2)

3 *V + Obj: to prepare.* If you . . . . a gun, a bomb etc., you prepare it so that it is ready to explode. (para. 4)

4 *V or V + Obj: to reinforce.* If you . . . . something that you have, you strengthen it so that it becomes more effective or secure. A formal use. (para. 5)

5 *V or V + with:* If two or more events . . . . , they happen at or around the same time. (para. 6)

6 *N Countable:* A . . . . is something good that you do not expect to get in addition to something else, although you are very glad to get it. (para. 7)

7 *N Countable:* When something is given a . . . . it increases and improves by a large amount. (para. 7)

8 *Phrase:* If you . . . . you become less efficient and less confident and less able to deal with things. (para. 8)

9 *N Countable:* An . . . . is something which people often say and which expresses a general truth about some aspect of life; an old-fashioned word. (para. 8)

10 *Phrase:* If something happens . . . . of something or someone, it causes harm or damage to them. (para. 9)

11 *V + Obj + over:* If you . . . . something such as a problem, you think carefully about it; used in informal English. (para. 11)

12 *V + Obj:* If you . . . . something that someone else has said, you repeat it, often without understanding what it means, rather than thinking what to say yourself. (para. 11)

Focus on Grammar: Review of conditionals 1 and 2

1

a **Say whether the following statements about conditional sentences are *true, partly true* or *false*.**

1 In conditional sentences, the conditional clause begins with *if* . . .
2 We use the first conditional to talk about possible future events.
3 In the first conditional, the verb in the main clause is *will* or *shall* , and the verb in the conditional clause is simple present.
4 We use the second conditional to talk about unlikely situations in the present and future.
5 In the second conditional, the verb in the main clause is *would*, and the verb in the conditional clause is in the past.

b **Now look at the following examples and compare them with the statements above. What extra information do they provide about conditional sentences?**

1 You can borrow the calculator as long as you bring it back tomorrow.
2 If you take an umbrella, it never rains!
3 If he tells you he's got no money, he's lying.
4 If I had the time and money, I'd travel the world.
5 If you tried harder, you might achieve more.

The meanings expressed by the first and second conditionals can be summarised as follows. There is a table in the Grammar File on page 93 showing the various verb forms which can be used in each case.

Type 1

a Conditions which are always true (common occurrences, general truths).
b Conditions which are very probable in the future.

Type 2

Conditions which are impossible or improbable in the present or future.

2 There are several examples of conditionals in the text (page 36). Classify the examples below as Type 1a, Type 1b, or Type 2.

Type

..... a Provided you have not cheated, you will notice something surprising.

..... b We would remember a lot more if we had more confidence in our memories.

..... c Things are more likely to be remembered if you are in exactly the same state and place as you were when you learned them.

..... d If you do not want to lose it, use it.

..... e If his mind is full of thoughts such as 'I'm sure I'm going to fail this test' ... he will not do as well as he should.

..... f ... just reading a book is no way to acquire information unless you happen to have a photographic memory.

Compare your answers with another student's.

Underline two other link words in the examples above. Can you think of any more? Refer to the Grammar File (page 93) for a list of conditional link words.

3 Match the two halves of the following conditional sentences.

a If you need to make a phone call,
    1 people would be more sympathetic.

b If you tidied your desk,
    2 leave a message with my secretary.

c If you didn't complain so much,
    3 everyone will be satisfied.

d Unless you've other plans,
    4 why would I be asking you?

e If there was an emergency,
    5 you wouldn't spend ages trying to find things.

f If I'm not here when you ring,
    6 you would have to interrupt the meeting.

g If I knew what the answer was,
    7 please keep it short.

h Provided you've done your best,
    8 I'd like you to have dinner with me.

4 Complete the following conditional sentences

a I find it hard to concentrate on studying if . . . .
b If I didn't have a dictionary, ...
c I can't learn a new word unless . . . .
d If I weren't studying English now, ...
e You learn more successfully if . . . .

STUDY BOX *although/ but; despite/ in spite of*

Despite and *in spite of* are prepositions and are followed by nouns (including *-ing* nouns) or noun phrases. **They cannot introduce clauses.**

Despite
In spite of | claims to the contrary, you cannot learn when you are asleep. (Text)

Although and *but* are conjunctions which introduce clauses. **Compare the following examples.**

Although there are claims to the contrary, you cannot learn when you are asleep. We slow down as we get older *but* we do not necessarily lose our intellectual faculties. (Text)

Mini-check: the prefix *under-*

Research shows we consistently *underestimate* our mental powers.

**The prefix *under-* is used with certain verbs (as in the example above), nouns and adjectives to suggest the meaning 'less than enough'. In most cases, the prefix *over-* can be used to give the opposite meaning.
Check that you understand the meanings of the words in italics in the examples below.**

I think you've *undercharged* me.
This meat is *underdone*.
The refugees were *undernourished**.
He was *underpaid* and overworked.
Much of the land is *underpopulated*.
She works with *underprivileged** children.

He's a much *underrated* poet.
The baby was *undersized* at birth.
The office is *understaffed* at present.
To call him rude was an *understatement*.
She felt *undervalued* by her boss.
The sports facilities were *underused*.

* These do not usually occur with the prefix *over-*.

Communication Activity: Your expectations

1 Factors in learning

How important do you expect the following factors to be in your English course? Put a number 1 by the most important factor, a 2 by the next most important, and a 3 by the least important.

your teacher   . . . .
your coursebook   . . . .
yourself   . . . .

Discuss your answers and your reasons with another student.

2 How can your teacher help you most?

Here are some possible ways your teacher can help you to learn (and you can add more if you like). Choose the *six* which you consider most important.

a by revising all major areas of grammar thoroughly
b by concentrating on areas of advanced grammar
c by working on your use of functional language
   (e.g. complaining/apologising)
d by explaining all new vocabulary clearly
e by giving regular tests
f by correcting every mistake you make
g by giving practice in pronunciation
h by setting regular homework
i by working through past examination papers
j by giving plenty of practice in speaking
k by giving practice in different types of writing tasks
l by getting students to work in pairs or groups
m by helping you to develop good learning methods
n ....
o ....

Compare your choices with the person sitting next to you.

3 How can you help yourself?

a **Here are 17 language learning habits. Tick things which you already do.**

1 translate from your own language before you speak or write
2 keep a vocabulary notebook and revise new vocabulary regularly
3 record new vocabulary in a short phrase or sentence
4 write new vocabulary with just a translation in your own language
5 use only a bilingual dictionary
6 use only a monolingual dictionary
7 use a grammar reference book
8 speak only English in the class
9 read English books, newspapers or magazines outside class
10 listen to spoken English outside class
11 translate every unknown word as you read
12 guess unknown words as you read
13 only speak in class when you're sure you won't make a mistake
14 ask questions in class
15 revise each lesson before the next
16 set yourself learning targets (e.g. 5 new phrasal verbs each week)
17 find out which areas of language you are weak in and give yourself
     extra practice in them

b **Some of the above habits may, in fact, be *unhelpful* in the long run. Which are they? (You will probably be able to find about five.) Compare your answer with another student's and discuss why certain habits might be helpful or unhelpful.**

c **Underline or highlight the good language learning habits which you will definitely try to adopt. Refer back to this page from time to time to see which good learning habits you have developed.**

Focus on Writing: Report / review

Task	You have been asked to write a short book review for a school/college English language magazine. Choose any book which you think might interest your fellow students. The book can be in any language and it could be of educational interest (a grammar or dictionary, for example), of practical interest (a guidebook or cookbook, perhaps), or purely for entertainment (a novel or biography, for example). Your brief is to include a clear description of the story/contents, to comment on what you think the most successful and least successful features are and to give an overall recommendation. Write 200 - 250 words.

Planning   **1 Which book?**

a **Make a list of three or four possible titles. They don't have to be new books (though it will be helpful if you have read them recently), and you don't have to have enjoyed them. Sometimes it's easier to pinpoint what you don't like about something than what you like!**

You could include a book connected to your English course (maybe even this book!), something connected with a hobby or interest, and something you've read for enjoyment. Remember, the books don't have to be in English.

b Work with one or two other students. Take it in turns to describe the books on your list and say what you like and dislike about them. This should help you decide which is easiest to talk about. Ask your colleagues which book they'd be most interested to read about.

2 What will you say?

When you've chosen your book, look at the instructions again. Underline the three parts of the task. Before you begin , refer to the notes on writing reviews in the Writing File, page 118.

English in Use 1: Editing skills

There is one unnecessary word in every line of the following text. It is either grammatically incorrect or does not fit in with the sense of the text.
Read the text, put a line through each unnecessary word, and then write the word in the space provided at the end of the line. The first line has been done as an example.

STRATEGY FOR SUCCESS: How to take notes

In an ideal world ~~the~~ revision would be part of everyday   1 . the . . . .
learning. At the end of each lesson you would be spend a few   2 . . . .
minutes by reading over what you had learned, thinking about   3 . . . .
it, and discussing about it with your friends. But it is far   4 . . . .
more than likely that you escape from the classroom with a   5 . . . .
sigh out of relief, and rush home.   6 . . . .
The importance of small doses of regular revision which is   7 . . . .
stressed by teachers, who may be round off lessons by summing   8 . . . .
up what they have been said, test you regularly on what you   9 . . . .
know, or distribute out copies of the key points of each   10 . . . .
lesson or topic.
The art of summarising - usually as known as 'taking   11 . . . .
notes'- is an important art when it comes over to revision,   12 . . . .
The best notes are those that you take them yourself; they   13 . . . .
are the ones most likely to can be related to the way you   14 . . . .
see things and make out sense of them. A helpful technique   15 . . . .
for subjects which require hard for learning is to note down   16 . . . .
things you really must not know on separate cards, which you   17 . . . .
keep in your pocket to learn at the odd moments. Vocabulary,   18 . . . .
for example, can easily be learned on the bus to school.

English in Use 2: Guided writing

As part of a project, you are going to interview a number of people on their approach to studying. You have made some notes to help you design a questionnaire which you can use during the interviews.

Write out the full questions by expanding the notes below. You must use all the words in the same order as the notes. You may add words and change the form of words where necessary. The first question has been completed as an example.

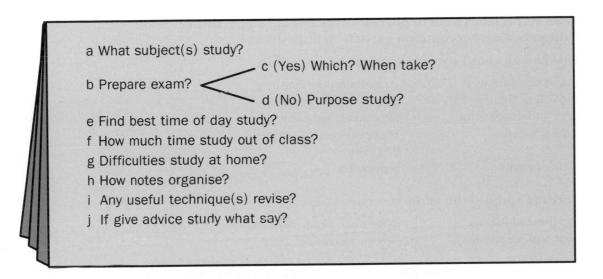

a What subject(s) study?

b Prepare exam?
    c (Yes) Which? When take?
    d (No) Purpose study?

e Find best time of day study?

f How much time study out of class?

g Difficulties study at home?

h How notes organise?

i Any useful technique(s) revise?

j If give advice study what say?

Questionnaire

a What subject or subjects are you studying at the moment?

b . . . .

c . . . .

d . . . .

e . . . .

f . . . .

g . . . .

h . . . .

i . . . .

j . . . .

Language Focus 3: Phrasal Verbs

1 Quiz

1 True or false?
Phrasal verbs tend to be 'colloquial' or 'informal' and it's best to avoid using them in written English.

2 True or false?
Phrasal verbs consist of a verb + a particle (e.g. *after, by, over*).

3 How many particles can be used to form phrasal verbs?
a 24   b 36   c 48

4 True or false?
Particles often have fixed meanings which can help us to understand the different combinations they are used in.

5 The commonest particles used in phrasal verbs are: *up/down, in/out on/off.*
Which of these is the *most* common particle in English?

<u>Clue 1:</u> This particle has 12 separate meanings including:

movement and separation
increase and intensification
improvement and preparation
fastening and restriction
approach
disruption and damage

completion and finishing
rejection and surrender
happening and creation
collection and togetherness
disclosure
separation

<u>Clue 2:</u> **Here are some of the verbs it occurs with:**

increase and intensification:
improvement and preparation:

brighten, speak, heat, liven
brush, make, set, swot

6 One particle only occurs in *one* phrasal verb in modern English. What is it?

<u>Clue 1:</u> **If you are taken .... by something, you are so surprised or shocked by it that you stop what you are doing and cannot think or behave normally.**

e.g. *I was a bit taken .... by this sudden reversal*

<u>Clue 2:</u> **It begins with 'a'!**

You can find the answers for the quiz on page 218.

2 Work with another student to answer the questions below.

1 Which verb?
Fastening and restriction: Which verbs could you use with the particle *up* to tell someone to do the following things?

2 Find the meaning

a Match each particle below to one of the meanings on the left. The first is done for you. (Note: each particle may have other meanings too.) Do not fill in the examples yet.

Beginning	*over* e.g. ....
Writing or recording	*back* e.g. ....
Getting rid of	*off* e.g. ....
Returning or retrieving	*on* e.g. ....
Spilling, overflowing	*away* e.g. ....
Continuing	*down* e.g. ....

b Find *two* verbs from the list below which will combine with each of the six particles above to make phrasal verbs with the meanings you have chosen.

| *boil* | *carry* | *copy* | *hand* | *jot* | *keep* |
| *pour* | *run* | *send* | *set* | *start* | *throw* |

3 Which particle?

a Choose one particle from the list on the right which fits each group of meanings.

1
```
Nearness, position, linking
Producing and organising
things
Groups and unity          [        ]
```

2
```
Following
Wanting
Similarity and imitation
                    [        ]
```

3
```
Movement past a person or thing
Visiting
Consistency and loyalty
                    [        ]
```

```
away
after
by
into
on
off
through
together
```

b Match each of the particles above with a group of verbs it can combine with.

1	*pass*	*push*	2	*chase*	*run*	3	*live*	*herd*
	drop	*call*		*inquire*	*go*		*throw*	*scrape*
	stick	*stand*		*take*	*name*		*hold*	*stick*

Learning Focus 3: Planning for writing

Introduction

1 If you wanted to do the following things would it be better to telephone or to write? Discuss your answers and the reasons for them.

a make a complaint about service in a restaurant

b thank someone for a present

c arrange a date to play tennis with someone

d report to your boss on a conference you've been to

e make a booking at a hotel

f let your customers know about a sale you are having

2 Decide which of the following points are advantages of writing and underline them.

More personal	Immediate feedback	Stress/intonation can clarify information
More immediate	More concise	Allows time for thoughts to be organised
Often more precise	More formal	Layout can clarify information
More convenient	Provides a record	

Basic decisions

1 We write for many reasons and there are several different factors which determine the kind of writing we choose to do. Think of some further examples to add to the following tables.

Subject and Purpose

General	Specific
e.g. to inform	e.g. to explain that you can't attend a meeting
to persuade	to encourage people to buy something
to invite	....
to apologise	....
....	....

Audience and Relationship

e.g. close family/friends
　　acquaintances
　　colleagues
　　potential employers
　　..................
　　..................

Special Circumstances

e.g. you want to catch people's attention
　　you want to make a very good impression
　　you want to clarify a number of details
　　you haven't got much time
　　this could be important legally
　　..................................

2 With these factors in mind, we need to decide about the following points

Format	**Style**	**Layout**
e.g. note	e.g. chatty/casual	e.g. formal letter layout
memo	informal	informal letter layout
postcard	neutral	heading(s)?
leaflet	formal	numbered points?
letter	humorous	eye-catching features?

Work with another student. Look again at the items in question 1 which you thought would be better expressed in writing. For each one, identify the audience and your relationship with them, and any special circumstances. Then select an appropriate *format, style* and *layout.*

Planning

1 **Which of the following approaches to writing a formal letter, report or exam composition seems most sensible, and why?**

> I write out the whole thing first in rough and then copy it out neatly or type it afterwards. That way I can correct most of my mistakes.

> I'm too impatient to do a rough version first. I think it's better to be spontaneous so I tend to start writing the final version immediately.

> I like to collect my ideas and make sure I haven't forgotten anything important so I make notes about what I want to say before I write out the final version.

2 *Making notes* before you start is a very good idea and essential in an exam.

How to make notes

- Make a list of all the points you want to include — so nothing is left out.
- Decide on the best order for the points — so the organisation is logical.
- Make a note of any useful expressions and vocabulary — so you make the most of your knowledge.

Remember: you can refer to the Writing File for notes on any special layout and language for particular types of writing.

5

Taking Off

Lead-in

1 When travelling alone by train or coach, which of the following are you most likely to do? Discuss with another student.

a sleep
b read a book or magazine
c listen to music
d watch the view
e talk to your neighbour

f work or study
g do a crossword or play a game
h nothing at all
i something else (say what)

2 Would your answer change if you were travelling by air?

Text

1 *Skim* the article fairly quickly in order to find out:

a why cameras are to be fitted in airliners
b where they will be located, and why
c what other purpose cameras might serve

2 *Scan* the text to find where the points below are mentioned and then read more carefully to say whether the following statements are *True* or *False*.

a Cameras will be clearly positioned to deter hijackers.
b Those passengers who object need not be filmed.
c The Japanese gangster intended to dispose of his grenade.
d The grenade failed to work properly.
e It will be possible to transmit pictures to the ground.
f A film recorded the VC10 captain's astonishment on waking.
g A camera could have prevented Richard McCoy's attempted hi-jack.
h The BA 747 captain's announcement exaggerated the danger of the situation.
i A camera could have prevented Dr Mobb's experience.

Compare your answers with another student's.

3 Vocabulary

a Look at the way the following words or phrases are used in the article, think about what parts of speech they are, and suggest another word which could be used instead, to give the same meaning.

a *dawned* (line 2)
b *install* (line 6)
c *get up to* (line 9)
d *combat* (line 12)
e *craftily* (line 21)
f *come into its own* (line 24)

g *tossed* (line 37)
h *beam* (line 45)
i *set his mind on* (line 64)
j *soared* (line 99)
k *lapse* (line 99)

b Compare your answers with another student's and then match each of the words above with one of the meanings below.

sink slowly   threw   fix   rose quickly   begun   was determined to   send/ transmit   fight against   cleverly   do/ get involved in   receive the attention which is really deserved

Watch it! Those mile-high dramas may be on film

A special report by Brian Moynahan, our Travel Correspondent

The age of inflight film-making has dawned.

Airbus Industrie, the European consortium of plane-makers, announced last week that it is offering to install tiny cameras on its airliners. This will allow the airlines to see what their customers and crews get up to at 30,000 ft.

Though the main purpose is to combat hijacking, it seems certain that film producers will be lining up to buy the offcuts[1]. Audience participation has never been seen on this scale.

There will be no hiding place for the camera-shy, since the whole aircraft, cockpit, cabin, lavatories and all, will be covered by the craftily concealed cameras.

The airliner loo, most underestimated of dramatic settings, will at last come into its own. A lot of things get flushed down them, false passports, drugs, love letters and, on October 26 last, on a Thai International Airbus, a hand grenade.

Film would have revealed a Japanese gangster entering the smallest room 160 miles out of Osaka on a flight from Bangkok. Deciding to rid himself of his hardware[2], he carelessly let pin become separated from grenade as he tossed it away. Explosion, decompression and consternation of gangster.

Cameras will also be placed in the cockpit and the crew will not be able to turn them off - a new factor in a hijack. There is technology to link the cameras with communications satellites that could beam terrorist movements to security on the ground, establishing the number of hijackers and possibly their identity.

International terrorism apart, some incidents clearly deserving immortality have failed to be preserved. The moment when a British Airways VC10 captain awoke on a night flight in the Far East to find his co-pilot sleeping gently next to him and the flight engineer snoring behind. Or the Filipino captain of a Swiftair DC3 who attempted to hijack his own aircraft while flying a payroll[3] to an oil field.

There is the case of Richard McCoy, who set his mind on hijacking a United Airline 727 on a flight from Denver. He went straight to the lavatory. Indeed a crewman was sent to get him out of it before the flight could take off. A camera would have recorded him changing into a dark black curly wig, a false moustache, a blue suit with red stripes, a large blue tie and silvered glasses - before presenting a hijack demand for cash.

No cabin full of extras[4] could recapture the faces on the passengers when Eric Moody, a British Airways 747 captain, 37,000 ft above an Indonesian volcano announced, 'Ladies and gentlemen, this is your captain speaking. We have a small problem and all four engines have stopped. We are doing our utmost to get them working again'.

He succeeded. Put that wonderful economy of dialogue on film and there wouldn't be a dry eye in the cinema.

Enough of hijackers and pilots. Ordinary passengers will be the main subjects for the camera.

A friend of mine was flying from Heathrow to Boston when he was taken violently ill with food poisoning. As his temperature soared, he began to lapse into unconsciousness. The steward told him 'Hang on, sir, there's a doctor on the passenger list. We're going to find him.'

A stewardess was giving my friend emergency oxygen by the time the steward returned. 'I'm afraid we can't find him, sir,' he said. 'What's his name?' my friend asked. 'Dr Mobbs.' 'Oh, my God,' said my friend. 'I'm Dr Mobbs.'

1 *offcuts* - piece of film left after the main part has been cut. (Also used of paper, fabric, wood, etc.)
2 *hardware* - weapon(s) (informal)
3 *payroll* - total amount of money paid to workers in a company
4 *extras* - actors who play very small parts - usually in crowd scenes

Focus on Writing 1: Leaflet

Task

It seems likely that cameras will be installed in most airliners before too long. Imagine, then, that this is now the case and that your local airport has decided to produce a small leaflet, in various languages, which will be handed to passengers when they check in. You have been asked to write a version in English.

Using the information in the article, explain the reasons for the cameras and how they work. Include a suitable heading and write about 250 words.

Planning

Work with one or two other students to discuss the following points.

a What is the *purpose* of the piece of writing? What must it achieve?

b What is the best *layout* to achieve the effects you decided on above? (numbered points? continuous prose? question and answer? etc.)

c What is the most appropriate *style* to achieve the effect you want? (very formal? very chatty? etc.)

Reminder: Plan your work in note form before you tackle the final version. You can refer to the notes on writing leaflets in the Writing File page 114.

Focus on Grammar 1: Past simple/past continuous

1 Look at the following examples. There are two verbs in each sentence. Say what the tenses are in each case and which action or event came first. Then match them to the correct diagrams below.

1 I was watching the news when the lights went out.
2 When the lights went out, I tried to find a candle.
3 As my eyes got used to the dark, it was easier to find my way around.

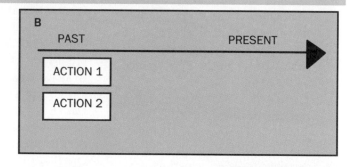

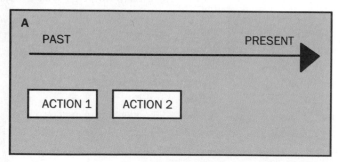

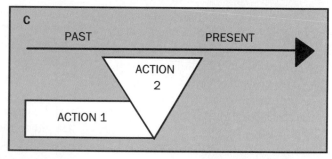

2 Fill in the names of the correct tenses in the explanations below.

In example 1, the . . . . tense is used to describe a longer action or event which was interrupted by a shorter one. (GF 2.2*)

In example 2, the . . . . tense is used to describe an action or event which followed immediately after another action. (GF 1.3*)

In example 3, the . . . . is used to describe two actions or events which happened in parallel. (GF 1.4*)

* Check your answers in these paragraphs of the Past Tenses section in the Grammar File (page 100).

3

Complete the following sentences with the correct forms of the verbs in brackets. The first three come from the text on page 48.

a A friend of mine (*fly*) from Heathrow to Boston when he (*be take*) violently ill.

b As his temperature (*soar*), he (*begin*) to lapse into unconsciousness.

c A stewardess (*give*) my friend emergency oxygen by the time the steward (*return*).

d When the police (*arrive*) at the scene of the accident, they (*take*) statements from a number of witnesses.

e He (*begin*) to make enemies as the business (*develop*) and he (*grow*) more powerful.

f One escaped prisoner (*be spot*) on the M4 motorway where he (*try*) to hitch a lift at midnight.

g I (*use*) the gears to control the car when the brakes (*fail*).

Focus on Listening 1

1 Towards the end of a flight, there is usually an announcement which gives passengers information which will be useful to them when they arrive at the airport. Work with another student and make a list of the kind of information which might be given in this situation.

2 You're on a plane which is about to land at Sydney's Kingsford Smith airport, and you are going to hear an announcement made by the Flight Service Director, Bob Mills. You need to listen carefully because it's the first time you've been to Australia, and the information will only be given *once*. *Before you listen*, look through the notes below to see what information is needed. *As you listen*, complete the information for Questions 1 - 12.

Arriving at Sydney

TRANSPORT

The airport is `1` .... kilometres from the city.

Taxis can be found `2` .... the terminal building.

The taxi fare is approximately `3` $........................... Australian.

The coach fare is `4` $ .... for adults and

`5` $ .... for children.

The Urban Transit Authority bus number `6` .... also goes to the city.

AIRPORT FACILITIES

`7` .... facilities are available outside the Customs Hall.

You can book `8` .... at the Travellers' Information Service.

Baggage lockers are `9` $........................... per locker per day or

`10` $........................... per locker for every day after that.

An outside `11` .... is also provided for $2 per day for each item.

OTHER INFORMATION

There is a `12` .... of $10 when you leave Sydney.

Focus on Listening 2

You are going to hear David B. Porter, one of the Customer Services Managers for the airline, Qantas, talking about letters of complaint and praise that the airline receives. *Before you listen*, look carefully at the notes below to see what information is required to complete them. *As you listen*, complete the notes by filling in the missing information.

1 When a complaint is received, the letter is acknowledged and then research and
.... take place.

2 From the Reservations Record System it is possible to find out .... a customer booked, and who the .... was who was involved in the booking.

3 If the airline was at fault, it will .... the fault and make restitution accordingly.

4 The airline may respond to complaints in one of the following three ways:
by .... the customer
by .... the customer
by .... the customer

5 The three main subjects which people complain about, according to Mr Porter, are:
...................., ..., ...

6 He gives an example of a problem which involved a businessman on a trip to South America whose .... did not arrive.

7 Letters of praise are taken very .... Copies are sent to the respective managements and the personnel concerned are .... The .... points go on the person's record.

Check: Phrasal verbs 1

Up = togetherness

In the text, we saw the expression *to line up*, to stand together in a queue. Here are some more verbs which combine with the adverb *up* with the same general meaning of coming together.

join team gang link pair meet

Complete each of the following sentences with one of the above verbs.

a We set off from Florence separately but .... up with the others by chance in Rome.

b I was unhappy because I felt everyone else in the class was .... up against me.

c The teacher asked each of us to .... up with another student.

d This computer can be .... up to other computers in the building.

e We .... up with a few other people to organise a waste paper collection.

f He stayed in the army for five years after .... up in 1950.

Focus on Grammar 2: Expressing the future

1

a There are a number of ways of expressing the future in English. One of these is the future simple tense. Look through the first few paragraphs of the text and underline any examples of the future simple that you find.

b Look at the possible uses of different future forms below and decide which one fits the examples you have underlined from the text.

Use	Form
1 Expressing a personal intention	. . . .
2 Expressing an opinion about the future	. . . .
3 Stating a future fact	. . . .
4 Making a prediction based on what you know or can see now	. . . .
5 Offering/promising/threatening to do something	. . . .
6 Talking about something you've arranged for the future	. . . .
7 Talking about a fixed future event (e.g. part of a timetable)	. . . .

c Look at the examples below and underline the verb forms in each. Match each sentence to one of the uses above and write the correct verb form in the space next to it.

1 They drive so fast round this bend that there's going to be an accident one of these days.
2 You don't get to Singapore till Friday, do you?
3 I'll see if I can get your car to start, if you like.
4 We're having some friends round for lunch on Sunday.
5 I'm going to try and arrange a skiing holiday this winter.
6 I doubt if the postman will come in this weather.

2 What do we call the verb form in this sentence from the text?

It seems certain that film producers will be lining up to buy the off-cuts.

This form is used: a) to talk about future actions which will not be complete (in the example above, it is suggested that a number of people will be involved over a period of time); and b) to talk about a future action in a neutral way, *without* the idea of personal intention in a statement, and without the idea of a request in a question.

e.g. I'll be seeing them at the weekend.
Will you be inviting Jim to your party?

For more information on this and other future forms, see the Grammar File (page 94).

3 Complete the following by putting the verbs in brackets into suitable verb forms and adding any other necessary words.

a A: Do you think Brazil (win) the World Cup this year?
   B: No, I don't think they . . . .
b A: Can you join us for dinner tonight?
   B: Thanks, but I (go) to the theatre with Andy.
c I (ring) you tonight at eight. Or you (have) dinner then?
d What time the plane (land)? I (meet) you at the airport, if you like.
e I've never seen him so angry; he looks as if he (explode)!
f It soon (be) illegal for back seat passengers not to wear seat belts.
g You (pass) the station on your way? If so, could you give me a lift?
h Have they decided what they (do) with their dog while they're on holiday?

Communication Activity: Faulty maps

"She said will passengers for somewhere I didn't catch go to gate number something or other."

In this activity, you and your partner will each have an incomplete plan of the Arrivals Hall at Hong Kong International Airport. Student A will have a plan with one half of the complete information, while Student B will have a plan with the other half of the information.

Do not show your plan to your partner. Work together to describe what you can each see in your plan and to find out what is missing. Mark any new information that your partner gives you in the correct place on your plan (there are about 11 missing points on each). Work as quickly as possible.

Student A should turn to the plan on page 214.
Student B should turn to the plan on page 216.

Focus on Writing 2: Instructions

Task	You have been asked to write a short feature in a popular English language magazine in your country. You are to give practical advice about travel in the form of eight 'rules'. One 'rule' should concern any documents that might be needed, for example. Write about 250 words in all.

Planning

| Packing |
| Money |
| Health |
| Hand Baggage |
| Insurance |
| Clothes for Travelling in |
| Choosing your Baggage |
| Guidebooks |
| Language |

1 Choose the seven other headings you want to write about from the nine listed on the left.

2 Decide on the order they should come in.

3 Make notes under each heading and check that no section will be too short or too long.

Notes

- Number each point and give it a heading.
- Give *dos* as well as *don'ts*, with reasons, where necessary.
- Include any personal tips of your own, and add a touch of humour if you wish.
- Refer to the information on writing instructions in the Writing File on page 121.

The following rule has been given to start you off. (You can put it in a different position in the list if you prefer.) Complete the other seven rules in the same way.

8
Rules
of
travel

1. Documents

Make sure you have a valid passport (or travel document) and any necessary visas for the countries you are visiting. If you need to apply for either, do so well in advance. Don't leave it until the last minute. Check that you've got your tickets and any other travel documents in a safe but reasonably accessible place for use during the journey.

English in Use 1: Cloze

Complete the following article from an airline magazine by writing the missing words in the spaces provided. Use *only one word* in each space.

UÇAĞIMIZA HOŞ GELDİNİZ
WELCOME ON BOARD

Taking (1) . . . . consideration the fact that you may be feeling a little nervous during the flight, we would like to remind you that flying today is the safest (2) . . . . of travel.

You may be disturbed by an unusual sound. The noise you hear immediately after take-off is the sound of the landing gear (3) . . . . pulled up as the plane lifts off and gets into flight position. While the plane is taking off it requires greater power than it (4) . . . . while cruising. In the same way, as it prepares to land, the reduced speed (5) . . . . . a change in the sound of the engines.

When the 'Fasten your seatbelts' and 'No smoking' signs light (6) . . . . a bell rings. This bell is also (7) . . . . when passengers ring for one of the cabin crew. During your flight, you may call the hostess by (8) . . . . the appropriate button.

CATERING SERVICE: On scheduled and charter flights special food is available for diabetics, vegetarians and others who, (9) . . . . reasons of health, religion or philosophy, are (10) . . . . to eat the regular meals. However, it is essential to inform Turkish Airlines (11) . . . . . this, well (12) . . . . advance, preferably when (13) . . . . your reservation.

We thank you for your trust (14) . . . . Turkish Airlines and wish you a pleasant flight. We look forward to (15) . . . . you again.

Reproduced by permission of Turkish Airlines Inc.

English in Use 2: Guided writing

You have been asked to write a series of brief profiles of people in particular jobs for an English language magazine. You have interviewed an Air Traffic Controller as the subject of the first profile and have made some notes.

You must use all the words in the same order as the notes. You may add words and change the form of words where necessary. Look carefully at the first sentence which has been done for you as an example.

a 12 years - Air Traffic Controller - Heathrow Airport.
b Began training - very tough - 17, and studied experienced controllers various airports.
c 3 ½ years gain basic Air Traffic Controller's licence - then specialised Aerodrome Control.
d Chose learn fly as well - understand pressures pilot.
e Works team ten - divided Visual Control and Approach Control.
f Wherever working - break every two hours - relieve concentration.
g If feel ill, another take over immediately.
h Retire 60 - Civil Aviation Policy all staff.
i Says life not full dramas - his job make sure don't happen.

Name: Roy Hendry
Age: 35
Married: no children
Occupation: Air Traffic Controller, Heathrow
Employer: Civil Aviation Authority
Lives: Bungalow in Crowthorne, Wokingham, Berkshire
Hobbies: Aerobatic flying, skiing, riding

Roy Hendry knows two important routes by heart. One is the M3 going north east from his home in Crowthorne to Heathrow Airport. The other starts on the tarmac at Heathrow Airport and stretches for about two miles, going up.

a *For twelve years, Roy has been an Air Traffic Controller at Heathrow Airport.*
b . . . .
c . . . .
d . . . .
e . . . .
f . . . .
g . . . .
h . . . .
i . . . .

Roy Hendry cannot imagine what a nine-to-five job would be like!

6 Language Matters

Lead-in

What do you know about the world's languages? Discuss these questions with another student.

1 Which language is spoken by most people as their first language or mother tongue?
2 Which language is the *official* language for most people?
3 How many languages are there in the world today?
  a 40   b 400   c 4,000
4 Two hundred years ago was the number of languages
  a more?   b the same?   c fewer?
5 The largest number of books translated from English into other languages are in the subject area of
  a Philosophy   b Applied Science   c Literature
6 Which author's work is most often translated into other languages?

Text 1

1 Find out if you were correct as quickly as possible by scanning the information in the text.

LANGUAGE - THE FACTS

Global talk

More people speak Chinese than any other language – though it is really a collection of eight different languages. The most widely spoken of these is Mandarin with about 700m speakers. English, however, is a more international tongue. It has official status in many countries where other languages are also spoken.[1]

MOTHER-TONGUE SPEAKERS

Below are the world's major languages ranked according to the number of people who have each as their first language – their mother tongue.

(millions)

1.	Chinese	1,000	11.	French	70
2.	English	350	12.	Punjabi	70
3.	Spanish	250	13.	Javanese	65
4.	Hindi	200	14.	Bihari	65
5.	Arabic	150	15.	Italian	60
6.	Bengali	150	16.	Korean	60
7.	Russian	150	17.	Telugu	55
8.	Portuguese	135	18.	Tamil	55
9.	Japanese	120	19.	Marathi	50
10.	German	100	20.	Vietnamese	50

FAMILY TIES

There are around 4,000 languages in the world today – 6,000 less than were spoken a couple of centuries ago. There were over 1,000 in the 'New World' before the colonists arrived – a number that has now dropped to around 400.[2]

Many languages clearly have a common source so it is possible to group languages into families of which the following[1] are the largest:

1. Indo-European *2,000m speakers*
Unlikely as it may seem, there are striking similarities between the major European languages and Sanskrit. These point to a common ancestor that probably originated in Eastern Europe 25 thousand years ago. The original 'proto' Indo-European language spread west and mutated into the present-day Romance languages like French and Spanish, and the Germanic, like English and German. As it moved south it took a wide variety of other forms from Kurdish to Hindi.

2. Sino-Tibetan *1,040m speakers*
The vast majority of the speakers of this group are in China but there are significant numbers of Chinese speakers throughout South-East Asia and even in the US.

3. Niger-Congo *260m speakers*
There are 1,000 or so languages in this group which are spoken in most of the southern half of Africa – below a line running roughly from Senegal to Kenya but excluding Namibia and South Africa. This includes Swahili which although the mother-tongue of only 4m people is probably used as a lingua franca by about 30m. Some of the other major languages include Rwanda (15m) and in West Africa Yoruba (17m) and Igbo (13m).

4. Afro-Asiatic *230m speakers*
Also known as the Hamito-Semitic group this is found across the northern half of Africa and in South-West Asia. The Semitic languages are the oldest, of which Arabic (150m) is the most significant and is the sacred language of Islam. Hebrew (4m) is the language of Israel – though the language spoken by Jesus Christ would have been Old Aramaic.

5. Austronesian *200m speakers*
Also known as Malayo-Polynesian, this is spoken over a vast area from Madagascar to Aotearoa(NZ) and includes at least 500 languages. They fall into two groups dividing on a line east and west of New Guinea.

MOST TRANSLATED AUTHORS

International reading tastes can be judged by seeing which authors are the most regularly translated.

	Author	Country	Translations	Translating countries
1.	V I Lenin†	USSR	321	12
2.	W Disney Productions	USA	274	10
3.	A Christie	UK	252	22
4.	J Verne	France	238	22
5.	B Cartland	UK	207	9
6.	H C Andersen	Denmark	159	21
7.	J Grimm	Germany	152	16
8.	E Blyton	UK	138	14
9.	K U Chernenko	USSR	122	8
10.	I Asimov	USA	108	12
11.	K Marx	Germany	103	16
12.	F Engels	Germany	96	10
13.	J London	USA	94	20
14.	W Shakespeare	UK	93	23
15.	A C Doyle	UK	91	18
16.	G Simenon	Belgium	90	16
17.	M Twain	USA	89	18
18.	C Dickens	UK	80	20
19.	F M Dostoevskij	USSR	78	16
20.	C Perrault	France	77	9

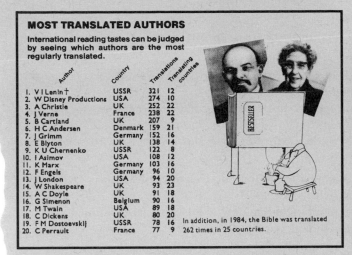

In addition, in 1984, the Bible was translated 262 times in 25 countries.

References

1 D Crystal, *The Cambridge Encyclopaedia of Language*, Cambridge University Press 1987. 2 Charles Berlitz, *Native tongues*, Panther 1983. 3 UNESCO, *Statistical Yearbook* 1990.

† Most translations from Russian take place into other languages used within the Soviet Union itself.

‡ This includes all languages from which translations were made. The next most popular source languages with the total number of translations were:
Latin (591); Arabic (536); Polish (477); Classical Greek (447); Dutch (416); Serbo-Croatian (405); Romanian (314); Norwegian (265); Bulgarian (265); Finnish (227).

TONGUE TO TONGUE

Translation from one language to another takes up a lot of intellectual energy. The figures below refer to the number of books translated in 1984, the latest year for which figures are available.[3]

The writing languages

Below are the languages most translated from, together with the subjects.

	Philosophy	Religion	Social Science	Pure Science	Applied Science	Arts	Literature	Hist/Geography	General	Total
1. English	1,301	1,116	1,545	1,184	2,548	956	12,826	1,024	224	22,724
2. Russian	119	55	2,180	769	424	229	1,996	434	24	6,230
3. French	401	351	421	133	408	328	2,925	411	44	5,422
4. German	347	318	413	200	537	346	1,737	378	35	4,311
5. Italian	88	171	106	75	129	181	637	146	11	1,544
6. Swedish	17	29	95	29	132	59	606	36	8	1,011
7. Spanish	33	81	69	7	35	42	521	46	5	839
8. Hungarian	8	9	110	65	109	126	170	53	29	679
9. Danish	34	7	28	25	47	20	457	28	5	651
10. Czech	14	–	96	68	151	50	224	27	5	635
TOTAL	2,676	3,169	6,212	2,787	4,940	2,608	26,454	3,114	445	52,405

The reading languages

Detailed below are the languages into which most translations went.

Original	English	French	Spanish	Russian	German	Italian	Japanese	Danish	Norwegian	Swedish
English	–	2,839	3,939	598	4,783	148	2,102	901	790	1,208
Russian	663	340	45	–	628	47	52	39	27	43
French	528	–	1,416	177	986	75	220	108	42	101
German	704	547	784	195	–	76	203	168	83	136
Italian	120	246	468	29	258	–	23	19	10	19
Swedish	102	35	28	9	165	2	5	194	178	–
Spanish	105	116	–	49	159	12	21	196	33	
Hungarian	246	41	17	73	171	5	2	0	2	2
Danish	69	28	90	17	112	0	6	–	58	127

Originally published in New Internationalist

OFFICIAL LANGUAGES

Listed here are the total populations of those countries where each language has official status – this will overestimate the number of speakers because only a relatively small number of Indians, for example, will actually speak English.

		(millions)
1.	English	1,400
2.	Chinese	1,000
3.	Hindi	700
4.	Spanish	280
5.	Russian	270
6.	French	220
7.	Arabic	170
8.	Portuguese	160
9.	Malay	160
10.	Bengali	150
11.	Japanese	120
12.	German	100
13.	Urdu	85
14.	Italian	60
15.	Korean	60
16.	Vietnamese	60
17.	Persian	50
18.	Tagalog	50
19.	Thai	50
20.	Turkish	50

2 **Now find answers to the following questions in the same way.**

a Which other language has the same number of first language speakers as French?

b How many major language groups are there?

c How many speakers of Afro-Asiatic languages are there?

d Which language are books in English most often translated *into*?

3 **These answers may take a little more finding, or thinking about!**

a How many people in the world have the language spoken in Brazil as their official language?

b How many Chinese languages are there?

c Where does the author of *Hamlet* come in the top 20 of most translated authors?

d In which subject were more books translated from Russian than English?

e Which language group does English belong to?

Text 2

More facts:

- The language with the largest vocabulary is English. It has 490,000 words plus another 300,000 technical terms.

- Educated English speakers use approximately 5,000 words in speech and up to 10,000 in written communication. Shakespeare used a vocabulary of 33,000 words.

- The largest English language dictionary in the world is the 20-volume *Oxford English Dictionary* which has a total of 21,728 pages.

1 **Discuss the following points:**

1 What are the advantages and disadvantages of

a a pocket-sized bilingual English dictionary?

b a large bilingual English dictionary?

c an English-English dictionary?

2 The 20-volume *New Grove Dictionary of Music and Musicians* is the world's largest specialist dictionary.

a How many different kinds of specialist dictionaries can you think of?

b Do you use a specialist dictionary of any kind?

c Would any specialist dictionary be useful for your future career?

3 Work on the Second Edition of the *Oxford English Dictionary* took 100 people 5 years to complete.

a How do people compile dictionaries? Where do examples of words come from?

b How can new technology help?

c What problems are there about including new words, popular colloquial expressions for example, in a dictionary?

Hurry, catch that word

Dictionary-making has come a long way since Dr Johnson had six Scottish clerks toiling away in his attic; the modern lexicographer uses computers, providing millions of words at the touch of a few keys, and employs a team of roving detectives to scour the countryside looking for new entries. Caroline St John-Brooks takes a look inside this competitive and secretive business

Dictionary-making, since computers took the drudgery out of it, has become fun. Hanks, the chief editor of Collins English dic-
5 tionaries, actually has his computer screen propped up on a facsimile copy of Johnson's dictionary, and plays with its keyboard enthusiastically.
10 He works from Birmingham University, leading an outfit which is rather off-puttingly known as Cobuild. It stands for the Collins and Birmingham University Inter-
15 national Language Database, and is housed in a handsome Edwardian mansion full of crumbling, leather-bound tomes in one of Birmingham's greener suburbs.
20 How do lexicographers find their words? Dr Johnson, whose citations were transcribed by six Scottish clerks working in the attic of his house, found most of them
25 from his own reading. Today, methods have changed. Cobuild has pioneered a huge electronic database, known as a "corpus",

containing 18m words — not, ot
30 course, all different. It includes complete novels, best-selling non-fiction titles, magazines and news-papers, transcripts of BBC programmes, casual conversations
35 and lectures. A particular word, together with its context, can be called up any time on the computer screen.

What's more, the team is build-
40 ing up a "monitoring corpus". Last year, it started inputting every issue of The Times, and the computer prints out new words on demand, giving the frequency with
45 which they appear.

We call up "greenhouse", from The Times database, and watch hundreds of references to the "greenhouse effect" fill the screen,
50 far outnumbering gardening references in relation to tomatoes and potplants.

But spoken language is important, too. A team of roving
55 word-detectives, based in Glasgow at Collins English Dictionary Unit, visits pubs and discos, hangs about in supermarkets and launderettes and listens to loud ladies on the
60 bus, in the race to pin down new words and meanings as soon as they are born. They scour shops for examples of new types of food and clothing. All finds are noted and go
65 straight into the computer.

The new dictionary's new words paint a picture of life in the late 1980s. Health hazards, environmental problems, computer jar-
70 gon, music argot, financial slang — it is all there.

Other words develop new meanings while retaining the old. "Dinosaur", for instance, now means "a
75 person or thing which is considered to be out of date," as well as its more familiar definition. One citation, in which Led Zeppelin are referred to as "dinosaurs of rock
80 and roll", was "overheard in Glasgow, 1988".

One of Hanks's favourite new words is "check it out" in the casual sense of "have a look at"
85 rather than "investigate" or "vet".

"We try to reflect English as it is really used today," says Hanks. "For instance, we identify the primary meaning of 'pylon' as 'a large
90 vertical steel tower-like structure supporting high-tension electrical cables'.

"In other dictionaries it appears first as an ancient Egyptian gate-
95 way.

Rosamund Moon, who has been working on the project for eight years, points out that deceptively simple words are often the most
100 complicated.

"Take 'take', for example. What is its core meaning? You may think it is something like 'to transport from place to place', but our moni-
105 toring shows us that this is not the most common use. It is much more often used in phrases such as 'take a look' or 'take a photograph'."

110 A key problem is which words to include. A new word could turn out to be ephemeral, no sooner frozen in print than disappeared from the street.

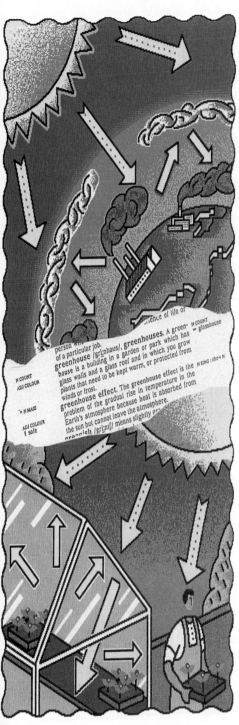

2 For the following questions, choose the answers which you think fit best.

1 From what we can tell, Dr Johnson
   A was an early dictionary maker
   B was a clerk in a Scottish office
   C works at Birmingham University
   D is a modern novelist

2 The writer thinks that the name Cobuild is
   A completely meaningless
   B difficult to pronounce
   C not very appealing
   D not quite accurate

3 A 'corpus' (line 28) is
   A a library of specialised books
   B a very advanced computer
   C a large collection of written material
   D a comprehensive dictionary

4 To 'input' (line 41) is a modern word which means to
   A save things to form a collection
   B analyse in great detail
   C feed information into a computer
   D check for mistakes

5 The interesting thing about the word 'greenhouse' (line 46) is that
   A it has recently changed its meaning completely
   B most people use the word wrongly
   C most people don't know what it means
   D its new meaning is more common than its original meaning

6 Examples of new spoken language are collected
   A at meetings held in Glasgow
   B in everyday social situations
   C by specially trained police officers
   D by ordinary housewives

7 The word 'dinosaur' (lines 73/74)
   A was first used by Led Zeppelin
   B originated in Scotland
   C is mainly used by journalists
   D has developed a new meaning

8 In some other dictionaries, the word 'pylon' (line 89)
   A is not explained
   B is only given one meaning
   C is given a very complicated explanation
   D is given the old meaning before the new one

9 The problem with new words is that
   A they tend to go out of fashion quickly
   B no-one agrees about what they really mean
   C there are too many to include
   D they tend to be slang

10 The article concerns the way that
   A dictionary makers record the spoken language
   B methods of dictionary making have changed
   C dictionaries used to be written
   D dictionaries are advertised and sold

STUDY BOX

1: no sooner ... than ..., hardly/ scarcely ... when ...

These expressions are used to mean that one action is followed very quickly by a second action. Look at these examples (the first is from Text 2 in this unit).

No sooner frozen in print *than* disappeared from the street.
I had *no sooner* paid one bill *than* another arrived!

We had *hardly* sat down *when* the doorbell rang.
They had *scarcely* set off *when* they had a puncture.

They are among a group of negative expressions which are sometimes followed by inverted word order for dramatic effect (see Grammar File, page 97). For example:
No sooner *had* I *paid* one bill than another arrived!

Vocabulary

The following words (A - F) are taken from the text. Look at the various definitions for each one that you would find in the dictionary and choose the definition which fits the context best. Then check your answers with another student.

A *outfit (line 11)*

outfit /ˈaʊtfɪt/ outfits. An outfit is   N Count
1. a set of clothes, especially one that you wear   = ensemble
for a special occasion.
2. a group of people who work together; a fairly   = team
informal use.
3. all the equipment that you need in order to   = kit
do a particular job.

B *citations (lines 21/22)*

citation /saɪˈteɪʃən/ citations; a rather formal   N Count
word. A citation is
1. an official document or speech which praises a   = commendation
person for having done something brave or special.
2. a summons to appear before a court of law; a
legal term.
3. a quotation from a book or other piece or writing.

C *roving (line 54)*

rove /rəʊv/ roves, roving, roved; a literary word.   V + OBJ or
1. If you rove around an area, or rove an area, you go   V + *around*
all around without going in any particular direction.   = wander
2. If your eyes rove around a place, you look   = scan
around there to see what you can find interesting.

D *scour (line 62)*

scour /skaʊə/ scours, scouring, scoured   V + OBJ
1. If you scour an area, book, etc. you make a   = search
thorough search of it because you are looking
for someone or something.
2. To scour a floor, pan, etc. means to clean its   = scrub
surface by rubbing it hard with something rough.

E *vet (line 85)*

vet /vet/ vets, vetting, vetted;
1. A vet is someone who is specially trained to   N Count
look after the health of animals.   = veterinary
                                                        surgeon
2. If you vet something, you check it carefully   V + OBJ
to make sure that it is acceptable.   = appraise

F *core (line 102)*

core /kɔː/ cores, coring, cored.   N Count
1. The core of a fruit is the hard central part   = centre
which contains seeds or pips.
2. When you core a fruit, you remove its core.   V + OBJ
3. The core of an object or place is its central   N Count
part.   = centre, heart
4. A core is also a group of people or things·   N Sing
that is always part of something, although the
other parts may change.
5. The core of something such as a problem or a   N Sing
proposal is its most essential part; a formal   = essence, heart
use.

Check: Phrasal verbs 2

A number of phrasal verbs are used in the text. To see if you remember them, complete the sentences below. Use a verb and particle from the following lists in each sentence. Make any changes necessary.

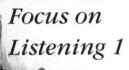

Verbs	Particles	Verbs	Particles
turn	about	check	up
prop	out	point	off
print	up	put	out
hang	out	call	out

a He was lying on the bed with his head . . . . on a pillow.

b I wouldn't have noticed the mistake if you hadn't . . . . it . . . .

c We're just waiting for the computer to . . . . a copy of the latest sales figures.

d Why don't we . . . . that new Indian restaurant in town?

e We used to spend our time . . . . at the Stage Door of the theatre, hoping to meet a star.

f He was able to . . . . the information he needed on the computer screen.

g I was going to go for a walk but the rain . . . . me . . . . the idea.

h This telephone answering machine has . . . . to be a most useful piece of equipment.

Check with the correct verbs in the Phrasal Verbs Reminder on page 66.

Focus on Listening 1

Six people were asked the following question: 'If you had the opportunity to learn a language that you had never studied before, which language would you choose?'

1 Listen to extracts from the six answers they gave and guess what languages they chose. Select your answers from the list below.

French Japanese Irish Arabic Portuguese Russian Spanish Chinese Greek

1 . . . .   3 . . . .   5 . . . .

2 . . . .   4 . . . .   6 . . . .

Discuss your answers and the reasons for them with another student.

2 You will now hear the recording again. Listen to the reason each person gives for choosing their particular language and match the reasons below with the correct extract number (1 - 6).

Reason	Extract
a to help their career	
b because it would be a challenge	
c because of curiosity about a country	
d for tourism	
e to understand the culture of a country	
f because the language is attractive	

Compare your answers with another student and discuss what you can remember about what the speakers actually said.

Focus on Listening 2: *Teach yourself Japanese*

You are going to hear a New Zealander talking about how he would go about learning Japanese.

1 Listen to what he says and be prepared to explain the main things he would do.

2 *Before you listen a second time*, read through the questions below and see if you can answer any of them. Discuss your answers with another student. *As you listen*, write short answers to the questions. You don't need to answer in the same words as the recording - you can use your own words.

a What aspect of Japanese would Brent *not* try to learn?..

b What would he concentrate on instead?...

c What two areas of language does he say he'd try to learn, in order to hold a

conversation?...

d Who does he think could help him to learn technical language?...............................

....

e What technique for learning does he think is important?...

....

f He has learnt some basic Japanese phrases already. Who from?...............................

....

g What kind of book would he definitely buy?...

h What advantage of one-to-one (private) lessons does he mention?...........................

....

i What advantage of learning in a class does he mention?..

....

j Which aspect of language does he think is most important? ....

....

Communication Activity

1 Read through the advertisement below and find answers to the following questions.

a What is being advertised?

b What can you achieve in three months, according to the advertisement?

c How long will you need to spend each day?

d What are the advantages of the system, according to the advertisement?

e What will happen if you fill in and send off the coupon?

f What special offer does the company make?

2 Choose a language that you would like to learn - it must be one that you have no knowledge of at present - and tick the box.

Work with another student. (First make sure they haven't chosen the same language as you.)

You think it would be a good idea to do the course with someone else. You could have extra speaking practice and it would also be more fun to work together, so try to persuade your partner to learn *your* chosen language with you. Think of good reasons for learning your language.

Focus on Writing: Informal letter

Task	Some English friends, John and Lesley Rippon, have written to you for advice. Their 20-year-old daughter, Gill, wants to get a job teaching English in your country. She's doing a teaching course at the moment, but she would like to learn something of the language before she comes. Apparently she's bought a 'Teach Yourself' book on your language, but they want to know if you have any other suggestions which would help her. It's quite some time since Gill studied a language at school so she would also be grateful for some general tips on learning a language.
	Write a letter to the Rippons giving advice and any helpful suggestions that you can. Write about 250 words excluding the address.

Preparation

Work with another student - one who speaks your language if possible.

1 Write down any general points about your language that you can think of. What are the things Gill will find most different from English and most difficult (pronunciation/writing system/tense system etc.)? Are there any things she should find quite easy? What will be the advantages of being able to speak a bit of the language when she arrives?

2 Make a list of things Gill could do to learn your language, e.g. go to evening classes (are they likely to be available?), do a language course in your country first, buy a cassette course etc. Think about pros and cons such as cost versus effectiveness. Decide which method is most realistic.

3 Write down any other things you can think of which could be helpful to her, e.g. reading simple books or magazines in your language (you could send her some), tuning into radio broadcasts, etc.

4 Write down any general tips on learning a language that you think would be helpful. Use your own experience as far as possible.

Planning

Working individually, make a plan for your letter. Decide on the ideas that you want to include and think about the best way to organise them. Jot down the main points for each section, the introduction, paragraph 1, paragraph 2 etc., and decide how to conclude the letter.

Note: Don't forget to start and finish appropriately for an informal letter. (See Writing File page 109.)

Focus on Grammar: Comparisons 1

1 There are several ways of comparing things in English. Underline the expressions of comparison in these extracts from texts in this unit.

a More people speak Chinese than any other language.
b The pronunciation would be the hardest part.
c You may think it is something like 'to transport from place to place'.
d ... the race to pin down new words and meanings as soon as they are born.

2 Comparatives and superlatives

a Comparatives of adjectives are formed with *-er* or with *more*. Superlatives are formed with *-est* or with *most*. Comparatives and superlatives of adverbs are normally formed with *more* and *most*, though there are some exceptions.

The rules are explained and the exceptions are listed in the Grammar File on page 92. Do the following exercise to test yourself. Then check the Grammar File if necessary.

b Complete the following sentences with suitable comparatives or

superlatives formed from the words in brackets. The sentences are based on information from the texts in this unit.

1 The (*widely*) spoken Chinese language is Mandarin, with 700m speakers.
2 English is a (*international*) tongue than Mandarin.
3 The Semitic languages are (*old*) of the Afro-Asiatic group.
4 Arabic is (*significant*) of the Semitic languages.
5 The table shows that Lenin was (*regularly*) translated author in the world in 1984.
6 Simple words like 'take' are often (*complicated*) to explain.
7 There are (*common*) uses of the word 'take' than 'transport from place to place'.
8 It is much (*often*) used in phrases like 'take a look'.
9 Japanese would probably be (*useful*) language of all for me to learn.
10 (*tricky*) thing would be to decide how to go about learning it.
11 Tourists seem to travel (*far*) and (*far*) these days.
12 Making a pronunciation mistake can be (*bad*) than making a grammatical mistake in Chinese.

3 As ... as ...

a Another way of comparing things is to use *as* (adjective/adverb) *as ...* The negative form is *not as ... as ...* or *not so ... as ...*

The structure can also be used with *much/many* , and words like *just, almost* and *nearly* can be used to qualify the comparison. See Grammar File pages 92 and 93 for details.

He was as busy as me   He's not as talented as his brother (is).
He was as busy as I was   It wasn't so hard as I thought.
Be there as early as you can. I haven't had so much mail as usual.

b *Work in pairs*. Make true sentences using *(not) as ... as ...* . Compare each pair in column A according to the topic in column B.

	A	B
a	You/a member of your family	1 tidiness
b	Two animals	2 lifespan
c	Your language/English	3 the sound of the language
d	Two sports/hobbies you've tried	4 enjoyment
e	Present/past	5 your appearance
f	Two newspapers in your country	6 international news
g	Two subjects at school	7 your performance
h	Reality/your expectations	8 a test/exam you've taken

c Complete the following common comparisons by choosing the correct words from the list below, using the information given to help you.

1 as quick as a . . . .   4 as blind as a . . . .
2 as light as a . . . .   5 as snug as a . . . . in a rug
3 as busy as a . . . .   6 as dead as a . . . .

bee: the population of a hive have to fly 80,000 km and visit four million flowers to make just half a kilo of honey.

bug: (an insect) There are up to 65,000 tiny insects called dust mites in every square metre of carpet.

flash: the fastest lightning travels at 140,000 km a second.

dodo: a bird which became extinct in the 17th century.

bat: bats use 'echo-location' to navigate and find food, though they can, in fact, see!

feather: a duck feather weighs 1.4 grams.

d Match each adjective in the list below with one of the animals illustrated.

as   brave   as a ...
       cunning
       fit
       free
       proud
       slippery
       strong
       stubborn
       weak
       wise

STUDY BOX

2: like v. as; alike

Like **is a preposition and is used before a noun or pronoun:**
Stop behaving *like* a child.

As **is a conjunction and introduces a clause:**
Do exactly *as* I say.
He got the job, *as* I thought he would.

Note: In American English, and sometimes in informal spoken British English, *like* **can be used before a clause e.g.**
Let's do it, *like* we agreed.

Alike **can be an adjective or an adverb. It is used:**
after a verb. The twins are so *alike* it's hard to tell them apart. (adj)
                 All the students were treated *alike*. (adv)

after a noun: The new tax laws will affect rich and poor *alike*. (adv)

English in Use 1: Editing skills

There is one word missing from every line of the following text. Read the text and mark the place where each word is missing with a line (/). Write the missing word in the space provided at the end of the line. The first line has been corrected as an example.

Apostrophitis

Punctuation is / politeness of printers. Punctuation marks   1...*the*...
are navigational aids, not scientific moral laws. But bad   2 ....
punctuation make a mess of your meaning. We are in a state   3 ....
of confusion about most insignificant of punctuation marks,   4 ....
the apostrophe. You cannot walk your local high street   5 ....
without seeing signs urging you 'ask one of our assistant's   6 ....
for advice', and not to 'take pram's inside'.

What is be done? I suppose we can help ourselves by   7 ....
remembering the origin of the apostrophe. It comes the   8 ....
Greek word apostrophos, means turning away; that is, it   9 ....
is the sign of omission. The apostrophe introduced to mark   10 ....
the possessive case in genitives where an 'e' originally   11 ....
been left out, as in fox's, James's. The genitives used be   12 ....
written foxes and Jameses. It was gradually extended all   13 ....
possessives, even where an 'e' had not previously written,   14 ....
as in man's, children's. This was not yet established 1725.   15 ....
But it is established and a lot of trouble it causes.   16 ....

Reproduced by permission of Philip Howard.

English in Use 2: Editing skills

1 **Skim the ten newspaper articles below to find out what the main topic is in each case. Answer the following questions by writing in the correct letters.**

1 Which three articles describe sporting events? . . . . . Can you say which sports are described?

2 Which article is an announcement from the Births, Deaths and Marriages section? . . . . .

3 Which article concerns a journey by air? . . . . .

4 Which article concerns a journey by sea? . . . . . What was the problem?

5 Which two articles concern politicians or political events? . . . . .

6 Which article concerns industry? . . . . . Which industry in particular?

7 Which article describes a charity appeal? . . . . . What is the money to be spent on?

A   Enkalon is to get £1,500,000 via the Northern Ireland Office to keep the textiles and carpet yarn factory open for another seven moths.
The Daily Telegraph

B   During the month of May, Henekey's steak bar will be supporting the Mayor's appeal for £45,000 towards an Emisonic Scanner for Windsor's King Edward VII Hospital
For every customer who dies in the bar during the month, 20p will be donated towards the fund.
Staines Informer

C   While sympathising with the miners and arguing the British government could have acted to end the strike, Jessica Larive-Groenendaal (Neth) said she and her Liberal colleagues could not support a strike called without a ballet.
European Parliament News

D   Perhaps the only disappointment of the championships from the British point of view was the defeat of Ade Mafe in the 200 metres at the hands of that good American sprinter Mel Lattany. It was in this Cosford stadium this time last year that Ade first hit the headlines by eating Lattany but yesterday he was not mentally tuned for another big race so soon after his silver medal performance in the world indoor games in Paris last weekend.
The Observer

E   Five thugs last night pulled the British passenger ship Capetown Castle clear of the sandbank on which she went aground at Flushing early yesterday.

F   Greg Norman, hot favourite for the Card Classic at Royal Porthcawl, missed a five-inch putt on the 11th green yesterday.
The blind Australian tried to tap in the tiddler one-handed but hit the ground with his putter and only just moved the ball.
Sporting Life

G   Lord Snowdon greeted Princess Margaret as she flew into Heathrow today with a welcoming hiss.
Evening Mail

H   United goalkeeper, Stepney, went full length to save from Hector and then, in the 18th minute, saved an almost certain goal when he bravely died at the feet of Davies.
The Gloucester Citizen

I   Greenwold, Florence May - Late of 163 Gerghold Road, Colchester. A simple, kind, and loving old lady who died with great dignity at 'Ambleside', Wood Lane, Fordham Heath, Colchester on Saturday, April 3, 1982, at 3.10 pm. Loved by her family and friends who knew her will.
Essex County Standard

J   What Mrs Thatcher's closest friends are wondering is whether as the signs suggest, she is beginning to suffer from metal fatigue.
The Guardian

Reproduced from an Advertisment from Epson (UK) Limited

2 You the Editor!

Each of the articles above contains one word which has been wrongly spelt with an unintentionally humorous result. *Scan* each article to find and underline the incorrect word, then write the correct version next to the article.

Phrasal Verbs Reminder

call up	instruct a computer to present information to you
check out	find out if something is suitable for a purpose
hang about	stay in the same place doing nothing, often waiting
point out	make somebody notice something
print out	reproduce on paper (using a computer or printing machine)
prop up	support something by putting something else underneath
put off	discourage someone from something
turn out	prove to be, be in the end

Language Focus 4: Vocabulary

What does *light* mean? How many meanings can you think of?

What is there to know about a word?

1 Meaning

a What *group of words* does this one fit into? For example, we can say *'light* blue'. What other adjectives can we use in front of colours?

b Does the word suggest a particular *positive* or *negative* attitude , or is it *neutral* in meaning? (connotation). How is *lightweight* used in these examples?

A *lightweight* suit; A *lightweight* intellectual

c Does the word occur in any *metaphors* or *idioms*? *Light-* can be combined with *three* of the following participles to make compound adjectives. Which are they and what do the adjectives mean?*

fingered	*faced*	*bodied*
handed	*headed*	*hearted*

2 Grammar

a What *part of speech* is it?

Some bicycles had no rear *lights*.
The fire took a long time to *light*.
You're standing in my *light*!
She was only wearing a *light* jacket.

b What are the *parts of the verb*?

to light, ... , ...

c Is the verb *transitive* or *intransitive*? Does any special pattern follow? Is the phrasal verb *separable* or *inseparable*?

light up. Can we say both 'Fireworks *lit up* the sky' and 'Fireworks *lit* the sky *up*'?

3 Use

a How *formal/informal* is the word or expression? (register/style)

Have you got a *light*?
In the *light* of recent experience, ...
As soon as I got into bed I went out like a *light*.

b What other words can it *combine with* (collocation)? Which of the words below can we use the adjective *light* with?*

colour	*headache*	*work*	*sound*	*meal*
cigarette	*sleep*	*wind*	*coffee*	*price*

c Is there a word which means the same (a synonym)? And one which means the opposite (an antonym)? Think of synonyms and antonyms for *light* in the examples from b above.

* You can find the answers to these questions at the bottom of this page and on the next page.

4 Word Formation

a What *other words* can be made from *light* (derivations)?

- What verb means 'to make something lighter'?*
- What is the difference between *lighting*, *lightning* and *lightening*?*
- What prefix can you add to the participle *lit* to make an adjective to describe a street with no lights, for example?

b How do you *spell* it?

Which of the following should be written a) as one word, b) with a hyphen, or c) as two words?*

light/bulb	*light/house*	*light/industry*	*light/year*

c How do you *pronounce* it? Which of these words have the same vowel sound as light / laɪt /?

trial	*height*	*straight*	*bite*	*buy*
weight	*fly*	*sieve*	*quiet*	

Now check your answers to the questions marked * above.

...ony ....ligh.. .....ern weapons. ...
EG ...a light railway eng..... ...ligh.. ...ern weapons.
18 Soil that is **light** is easy to dig, because it has a ADJ QUALIT = friable
loose texture and is not sticky or solid.
19 Light colours are very pale. EG *He was wearing a* ADJ QUALIT
*light blue shirt... Her skin is lighter than the rest of
her family.*
20 Light winds and breezes blow gently. EG *A light* ADJ QUALIT ⇑ gentle
breeze got up.
21 A **light** sleep is one that is easily disturbed and in ADJ QUALIT : ATTRIB = shallow
which you are often aware of the things around you.
▶ used to describe people who sleep lightly. EG
Actually, I'm a very light sleeper. ◊ **lightly.** EG   ◊ ADV WITH VB
...lightly dozing in front of the fire.
22 A **light** sound is one that is not loud. EG *A light rap* ADJ QUALIT
sounded at the door. ◊ **lightly.** EG *She tapped lightly* ◊ ADV WITH VB
at the door.
23 A **light** meal is small in quantity. EG *...a light lunch.* ADJ QUALIT
◊ **lightly.** EG *After lunching lightly at Queenie's he* ◊ ADV WITH VB
slipped into the National Gallery.
24 If food is described as **light**, **24.1** it contains a lot of ADJ QUALIT
air. EG *Your cakes are always so wonderfully light.*
24.2 it has a delicate flavour and is easy to digest. EG ADJ QUALIT
She had made a very light tomato soup.
25 Light work does not involve much physical effort. ADJ QUALIT
EG *The children help with light housework.*
26 Movements and actions that are **light** are grace- ADJ QUALIT
ful or gentle and are done with very little force or

country.

light bulb, light bulbs; a' 'o spelled with a hyphen N COUNT
and as one word. A **light bulb** is the round glass part
of an electric light or lamp from which light shines
when the lamp or light is switched on.

lighten /laɪtə°n/, **lightens, lightening, light-**
ened. 1 When something **lightens** or when you   V-ERG
lighten it, it becomes brighter or less dark in colour.
EG *After the rain stops, the sky lightens a little...*
Constant exposure to the sun had lightened my hair.

2 If you **lighten** something such as a load or burden,   v+o
you make it lighter by removing some of it. EG *By*   ⇑ ease
doing this you are lightening the load of hospital   = alleviate
doctors.

3 If someone's face or expression **lightens**, it be-   v
comes more cheerful, happy, and relaxed. EG *Her*   = lift
whole expression lightened.

4 If you **lighten** an object, you make it less heavy. EG   v+o
Almost immediately they began to lighten their
products in an effort to increase sales.

lighter /laɪtə/, **lighters.** 1 **Lighter** is the comparative of **light.**

2 A **lighter** is a small device that produces a flame   N COUNT
which you can use to light cigarettes, cigars, pipes,   = cigarette
etc. EG *Can I just use your lighter? I've run out of*   lighter
matches. ● See also **fire lighter.**

light-year, light-years. 1 A **light-year** is the   N COUNT
distance that light travels in a year; a technical term
in astronomy. . . .

matches. ● See also **fire lighter.**

light-fingered. Someone who is **light-fingered**   ADJ CLASSIF
steals things, for example out of people's pockets; a
rather old-fashioned word.

light-headed. If you are **light-headed**, you feel   ADJ QUALIT
rather dizzy and faint, for example because you are   ⇑ unwell
ill or because you have drunk too much alcohol. EG *I*   = giddy
was light-headed; I had not slept and I was very
hungry.

light-hearted. 1 Someone who is **light-hearted** is   ADJ QUALIT
cheerful and happy. EG *He was in a light-hearted*   = carefree
mood. ◊ **light-heartedly.** EG *She flirted with them*   ◊ ADV WITH VB
light-heartedly and enjoyed herself enormously.   = gaily

2 Something that is **light-hearted** is entertaining or   ADJ QUALIT
amusing, and not at all serious. EG *Let me finish with*
a slightly more light-hearted question... ...a light-
hearted remark.

lighthouse /laɪthaʊs/, **lighthouses.** A lighthouse   N COUNT
is a tower containing a powerful flashing lamp that is
built on the coast or on a small island or rock in the
sea. Lighthouses are used to guide ships or to warn
them of danger. EG *She walked down the quay*
towards the lighthouse.

light industry, light industries. Light industry   N COUNT/
is industry in which only small items are made, for   UNCOUNT
example household goods and clothes, and in which
large heavy machinery is not used.

lighting /laɪtɪŋ/. 1 The **lighting** in a place is the   N UNCOUNT
way that it is lit, for example by electric lights, by   ⇑ system
candles, by windows, etc, or the quality of the light in
it. EG *They walked along the corridor, with its*
artificial lighting, towards the department office...
...poorly designed street lighting... The lighting was
restful.

2 The **lighting** in a film or play is the arrangement of   N UNCOUNT
electric lights that are used to light the film or play.

lightning /laɪtnɪŋ/. 1 **Lightning** is the very bright   N UNCOUNT
flashes of light in the sky that happen during
thunderstorms. EG *...a flash of lightning... He was*
struck by lightning, and nearly died. ● See also
forked lightning, sheet lightning.

2 **Lightning** describes things that happen very quick-   ADJ CLASSIF:
ly or last for only a short time. EG *Terry and I*   ATTRIB
exchanged lightning sidelong glances... He drew his
gun with lightning speed.

lightning conductor. light-'

Learning Focus 4: Developing editing skills

1

When do you edit?

One of the most important stages of writing is the
polishing stage. This is when you look through
what you've written, with a critical eye, so that you
can correct any mistakes you see and make any
other changes which you think would improve
your work.

Why edit?

It's not always easy to spot mistakes, especially if
you are thinking about meaning rather than
grammar. But careless mistakes will give the
reader a bad impression and may cost you marks in
an exam, so it's worth working to improve your
editing skills.

Improving your editing

There are several things you can do to help
yourself. In the first place, there are probably a few
mistakes which you make frequently in your
written work. It could be omitting particular
prepositions, or mis-spelling certain words, or
forgetting to use paragraphs, for example. Make a
note of them and check these points first when
you're reading through your work. Eliminate the
predictable problems first!

After that, check your work systematically. What
you look at will depend on the type of writing, but
here are some suggestions:

Agreement	- Do all the verbs agree with their subjects?
Time	- Is your use of tenses correct for the context?
	- Is your use of tenses consistent (or do you sometimes slip from past into present in a narrative, for example)?
Articles	- Are definite and indefinite articles used correctly?
Linking	- Have you overused *and* and *but*? Could you make more use of words and expressions like *while/ whereas, despite, as a result,* and so on, to link ideas?
Capitals	- Have you used capital letters where necessary? (See Grammar File page 104.)
Layout	- Have you used the correct layout for the document (e.g. formal letter)? Have you used paragraphs appropriately?

2 You have already had some practice editing other people's writing in several exercises in the English in Use sections. The examples below, which all come from real life, contain a variety of types of mistakes. Use your knowledge and experience to identify and correct them.

A Wrong word!

1 Lady Di arrived alone at the restaurant at 9 o'clock. She wore a nice red night-dress and showed a good suntan.

2 Sydney Opera House: "One of the most beautiful examples of modern agriculture in the world."

3 Applicants for this post should write enclosing a detailed post mortem.

(Language students' work, Australia)

4 Doner Kebap: Pieces of lamb packed tightly round a revolting spit.

('What to eat?' section in a Turkish city guide)

B Unintended meaning!

1 If this is your first visit to the USSR, you are welcome to it.

(Hotel notice, Moscow)

2

(Nassau newspaper)

C Various mistakes

1

PRATICAL ADVICES FOR THE CLEANNESS
To wash your pots, do never use steel wool or abrasive products because you would damage the best bright finish which allows you an easy and quick cleanness also in the dishwater. On the contrary you will use a normal sponge with a liquid detersive or a specify produc for steel's cleanness. The eventual pots left by the food will disappear easily polishing them with few drops of juice vinegar or lemon. After the rinsing in the hot water, your pots will shine again.

2   Check-out: 12.00 noon.

The Management asks you to place valuables in the safety deposit boxes, available free of charge at the chasier's desk. Otherwise we are sorry but can not take any responsibility for losses or damages in your valuables in the hotel. Please contact the Concierge for theatre tickets, table reservation, newspapers and for taxi as well. After arrival please take over your luggage in your room from the bellboys personally and upon departure always give it to them or leave them in your room.

(Hotel brochure, Vienna)

3

BEKRİ BAR OF ETAP İZMİR HOTEL

A warm, dim, comfortable and the music played by a Spanish guitar embraced us as we entered the Bekri Bar of Etap İzmir Hotel.

You may listen to a highly qualified music performed by a guitarist every day- exept Sundays- begining from 6.00 p.m. extending to late night hours.

Of course Mr. Isıklar prepares a sweet coctail to us named "Mr. Bekri". We learn that this coctail, which we found to be very delighful, is a specialty carrying the name of the bar.

3 Underline the mistakes you find in the student's composition below, and then discuss with a partner the best way to correct them.

The Australian   No. 7

The Australian are different from the Japanese. It has both advantages and disadvantages. First, I remark advantages of the Australian.

When I lived in Japan, I was tired from my work every day because many Japanese companies compel us to work for many hours. But in Australia, almost companies finish work at 5 o'clock and take two days holidays per week. Usually, there is no rush hour such as Japanese I think that the Australian treasure each individual life and it is very important for human beings.

Next, I remark disadvantages of the Australian. If I want to go shopping, I must go a store till at 5 o'clock. It is very inconvenient and it is the reason why there is no development of the Australian economy. I think that indivisualism is very important in Australia, so the Australian society is slow.

Finally, I remarked advantages and disadvantages of the Australian, but both have common ground that the Australian is indivisualist. I understand that advantages and disadvantages usually have a common factor, and it is easy to grasp a characteristic.

7

The Ages of Man

Lead-in

1 Look at the eight photographs below. How old would you say each person is? (Each represents a different decade.) Find out what other students think too.

A

C

E

G

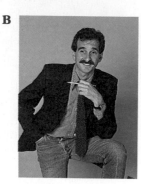

B

D

F

H

Did you find that any of your guesses were very different from those of other students? If so, which ones?

2 On the whole, we seem to be able to assess age very accurately, even from a poor photograph. How do we do it? *Discuss with a partner* the factors that we take into account. (It may help to compare one or two of the photographs again.)

3 What changes does the process of ageing bring about? Consider the *whole* body. *With a partner*, make a list of the various effects in the following areas:

skin   senses   posture   balance   body   shape   appetite   hair etc.

4

a What can we do to disguise the effects of ageing? Discuss with your partner.

b Do you think we should try to disguise the ageing process? Why/why not?

Text: Part 1

1 From the title of the text, what would you expect to find mentioned in it? What *are* the secrets of a long and healthy life? *Work with a partner* to make a list.

2 Now read Part 1 of the text in order to see how many of your ideas are mentioned.

Secrets of the oldest man in the world

● On Saturday, Shigechiyo Izumi (right) will be 120 years old, the highest human age ever authenticated. But Izumi is only the most spectacular illustration of a trend that has now made the Japanese the longest living people in the world. What is the secret? To find out, OLIVER GILLIE, Medical Correspondent, visited Izumi at his remote coral island home, Tokunoshima, which hangs off the tip of Southern Japan.

SHIGECHIYO Izumi walked forward to greet us. He was bent almost double, with watery eyes, wispy white beard 5 and deeply wrinkled skin.

His mind is still vigorous. Talking in the local dialect through interpreters, he could remember both his childhood 10 more than 100 years ago and the people he had met the day before. Most important, he still enjoys life which, he said, has never ceased to be a 15 pleasure.

His eyesight is still functional although one eye was damaged by a flying chip of wood when he was in his 60s. 20 He also hears well although it is necessary to speak loudly and distinctly. Since his 80s he has had no teeth. He obtained a denture 30 years ago but has 25 never used it.

In Izumi's lifetime, Japan has changed from a traditional agricultural economy to one of the world's leading industrial 30 countries. But life on Tokunoshima has changed little. Izumi, who has always worked as a small farmer, says the monotonous 35 life is good.

His day generally begins with a walk round the garden.

As recommended by the Buddhist sages, he contem-40 plates nature as he walks. But he is practical too: if he sees a weed, he roots it out.

In the past six years Izumi's heart has weakened. But he 45 has little cholesterol or fats in his blood and no signs of atherosclerosis, the condition that causes heart disease in Western people.

50 Izumi's doctor for the past 30 years, Yoshinobu Moriya, says: "He has difficulty in breathing, and swelling of his legs. This is because his heart 55 is aging and is no longer pumping well.

However, Izumi has had few serious illnesses. In 1982 he had a bad bout of 60 pneumonia but rapidly got better with antibiotics and oxygen. "An old man like this is very responsive to drugs," says Dr Moriya.

65 Izumi smoked three or four cigarettes a day until he was 116 when he gave it up on doctor's advice. Until he was 70 he drank very little. Then 70 he developed a taste for *shochu*, a type of white rum made from sugar cane, which contains 40% alcohol. Each evening he drinks a third of a

75 pint, always diluted, six or seven parts of warm water to one part spirit.

The local *shochu* manufacturers have launched a special 80 brand of Longevity Liquor bearing Izumi's portrait. But Dr Moriya says: "Izumi's kidneys are not strong. I have advised him to stop drinking. 85 I don't think *shochu* provides a recipe for long life."

Izumi, however, says: "Without *shochu* there would be no pleasure in life. I would 90 rather die than give up drinking." And he presses more of the drink on his visitors with a smile.

WHY HAS Izumi lived so 95 long? Clearly his zest for life has helped. But his physical fitness as a young man and his diet throughout life are probably the key.

100 As a young man Izumi was very fit. He was a local champion in sumo wrestling. But he did not have to train specially. His fitness came 105 through hard work on the farm and tasks such as carrying potatoes to market on his back. Such hard exercise is now known to be very 110 effective in lowering harmful types of cholesterol in the blood.

And population studies have shown that sedentary people 115 have an increased mortality from heart disease. Exercise

helps to retard aging processes.

As for diet, for most of his 120 life Izumi has lived on vegetables from his farm – potatoes, sweet potatoes, beans, tomato, aubergine, cucumber, carrots, spinach 125 and cabbage.

Izumi ate meat only on festival days. There was, anyway, little meat to be had on his island and his simple, 130 largely vegetarian diet, changed little during his first 100 years.

BUT Izumi's age is only the spectacular peak of a trend towards longevity in Japan. 135 The life expectancy of the Japanese has risen by eight years since 1960. It is now the highest in the world: 74 for men, 80 for women. This 140 compares with UK figures of 71 for men and 77 for women. The Japanese now live longer on average than people in Sweden, Canada, Iceland and 145 France, which formerly led the world in longevity.

The reason for Japan's improvement is almost certainly a low incidence of 150 coronary heart disease. Some 27% of people in Britain die of coronary heart disease compared with only 6.7% of people in Japan.

155 IZUMI himself does not like to be asked what the secret is of his longevity. He feels that he just happens to have had a long life and that there is no 160 special reason for it.

Pressed for an answer he says: "Only God knows. God will decide how long I am here."

165 When I asked if he had a message for the world he sang another island folk song which instructs people what to do at each stage of life. The song 170 kept returning to a theme: "*So long as we live, as far as we survive, we can do anything. Life is more precious than anything else.*"

3 What *were* the secrets of Izumi's long life?

4 **Answer the following questions in your own words, without looking back at the text.**

a In what ways is Izumi still in good health?
b What health problems does he have?
c What bad habits has he had?

Check your answers with another student and then look back to see if you left out any points.

5 **Vocabulary**

Do the following exercise *without looking back at the text* first of all. The first letter of each word is given to help you. Which words or phrases were used:

a   to describe Izumi's eyes (Adj)?   *w* . . . . .

                 beard (Adj)?   *w* . . . .

                 skin (Adj)?   *w* . . . .

b   to describe his reaction to drugs (Adj)?   *r* . . . .

c   to describe what happened after he first tried shochu (phrase)?

        he . . . .

d   to describe what the shochu manufacturers did with a new brand of the liquor

        (Vb)?   *l* . . . .

e   to mean 'living to a great age' (N)?   *l* . . . .

f   to describe his enthusiasm for life (N)?   *z* . . .

g   to describe people who are inactive, or who spend a lot of time sitting down

        (Adj)   *s* . . . .

h   to describe what exercise does to the ageing process (Vb)?

                                         r . . . . .

i   to mean 'a high point' (N)?   *p* . . .

Compare your answers with another student's and then check them by looking back at the text.

Focus on Grammar 1: Comparisons 2

1 Look at table 1 on the next page which shows a comparison of Japanese and British diets.

a Name *two* foods which the Japanese eat in far greater quantities than the British.
b Which foods do the British eat in greater quantities than the Japanese?

2 Using expressions from tables 2 and 3 on the next page,

compare the Japanese and British eating habits for the following foods:

a fruit and nuts   e citrus fruits
b dairy foods   f rice
c oils   g total sugars
d fresh fish   h meat

e.g. The Japanese eat far more eggs than the British (do).
The British eat over twice as much meat as the Japanese (do).

Table 1

Japan and Britain: Comparison of diets (grams per person per day)	●	🇬🇧
CEREALS		
rice	218	4
wheat products	121	217
VEGETABLES		
potatoes	63	165
beans	90	20
green vegetables	100	55
other vegetables	167	81
FRUIT AND NUTS		
citrus fruits	78	19
other fruit and nuts	89	71
FISH, SEAFOOD, MEAT AND EGGS		
fresh fish	42	7
shellfish	18	0.5
other seafood	34	13
meat	71	153
eggs	40	28
FATS AND OILS		
butter	1	13
margarine and solid fats	2	26
oils	10	4
DAIRY FOODS		
milk	120	297
other dairy foods	9	56
SUGAR AND JAM		
jam	1	8
total sugars	60	120

Resarch by Caroline Walker

Table 2

slightly much/far considerably	more / less / fewer
a great deal	

Table 3

nearly about exactly over	twice half five times etc.	as	much many	as

---

Text: Parts 2 and 3

1 **What do we know about the effects of vegetables on our health? And which vegetables are the best for us? Read Part 2 to find out, and then answer the questions below.**

a According to recent research, what *is* the effect of eating certain vegetables daily?
b Which vegetables would *not* have this effect?
c Why has heart disease in Japan increased recently?
d Why do vegetables and beans help to protect our health?
e What is 'Project Popeye'?

As with Izumi, the population as a whole seems to benefit from its diet – particularly the low consumption of animal fat and the high consumption of vegetables and fish. Significantly, heart disease has increased among the Japanese since they began to switch to a Western diet containing more meat and dairy products.

But the Japanese still eat almost twice as much vegetables, including beans, as the British. Vegetables and beans contain soluble fibre which helps to lower blood cholesterol and thus reduce the risk of heart disease.

The crucial importance of green and yellow vegetables in the diet has been demonstrated by a major research project which is just coming to fruition in Tokyo. Dr Takeshi Hirayama, of the National Cancer Centre Research Institute, has studied the lifestyle of more than 122,000 Japanese men over a period of 16 years. He has found that men who have a daily helping of green or yellow vegetables, such as spinach, lettuce, green pepper or carrots, have half the average risk of developing heart disease, cancer and peptic ulcer.

The National Cancer Centre in Tokyo now has a campaign called "Project Popeye," which aims to persuade people to eat more vegetables such as spinach.

© *Times Newspapers Ltd.*

2 English in Use: Cloze

Now complete Part 3 of the text by writing a suitable word in each space.

As (1) . . . . seafood, the Japanese eat about three ounces a day (2) . . . . . . average - more than the (3) . . . . of meat they eat. (4) . . . . contrast, the British people do not eat three ounces of seafood a week. The (5) . . . . of fish in the diet has been (6) . . . . recently by doctors and scientists at the University of Leyden in Holland. They studied the diet of Dutchmen in a small town (7) . . . . a period of 20 years and found that an intake of an average of one ounce of fish a day, equivalent (8) . . . . . . two or three fish meals a week, (9) . . . . against heart disease and sudden death.

It has long been (10) . . . . that Eskimos, who traditionally have a mainly fish diet, are relatively (11) . . . . from heart disease. But it (12) . . . . as a surprise to the scientists that even small amounts of fish (13) . . . . be beneficial. Dutchmen who ate fish only once a week seemed to obtain health benefits compared (14) . . . . men who (15) . . . . ate fish.

STUDY BOX ▶ *would rather*

1 ***would rather*** + inf: **This means the same as *would prefer to* + inf and is normally followed by *than* ... in a statement, and by *than* ... or *or* ... in a question.**
I *'d rather die* than give up drinking.
Would you *rather go* to the cinema or the theatre?

2 ***would rather*** + clause: **This expresses a wish or preference about someone or something else. It takes a verb in the past when referring to the present or future, and a verb in the past perfect when referring to the past.**
She *'d rather* he *didn't smoke* in the house.
Would you rather I came back later?
I *'d rather* you *'d told* me the truth in the first place.
Would you *rather* I *'d stayed* in a hotel?

Focus on Writing: Article

Task   You have been asked to write a short article in an English language magazine for children aged 12 - 16 in your country.
You have decided to use some of the information from the texts in this section and to call the article 'Project Popeye'.
Your article has to be between 250 and 400 words in length, and you have been told that it should be entertaining as well as informative!

Planning

1 Decide (and write down!) what the *main theme* of your article is to be.

2 Think about the best way to appeal to young people of this age. What aspect(s) of the subject would interest them or catch their imagination?

3 Decide on a suitable heading and make a list of paragraphs showing which topics you will cover in each one.

4 Think about the best *style* to use. Put yourself in your readers' place. What approach would keep *you* reading?

For notes on writing articles, see Writing File page 116.

Popeye was a popular American cartoon character. He was a sailor who could perform extraordinary feats, but only after eating a tin of spinach!

Focus on Grammar 2: Present perfect

1 The following terms are often used when describing the use of particular verb forms:

action/event   habitual action   state

Find **two** examples for each of the terms in the verb forms below:

They live in New Zealand.
He hit me!
Have you ever been a smoker?
I cycle to work.
I've always hated sport!
It began to rain.

2

a Which of the descriptions below represent uses of the present perfect?

1 An action or event which was completed at a specific time in the past.
2 A habitual action in the past.
3 An action in the recent past which has a significant result in the present.
4 An action in the past where the time is unknown or unimportant.
5 A habitual action which began in the past and still continues.
6 A state which began in the past and still continues.

b Look carefully at the verb forms in the following extracts from the text in this unit. Match each one with one of the uses described above.

Example

a I *have advised* him to stop drinking.
b Since his 80s he *has had* no teeth.
c In 1982 he *had* a bad bout of pneumonia.
d Izumi *smoked* three or four cigarettes a day until he was 116.
e For most of his life, Izumi *has eaten* vegetables from his farm.
f The benefit of fish in the diet *has been shown* recently by doctors and scientists.

Use

c An important point to remember about the present perfect tense is that there is a strong link with the present. When Izumi's doctor says *'I've advised him to stop drinking'* , he means that Izumi now *knows* what his doctor's advice is. When, or how, or how many times he advised him is not important.

d Say what the present result is in the following examples of the present perfect, which are also from the text. The first one is done as an example.

The benefit of fish in the diet has been shown recently ...	Scientists and others now know the value of eating fish.
In the past six years, Izumi's heart has weakened.	
Dr Takeshi Hirayama has studied the lifestyle of 122,000 Japanese men ...	
The life expectancy of the Japanese has risen by eight years since 1960.	

3 The present perfect continuous tense

a Study the following pairs of examples and say what the differences in use between the present perfect simple and continuous are.

I've worked for the Wessex Bank since I left school.
I've been working for the Wessex Bank since the summer.

He's typed three pages of his report this morning.
He's been typing his report this morning.

I've waited long enough. I'm going home!
I've been waiting for three hours!

b Which of the following statements are true about the present perfect continuous tense?

a It is often used for more temporary actions.
b It is often used for more permanent actions.
c It is used when the quantity of actions or finished products is mentioned.
d It is used when an action has not yet been completed.
e It suggests the completion of an action.
f It emphasises how long an action has been going on.

Note: There are certain verbs which are not usually used in the present perfect continuous and these are listed in the Grammar File on page 106. For more information about the present perfect simple and continuous, see Grammar File pages 101 and 102.

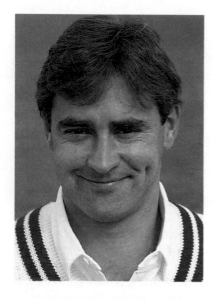

4

The following text describes the feelings of Chris Cowdrey, a well-known English cricket player, on reaching the age of thirty. Complete the text by putting the verbs in brackets into the correct tense, past simple, present perfect simple or continuous. Make any necessary changes to word order.

'I (1 *not mind*) when I (2 *become*) 30 at all except that in cricket terms it does mean I pretty much (3 *reach*) the last stage of my sports career. It used to be possible to carry on until you (4 *be*) 40 but nowadays, people burn themselves out more quickly. Since my late twenties it (5 *get*) slightly harder to keep fit.

'Sport used to come above all else for me, but that is changing as I get older. Also, I just (6 *return*) from my honeymoon in Europe where we (7 *go*) to the opera and ballet and I (8 *love*) it. I also (9 *change*) in that I now try and see more of my family than I used to. It (10 *be said*) that I have a bad relationship with my father but that's not true, it's just that as a child I hardly ever (11 *see*) my father; for 17 out of 20 Christmases he (12 *be*) away.

'When I (13 *reach*) my late twenties I (14 *feel*) the need to settle down and (15 *be*) lucky to meet the right person. If I'd married the girls I (16 *like*) in my early twenties, I'd have taken a chance. It'd have gone wrong because I (17 *mature*) and (18 *change*).'

Focus on Listening 1

Five different people, who each represented a different decade between teens and 80s, were asked how they felt about being the age they were.

1

Listen to what they say and try to decide how old each one is. Write your answer in the space below and add any information that you hear which helps to make your decision. Then discuss your answers with another student.

Speaker	Age	Reason(s)
1		
2		
3		
4		
5		

2 Listen to the recording again and answer the questions below by writing the number of the correct speaker (1 - 5) in the space on the right. Two questions have no correct answer and you should leave these blank.

Which speaker:

a speaks most positively about their age?

b seems surprised at how quickly they've aged?

c has no regrets at all about growing older?

d has noticed a change in other people's attitudes to them?

e says they would like to change their age?

f doesn't think they've changed much physically?

g seems concerned about small changes in their appearance?

Focus on Listening 2

You are going to hear a short talk on the way life expectancy in the West has changed over the ages. *Before you listen*, look carefully through the table of information below. *As you listen*, fill in the missing information for Questions 1 - 6 in the table below. See if you can complete this task after *one* hearing only.

© *The Observer*

	1	120 AD	1400 AD	1990's
	Classical Greece	(Imperial Rome)	**2**	(Today)
Male life expectancy	45	40.2	37.7	70
Female life expectancy	36	**3**	31.1	**4**
5	4.3	3.7	4 +	**7**
Number of survivors	2.7	2.0	**6**	2

English in Use: *Discourse cloze*

Choose the best phrase or sentence (given below the text) to fill each of the blanks in the following text. Write one letter (A - H) in each of the numbered spaces. Two of the suggested answers do not fit at all.

PARENTS WHO COPY TEENAGERS 'ARE EMBARRASSMENT'

By JOHN IZBICKI Education Correspondent

A leading psychiatrist has come out in defence of teenage aggression and the generation gap and advised parents and teachers to stop copying adolescents in dress, speech and action.

Dr Martyn Gay, consultant psychiatrist at Bristol Royal Hospital for Sick Children, told senior public school heads meeting at Cambridge yesterday: 'Parents who dress like their adolescent children are an embarrassment to them. (1) .... where parents invited rather than avoided problems with their children.

(2) .... who would dress up in jeans and a tee-shirt to accompany her adolescent daughter to a discotheque. The daughter was almost certain to end up finding a boyfriend and marrying long before her mother gave up going to discos. 'Her daughter will grow up and achieve maturity before her mother,' said Dr Gay.

(3) .... who joined his son in leather-jacketed motorbike convoys and for teachers who constantly copied their pupils in dress and mannerisms. (4)............. being scorned by the youngsters.

(5) .... pointed out that adolescents need and respect a degree of pressure and control from parents (6) ...., and he advised parents and teachers to set and stick to rules that are firm and fair.

© *The Daily Telegraph plc.*

A One example was that of a middle-aged mother

B even though they will bitterly resent it

C They would end up

D because they dislike them

E The same went for the father

F Dr Gay, father of four teenage children

G Another example was that of a parent

H And he outlined some of the most common cases

Communication Activity

1 Ages of Excellence

What are the ideal ages for the following occupations? Work with a partner to match the occupation to the ideal age.

racing driver	14	
surgeon		25
gymnast	30	
marathon runner		30
judge	45	
airline pilot		50
footballer	65	

You can check the answers which were given in a recent UK survey on page 218.

2 Ideal Ages

Discuss with your partner the ideal ages for the following stages of life.

a the age at which you start school

b the age of majority - the age when you are legally an adult

c the age at which you leave home

d the age at which you have your first child

e the age at which you retire from work

Wish You Were Here ...

Lead-in

"For Gods sake, Gerald, unwind gradually!"

1

a Write down all the places that people can stay in on holiday. (Think of as many different *types* of holiday as possible!)

b Tick those places on your list that you have stayed in yourself.

c *Work with another student.* Compare your lists. Then choose *one* of the places your partner has ticked and find out as much as possible about the holiday(s) concerned as possible.

2

a Why do people take holidays? The usual reason given is 'rest and relaxation'. How many other reasons can you think of?

b How restful and relaxing are holidays *really*?

3
Think about the best and worst holidays you ever had. Where were they, and what made them so good or so bad? Tell your partner.

Text

1 Now read the text on the next page in order to find out:

a what recent evidence suggests about the effects of holidays
b what reasons there might be
c what the results of further research could be

2 *Without looking back at the text yet*, say whether the following statements are *True* or *False*.

a Psychologists have proved scientifically that holidays are stressful experiences.
b Professor Kerry Cooper has had personal experience of a stressful holiday.
c A change of routine is harmful to the health.
d People need longer than two weeks in order to relax properly.
e People always tend to say they've enjoyed their holiday.
f Family holidays are the least stressful.
g Those who have had good holidays are better able to face work again.
h Holidays can lead people to ignore problems in their lives.
i The purpose of the research is to identify those people who need a holiday, and those who don't.

Now check your answers by looking back at the text. Be prepared to give reasons for your answers.

"I still can't get over that one of you in your bikini."

3 Answer these questions *in your own words.*

a How will it be possible to test the stressful effects of holidays scientifically?
b How does Professor Cooper feel after his holiday with his children?
c What is the difference between Type A and Type B people?
d Why can't a Type A person relax during a two week holiday?
e Why are people unwilling to admit that they've had a bad holiday?
f What kinds of problems can arise during family holidays?

Give us a break – from holidays

by Paul Martin

WARNING: Holidays can damage your health. Psychologists believe that many of the millions of Britons returning to work this week would have been better off staying at the office instead of taking their annual break.

Increasing evidence that holidays can cause harmful stress rather than provide welcome rest and reinvigoration is to be scientifically tested later this year.

Researchers from the University of Manchester's institute of science and technology plan to attach telemeters, small instruments that measure stress intake, to a selected sample of holidaymakers before, during and after their yearly break.

Kerry Cooper, professor of organisational psychology at the institute, is even more determined to go ahead with the project after taking his two children to Disneyland on a study tour in the United States last week.

'I'm shattered. I'm exhausted,' he told The Sunday Times from Los Angeles. 'It's been very stressful indeed; so much so that I'm looking forward to a business breakfast tomorrow.'

Cooper maintains that even the most smooth-running holiday produces stress simply by being a change in routine. Whether the stress builds up to health-harming levels depends, he says, on your personality, on the relationships within the family, and on the type of holiday you take.

Type A people, the more dynamic, goal-oriented, hard-driving, take far longer to unwind than the more relaxed less ambitious type B group.

A two-week holiday would often not relax a type A person who would spend the time worrying about work he could have been doing at the office, the cost of the holiday, or whether their home is being broken into. As one holidaymaker put it: 'I spent the first part of my holiday worrying if I locked up the house properly, and the rest of the time worrying if it'll still be safe when I come back.'

One reason why the hazards of holidays had until recently escaped the attentions of stress researchers is the bland response most people give when asked how they enjoyed it.

'People have invested so much time and energy into a holiday that if they had a bad time they won't admit it, even to themselves,' said Vanja Orlans, of the stress research and control centre at London University's Birkbeck College.

Professor Cooper pointed out that family tensions, kept at bay during the rest of the year, often erupt when the family is thrust together incessantly.

The vacation itself may cause conflicts through each holidaymaker preferring a different sort of activity, or inactivity, the 'museums versus sandcastles' syndrome, added Vanja Orlans.

Even those who said they had a successful holiday came back worried. 'I was depressed at the thought of going back to work,' said Lynn Hatley, a part-time secretary in a garage. 'When I walked in my front door I felt a pain right round my head as all the pressures piled back on me.'

The stress specialists debunk the notion that a good holiday necessarily helps people start work with renewed enthusiasm.

'People who come back from a terrific holiday are often disorientated and can't work well,' Orlans said.

She added that the fixed yearly holiday period has big drawbacks: people may postpone dealing with things that are getting them down at work or at home, believing the holiday will be the cure.

Cooper believes new research could help provide guidelines for people to design the right sort of holiday for their personality, family structure and work position. Some may need passive ones, others active, some short, some long. Going on holiday when work stress is affecting you, or taking several short ones during a year, often meets the individual's needs better.

4

a Look at the way the following words or phrases are used in the article and suggest another word or words which could be used instead, to give the same meaning.

1 *better off* (line 5)
2 *maintains* (line 35)
3 *unwind* (line 46)
4 *bland* (line 64)
5 *kept at bay* (line 76)

6 *erupt* (line 77)
7 *debunk* (line 95)
8 *are ... disorientated* (lines 100/101)
9 *drawbacks* (line 104)
10 *getting them down* (line 106)

b Compare your answers with another student's and then match the words or phrases above with one of the meanings below.

relax *reveal the truth about* *disadvantages*
happier/in a better state *making them depressed*
gentle/unemotional *are confused/lose their sense of direction*
avoided *argues* *break out/explode*

Focus on Grammar 1: Modal verbs 1

For general information about modal verbs, and detailed information about the verbs below, see Grammar File pages 97 - 99.

1 Ability: can, could

Holidays *can* damage your health.
A Type A person would spend time worrying about work he *could have been doing* at the office.

a The table below has been filled in for the ordinary verb *see*. To show how modal verbs differ from ordinary verbs, fill in as many parts of the table as possible for *can*.

	see:	*can:*
Inf.	*see*	
Present	*see/sees*	
Pres. Part.	*seeing*	
Past	*saw*	
Past Part.	*seen*	
Negative	*doesn't see* *didn't see*	
Question	*do you see?* *did you see?*	

b Complete the following sentences using suitable verb forms expressing ability.

1 With the help of a passer-by, I . . . push the car to the side of the road.
2 I'm sorry I'm late. I . . . find a parking place.
3 If you'll be sitting at the back of the theatre, . . . hear clearly?
4 She was such a clever child that she . . . read by the time she was four.
5 He was so good at science at school that he . . . a doctor, but he went into politics instead.
6 He used to . . . run a marathon but he's got less stamina now.

2 Possibility: could, may, might

The vacation itself *could* cause conflicts.
New research *could* help provide guidelines for people.

Complete the following sentences using suitable verb forms expressing possibility.

1 I thought he would telephone but he . . . .
. . . .
2 Don't touch it! It . . . .
3 Now that there's a shortage of oil, prices . . . .
. . . .
4 I don't know who telephoned but it . . . .
. . . .
5 I gave her such good directions that she . . . .
. . . .
6 The exam was so easy, nobody . . . .
. . . .

Communication Activity 1: What kind of traveller are you?

Imagine that you have booked a two week package holiday in a seaside resort. *Work with a partner* to discuss the following questions. In each case, mark the answer you would choose. (Your partner's answers may be different, of course.)

1   There is no sign of your luggage when you arrive at your destination in the middle of the night. Do you:
a   think what a terrible start to the holiday and decide to stay at the airport until it turns up?
b   take a telephone number and ring back in the morning?
c   do nothing and wait for the courier to sort things out?
d   grab a taxi and tell the driver to take you to the nearest all-night discotheque?

2   At the hotel, you are shown a room which has neither the balcony nor the sea view which you've asked for and paid for. Do you:
a   take what you're offered for the moment, but determine to get what you want in the morning?
b   refuse to accept the room and camp in the lounge?
c   smile and turn up the volume on your personal stereo (you knew things would go wrong)?
d   take the room, certain you'll be able to swap it later?

3   The restaurant at your hotel turns out to be ridiculously expensive. Do you:
a   a eat without worrying because, after all, you <u>are</u> on holiday?
b   pay up, but moan continuously?
c   decide to go on a diet for the duration of the holiday?
d   find a cheaper restaurant a couple of streets away?

4   The weather is awful. Do you:
a   see if there's any chance of an earlier flight home?
b   stay in your room and listen to music on your personal stereo?
c   organise trips to museums and art galleries until it gets better?
d   make for the beach anyway? (You once read an article that said the sun can tan you even through thick clouds.)

5   When you arrive at the beach, you find it's covered in tar and there's a plague of jellyfish. Do you:
a   spend the fortnight lying on your balcony?
b   look into the possibility of transport to another beach?
c   complain bitterly to the courier and ask why nothing was said about this in the brochure?
d   use the beach regardless - a jellyfish sting can't be all that bad.

6   Doing the accounts at the end of the day, you realise that you handed over a 200 instead of a 20 denomination note for lunch. Do you:
a   go back to the restaurant, certain they'll give you a refund once you explain what's happened?
b   curse all foreigners and never leave another tip all holiday?
c   shrug your shoulders and write it off to experience?
d   have an enormous meal at an expensive restaurant to show that you won't let your holiday be spoilt by a little thing like money.

7   Having tried all the restaurants, you are forced to acknowledge that the local cuisine is appalling. Do you:
a   feel thankful that at least the fruit and salads are delicious, and resolve to stick to them?
b   complain bitterly, and eat lots of ice-cream and sweets between meals - even though neither is particularly appetising?
c   give up on the local cuisine and go on a crash diet?
d   reckon you've just been unlucky so far, and give the restaurants another try?

8   You go on a whole-day coach trip with regular stops for drinks, meals and sightseeing. The rest of the party don't look like the sort of people you'd mix with at home. Do you:
a   talk only to your holiday companion and feel glad you both brought books?
b   bitterly regret your mistake and spend the day in a bad mood?

c single out anyone who looks in the least bit 'your type' and see if you can start a conversation?

d make yourself the life and soul of the party?

9 **Too late, you discover that the local tourist police are strict on illegally parked hire-cars. You are asked to accompany them to the police station. Do you:**

a suggest they ring your hotel so that the receptionist can vouch for you and help overcome the language problem?

b rely on your own charm to deal with the situation?

c fold your arms, smile and wait for them to get bored?

d insist that they send for your consul, refuse to answer any questions until he arrives, and resolve to go to jail before you'll pay the smallest fine?

10 **When you go away on holiday, do you:**

a hardly think about what's going on at home from the moment you arrive until the moment you return?

b know there's absolutely no point in worrying about things at home because there's nothing you can do about them?

c wake up most mornings worrying about how on earth they are managing at home without you?

d send postcards to a few close friends during the second week?

Interpretation

There are at least four different ways of behaving on holiday. From the possible answers above, can you tell what they are? Discuss your ideas with another student.

Now check your own results following the instructions below.

Scoring

For *question 1* note down the letter Z if you chose answer a, W if you chose b, X if you chose c, Y if you chose d.

Treat the other questions in the same way:

2	a W	b Z	c Y	d X
3	a X	b Z	c Y	d W
4	a Z	b Y	c W	d X
5	a Y	b W	c Z	d X
6	a X	b Z	c W	d Y
7	a W	b Z	c Y	d X
8	a Y	b Z	c W	d X
9	a W	b X	c Y	d Z
10	a Y	b X	c Z	d Z

Though we may display elements of more than one type of behaviour, each of us has a particular tendency.

W - If you chose a large number of W options, it shows you are a Good Holiday Person - flexible, adaptable and capable of coping in awkward situations, everyone's ideal companion.

X - A large number of X options reveals a Blind Optimist - if you're lucky, your blindness to reality may work for you, but you tend to be a tiring holiday companion.

Y - A majority of Y's indicates a Selfish Pleasure-seeker - determined to carry on with what you want to do, no matter what's happening around you. While you are capable of having a good time on even the most disastrous holiday, you do not contribute to anyone else's enjoyment.

Z - if Z answers predominate, you are a Self-destructive Grumbler - seeing trouble where none exists, and biting off your nose to spite your face.

"I've a nasty feeling we've had burglars"

Check: Phrasal verbs 3

1 There is at least one phrasal verb in each of the ten sections of the questionnaire. Underline the ones you can find and then compare your answers with another student's.

2 Ten of the phrasal verbs from the questionnaire are needed to complete the sentences below. Use a verb and a particle from the following lists in each sentence.

Verbs		Particles	
make	*stick*	*up*	*off*
send	*single*	*into*	*up*
turn	*turn*	*to*	*for*
pay	*write*	*out*	*out*
look	*sort*	*up*	*for*

a   We had to wait 20 minutes before the coach . . . . to collect us.

b   The travel agent managed to . . . . the problems about my ticket.

c   If you . . . . the centre of town, you should be able to find a hotel there quite easily.

d   The customs officer . . . . me . . . . from the group, for some reason, and examined every bit of my luggage.

e   They can fine you on the spot for speeding, and if you don't . . . . they arrest you!

f   They . . . . the music . . . . so loud that we couldn't hear each other speak.

g   If her temperature hasn't gone down in the morning, I'd advise you to . . . . a doctor.

h   I don't like spicy food, so I'm . . . . salads and fruit.

i   The travel company won't refund the deposit we paid. There's nothing we can do, I'm afraid. We'll just have to . . . . the money . . . .

j   They're . . . . the possibility of renting a villa in the Algarve this summer.

"You didn't say anything about sharing"

Check with the correct verbs in the Phrasal Verbs Reminder on page 87.

Mini-check: *-ing* or infinitive?

In these extracts from the text on page 81, change the verbs in brackets into the correct form: *-ing*, *to* + *inf*, or plain infinitive.

a   Many people would be better off (*stay*) at home.

b   Holidays can cause stress rather than (*provide*) welcome rest.

c   Researchers plan (*attach*) small instruments . . .

d   Kerry Cooper is determined (*go ahead*) with the project . . .

e   A holiday can produce stress simply by (*be*) a change in routine.

f   Type A people take far longer (*unwind*) than . . .

g   A person who would spend time (*worry*) about work . . .

h   I was depressed at the thought of (*go*) back to work.

i   People may postpone (*deal*) with things . . .

j   New research could help (*provide*) guidelines . . .

Communication Activity 2: Travelspeak

1 What the brochures say ... and what they mean.

Your Hotel

Luxury:
Expensive.

Exclusive:
Expensive and smaller.

De-luxe:
Extremely expensive and huge.

Unique:
Something wrong with it.

Elegant:
Fifty years old.

Up to date:
Twenty years old.

Modern:
Unfinished.

Charming:
Run down.

Picturesque:
Falling down.

Delightful:
Odd.

Ideal for families:
Already a mess.

Very friendly, personally run:
They can't afford staff and call you by your first name.

2 Now match the following descriptions to their 'translations'. *Work with another student.*

Your Resort:

1 Unsophisticated

2 Deserted beaches

3 Fantastic marine paradise

4 A few minutes' stroll from your hotel

Amenities

5 Flourishing tropical garden

6 Free watersports

7 Babysitting available

8 Radio

9 Dancing by moonlight

10 Weekly barbecue

11 Games room

12 Table tennis

13 An optional excursion

a Half a pack of cards

b Kids scream all night

c Jungle

d Water rationing and frequent power cuts

e Escape

f Beach

g Take a packed lunch and compass

h Sharks

i Half a table; no balls, no bats

j A beach is nearby

k There's no roof

l There's no TV

m Burn your own dinner on the staff's night off

"*For once the brochures were right - it is a deserted beach*"

Translations by William Rushton

3 Look at the following brochure descriptions. *Work with another student to 'translate' six of them.*

Ambiance

Helpful staff
Simple yet cosy accommodation
Old fashioned comfort
Most of the rooms have a sea view

Your Entertainment

Cultural Shows
Disco
An unforgettable night out

Your Hotel Restaurant

Relaxed, informal decor
Generous hospitality
Seafood delicacies
Fun-filled atmosphere

4 Now *work with another pair*. Take it in turns to read out one of your translations. The other pair should see if they can guess which of the brochure descriptions it refers to.

Focus on Grammar 2: Review of reported speech

For detailed information about reported speech see Grammar File pages 103 and 104. There are also lists of the various reporting verbs on page 106.

1 Reporting Statements and Questions

a Match each statement below to a suitable reporting verb on the right and then put each statement into reported speech.

1 I'm a superb cook.	confirmed
2 I'll phone as soon as I have any news.	estimated
3 OK, it's true that I've told some lies.	insisted
4 The meal you served us was totally inedible.	boasted
5 If you don't leave immediately, I'll call the police!	added
6 You must stay and eat with us this evening.	promised
7 I really don't think he needs help.	complained
8 We're definitely getting married next April.	admitted
9 ... and it wasn't expensive either.	threatened
10 It might well cost £1,000 to repair the damage.	doubted

b Change the following into reported speech (the first three examples come from the text in this unit). Use suitable reporting verbs in each case.

1 'I'm shattered. It's been very stressful indeed; so much so that I'm looking forward to a business breakfast tomorrow.' (Professor Cooper)
2 'I spent the first part of my holiday worrying if I had locked up the house properly and the rest of the time worrying if it'll still be safe when I get back.' (Holidaymaker)
3 'People who come back from a terrific holiday are often disorientated and can't work well.' (Vanja Orlans)
4 'Where have you come from? How long have you been away? What did you buy while you were on holiday?' (Customs officer)
5 'Did you have a good time? Would you go there again?' (Friend)

2 Reporting Orders, Requests, Suggestions etc.

Change the following into reported speech using a *to*-infinitive or a *that*-clause with *should*, as necessary. Use suitable reporting verbs in each case.

1 'I'd look for another job, if I were you.'
2 'Please, please do everything you can to help me.'
3 'You mustn't touch anything in this room.'
4 'You could always advertise for a flat.'
5 'Don't drive too fast. The roads are really icy.'

Phrasal Verbs Reminder

look into	investigate
make for	go in the direction of
pay up	pay in full
send for	ask or order someone to come
single out	select or separate from a group for special attention
sort out	deal with or solve a problem
stick to	continue with something, not change from it (e.g. a diet, a promise)
turn up	increase the volume
turn up	appear/arrive
write off	recognise that something is a loss (e.g. a bad debt)

Communication Activity 3: Roleplay

For this activity you need to work in pairs. Student A will be a hotel guest and Student B will be a courier working for a travel company.

Decide which roles you want to play and turn to the instructions at the end of the book.

Student A should turn to page 214.

Student B should turn to page 216.

Focus on Writing: Letter of complaint

Task

Imagine that the person who had Role A on page 214 has just returned from the holiday with Cheapotours Ltd. The courier was unable to solve the problem about the room and that is A's main complaint, although there were a few other problems as well.

Write A's letter of complaint to the travel company, describing the problems in as much detail as possible (fortunately, there is a photograph showing the balcony of A's room, which can be enclosed - see page 214) and suggesting what action you think the company should take.

Planning

1 Decide on certain details so that your letter can be realistic:

the writer - name (your own or an invented one); how did you travel - alone? with a friend? with your husband or wife? with children?
the holiday - dates; place; name of hotel; name of courier.

2 Make a list of the problems you experienced during the journey and at the hotel. Number them in order of importance.

3 Remember that it isn't very useful if you merely complain. You will need to suggest what action you think the company should take. Think carefully about this. Could you reasonably expect a refund for the whole cost of the holiday, for example? If not, what price can you put on your loss of enjoyment? Would you be satisfied with an apology? Decide, too, whether to mention any action you intend to take if the company ignores your letter or refuses to take your complaint seriously.

4 If you took part in the role play, use details of the conversation you had. If you report what was said by the courier, hotel staff etc., don't forget to use appropriate reporting verbs and correct tenses for reported speech. (See Grammar File pages 103 /104 and 106.)

For guidance on the layout and structure of this kind of letter, and for examples of useful language, see Writing File pages 111 and 112.

English in Use 1: Cloze

Read the article below and circle the letter next to the word which best fits each space. The first answer has been given as an example.

Oh No! Not Again...

The blow fell, as I suspected it (1) . . . . Nine short words that were (2) . . . to spoil the afternoon. Quite innocent words (3) . . . as our hostess offered us a cup of tea and a plate of chocolate biscuits. 'Would you (4) . . . to see our latest holiday photos?' said Rokiah with a smile.

Whenever I visit family, friends, acquaintances, colleagues, or even comparative strangers, I am (5) . . . to what I call the ordeal by viewing. (6) . . . come the photos which either chronicle the family's history from the black and white days to the glorious technicolour present, or (7) . . . toothy grins superimposed on well-known beauty (8) . . . . Now, to be perfectly truthful, there is nothing I enjoy more than a large book of professional photographs showing mountains (9) . . . in mist or close-ups of baby gorillas. And when I see scuba divers picking up corals from the sea (10) . . . or parachutists spread-eagled above the clouds, my heart misses a (11) . . . . But family snapshots, no thank you. I know the scene too well.

The family group photo, wherever it is taken, (12) . . . from one basic fault. The problem is this: everyone must be (13) . . . his or her best at the same given moment. This is asking for a miracle. Little Ali pulls his socks up. Mak Chick (14) . . . a fly away from her nose. Ani squints as sunlight is (15) . . . from the windscreen of a passing car just as the photographer presses the button.

Reproduced by permission of Roy Flindall and 'Wings of Gold' (Malaysian Airlines magazine)

"This one shows us at Gatwick for three days during the air controllers' strike"

1	A might	B should	C did	D will
2	A insured	B proved	C guaranteed	D promised
3	A suggested	B mentioned	C told	D spoken
4	A want	B care	C mind	D desire
5	A subjected	B punished	C obliged	D involved
6	A Away	B Off	C Up	D Out
7	A describe	B discover	C develop	D display
8	A places	B sites	C spots	D points
9	A enveloped	B closed	C contained	D surrounded
10	A floor	B bed	C base	D bottom
11	A pound	B tick	C beat	D strike
12	A undertakes	B faces	C suffers	D bears
13	A on	B at	C in	D by
14	A brushes	B rubs	C scratches	D catches
15	A shone	B directed	C reflected	D beamed

English in Use 2: Text completion

You work for a travel company. A colleague of yours has recently written an informal report on some new accommodation which your company intends to include in its new brochure. Use the information to complete the entry for the brochure by writing the missing words in the spaces provided on the right. The first answer has been given as an example.
Use *not more than two words* in each space.

CONFIDENTIAL REPORT
The Palm Hotel
This is quite a nice hotel, if a bit on the small side.
It's in the new part of town which is hardly pretty but handy for the shops. It takes 15 minutes to walk to the beach (I timed it!). The rooms (all 26 of them) have twin beds and most have a balcony. You can see the harbour from the balconies (if you've got good eyesight!) – don't forget to mention this. There's no hotel restaurant but you only have to walk a short way to find plenty of local eating places. The one drawback I think it's worth mentioning is that with all the restaurants and bars, the centre of town does get quite noisy at night (and into the early hours!).

Seagull Studios
Three mini apartments along the road a bit from the Palm and above a bar which could get rather noisy late at night. (I think you'd better mention this specifically so there's no chance of complaints.) Every studio has twin beds (with a toilet and shower) and a private balcony (looking on to the road). The so-called kitchenette has a tiny cooker and fridge and only very basic equipment – just about enough to peel an apple – so warn people that they shouldn't expect to cook gourmet meals!

Signed: *T. Rowland*

Palm Hotel
A small, comfortable hotel which (1) . . . in the newer part of town, close to the main shopping area and only a (2) . . . stroll from the beach. There are 26 rooms, all (3) . . . are twin-bedded. Most rooms have a balcony with a (4) . . . the picturesque harbour. (5) . . . the hotel has no restaurant, there is a wide (6) . . . of places to eat, all (7) . . . a few minutes' walk. (8) . . . its central position, this accommodation will not (9) . . . those looking for peace and tranquillity.

Seagull Studios
A little (10) . . . down the road from the Palm Hotel, 3 twin-bedded studios, (11) . . . with its own en suite toilet and shower, and balcony. The kitchenettes are basically (12) . . . with a small cooker and fridge, and are not (13) . . . preparing full meals. Some late-night noise from the bar below is (14) . . . and we do not (15) . . . this accommodation for those who like early nights!

1 *is situated* . . . .
2 . . . .
3 . . . .
4 . . . .
5 . . . .
6 . . . .
7 . . . .
8 . . . .
9 . . . .
10 . . . .
11 . . . .
12 . . . .
13 . . . .
14 . . . .
15 . . . .

Grammar File

Order of adjectives

When there is more than one adjective in front of a noun, the general order in which they occur is as follows:

1 Qualitative Adjectives	2 Colours	3 Classifying Adjectives
Adjectives describing particular qualities a person or thing has.	e.g. *red, yellow, blue* etc.	Adjectives describing what class a person or thing belongs to.
e.g. *big, heavy, happy, clever angry, cold, sweet, strange*		e.g. *medical, industrial historical, golden, natural,*

A more detailed breakdown of the most usual order of adjectives is as follows:

Opinion	Size	Age	Shape	Colour	Origin	Material	
lovely	*tiny*	*young*	*round*	*grey*	*Chinese*	*cotton*	
horrible	*big*	*old*	*square*	*brown*	*American*	*steel*	+ NOUN
strange	*huge*	*ancient*	*oblong*	*orange*	*Parisian*	*gold*	

Comparison

1 Comparatives and superlatives

1.1 Adjectives

Adjectives of one syllable add -*er* and -*est*. If the adjective ends in -*e*, -*r* and -*st* are added. If the adjective ends in a consonant -*y*, this changes to -*ier*, -*iest*. If the adjective ends in a single consonant after a single vowel, the consonant is doubled (see Grammar File page 105).

e.g. *strong, stronger, strongest*   *wise, wiser, wisest*
rich, richer, richest   *dry, drier, driest*
thick, thicker, thickest   *hot, hotter, hottest*

The following have irregular forms:

good, better, best   *far, farther* (or *further*), *farthest*
bad, worse, worst   (or *furthest*)

Adjectives of two syllables which end in -*y* add -*er* and -*est*. Most other two-syllable adjectives take *more* and *most*.

e.g. *funny, funnier, funniest*
modern, more modern, most modern

The following two-syllable adjectives can form superlatives with either the endings -*er*/*est* or with *more*/*most*.

common	*handsome*	*narrow*	*shallow*
cruel	*likely*	*pleasant*	*simple*
gentle	*mature*	*polite*	*stupid*

Adjectives of more than two syllables take *more* and *most*.

e.g. *interesting, more interesting, most interesting*

1.2 Adverbs

Most adverbs form comparatives and superlatives with *more* and *most*.

e.g. *easily, more easily, most easily*

Adverbs with the same form as adjectives form comparatives and superlatives in the same way as adjectives.

e.g. *fast, faster, fastest*   *straight, straighter, straightest*
hard, harder, hardest   *early, earlier, earliest*

The following have irregular forms:

well, better, best   *badly, worse, worst*

1.3 Qualifying comparatives and superlatives

He's	*no*	*older*/ *more intelligent* etc.
	hardly any	
They go	*a little*/ *slightly*	*faster*/ *more smoothly* etc.
	(quite) a lot	
	lots *much*/ *far*	

2 as ... as ...

2.1 This structure can be used with adjectives and adverbs, and also with *much* and *many* + noun. The second *as* can be followed:

a	by a noun, noun phrase or object pronoun	*He's as tall as his father.* *He thinks nobody knows as much as him.*
b	by a clause	*He's as tall as his father is.* *He thinks nobody knows as much as he does.*
c	by *possible* or *ever* or *usual*	*I'll stay as long as possible.* *He looked as handsome as ever.*

The negative is formed with *not as ...* or *not so ....*

e.g. *She's not as careful as she should be.*
He didn't do as well as he had hoped.
We haven't had so much rain as last year.

2.2 Qualifying comparisons with *as ... as ...*

A	is	just	as hard-working as B (is).
		almost	
A	works	nearly	as hard as B (does).
		quite	
		twice	
A	is	not nearly	as hard-working as B (is).
		not quite	
		not half	
A	doesn't work	nearly	as hard as B (does).
		quite	
		half	

For the use of the expressions *half/twice/three times as ... as ...* , with *much/many* , see Focus on Grammar page 74.

2.3 Special word order: *as* + adjective + *a / an* + noun + *as ...*

> e.g. *A is as hard a worker as B.*

This is an alternative and slightly more formal way of expressing the meaning of *A works as hard as B* . In this structure, it is essential to place an indefinite article before the noun. The negative is formed with *not as ...* or *not such ...*

Further examples:

> *That was as fine a game as I've ever seen.*
> *It wasn't as windy a day as had been forecast.*
> *I'm not such an expert player as you are.*

Conditionals

1 Summary of forms

Type 1: Conditions which are always true (A) or very probable in the present or future (B).

A	*If*	present form	present form or imperative
	When		
B	*If*	present form	future form or imperative

> e.g. A *When you put salt on ice, it melts.*
> *If you see her, give her my love.*
> B *If I leave now, I'll miss the rush hour.*

Type 2: Conditions which are improbable or impossible in the present or future.

| *If* | past simple or | *would, could, might* + infinitive |
| | past continuous | |

> e.g. *If you met the President, what would you say to him?*
> *If they lived a bit nearer we might see them more often.*

Type 3: Unreal conditions in the past.

| *If* | past perfect simple | *would/should/could/might* |
| | or continuous | *have* + past participle |

> e.g. *If the telephone hadn't woken me, I'd have been late for my appointment.*
> *She could have gone to university if she'd wanted to.*

Mixed conditionals: Conditions in the past with a present or future result.

> e.g. *If they hadn't agreed to baby sit, they'd be here.*
> *You might be a star now if you'd got that part in the film.*
> *If she hadn't decided to change jobs, she would be going to China next month.*

2 Special points

2.1 *Conditional Links*:

Apart from *if*, the following links can be used to introduce conditional clauses:

> unless   as / so long as   suppose / supposing (that)
> providing / provided (that)   on condition (that)

2.2 *Punctuation*:

When the *if* clause comes first in the sentence, it is followed by a comma. When the main clause comes first, no comma is used.

2.3 *Should*:

Using *should* + infinitive (without *to*) in the *if* clause makes the condition less likely.

> e.g. *If you should need any help, just let me know.*

In formal contexts, *should* can replace *if*.

> e.g. *Should you need any help, please don't hesitate to contact me*

Expressing the future

Form	Use
Going to	
e.g. *We're going to have a party.* *Are you going to invite John?*	1 To express personal intention. The action has usually been considered in advance and some arrangements may have been made.
e.g. *I think I'm going to faint.*	2 To make a prediction based on what you know, feel or can see.
Future simple	
e.g. *He'll be forty in June.* *Tomorrow will be cold and wet.*	1 To express a future fact or prediction.
e.g. *I know, I'll phone for a taxi.*	2 To express a sudden decision.
e.g. *Shall I give you a lift?* *Will you help me with this bag?*	3 To express an offer or request.
e.g. *I'll hit you if you do that again.* *Don't worry, I won't be late.*	4 To express a threat or a promise.
e.g. *I suppose you'll be pretty busy.* *Do you think he'll come?*	5 To express an opinion about the future after verbs like *think, suppose, expect, doubt if* and also with *probably*.
e.g. *There's a car pulling up outside.* *Oh, that'll be Jim.*	6 To express strong probability.
Present continuous	
e.g. *What are you doing this evening?* *The car's being serviced tomorrow.*	To express a pre-arranged future action. Similar in meaning and use to *going to* but with less sense of personal intention.
Present simple	
e.g. *What time do you arrive at Heathrow?* *We call at Venice and Athens.*	To express the certain future, a fixed future event usually based on a timetable or programme.
Is to	
e.g. *You are to do exactly as I say.*	1 To express an instruction or order
e.g. *The President is to visit Rome.*	2 To talk about an action or event which has been arranged, often officially.
About to/ due to	
e.g. *The building is due to be completed in 1995.* *He's about to announce the result.*	To talk about actions or events which are expected to happen, usually fairly soon.
Future continuous	
e.g. *It's awful to think I'll be working this time next week!*	1 To talk about an action which will be in progress at a point in the future.
e.g. *The big stores will be having their winter sales soon.*	2 To talk about an action or event which will happen as a matter of course.
e.g. *Will you be checking out today?*	3 To express a request for information rather than a request for action.
e.g. *Where's Nigel tonight?* *He'll be performing somewhere with his band, I expect.*	4 To express strong probability.

Future perfect

e.g. *They will have received our*   To talk about a future event
letter by Monday.   which will be complete by a time
which is further in the future.

Future perfect continuous

e.g. *I'll have been working in this*   To talk about the duration of an
company for 10 years next April.   action, as seen from a point in the future.

Infinitive

1 The *to*-infinitive

The *to*-infinitive is used:

1.1 to express purpose.
e.g. *There's a reporter here to interview you.*
I go swimming to try and keep my weight down.

1.2 after certain verbs (there is a list of the main ones on page 105).
e.g. *We can't afford to go out much.*
Don't hesitate to contact me if you need help.

1.3 after the objects of certain verbs (there is a list of the main ones on page 105).
e.g. *You surely don't expect me to come with you?*
Could you remind me to post this letter?

1.4 after the auxiliary verbs *be* and *have*.
e.g. *Does she have to be so aggressive all the time?*
The police are to start towing away vehicles soon.

1.5 after adjectives.
e.g. *They're bound to want something to eat when they arrive.*
Fortunately, it's not likely to happen.

1.6 after *too* + adjective and adjective + *enough*.
e.g. *It's just too hot to eat.*
Are you fit enough to take part in the race?

1.7 as the subject of a sentence.
e.g. *To spend so much money would be foolish.*
To err is human, to forgive divine.

2 Infinitive without *to*

The infinitive without *to* is used:

2.1 after modal verbs.
e.g. *We could telephone to see how she is.*
Why can't you be more considerate?

2.2 after the objects of certain verbs.
a   *make, let,* and sometimes *help.*

e.g. *She wouldn't let me pay for the damage.*
You can't make me go.
The porter will help you carry your cases.

b   *hear, see, feel, notice, watch* when used in the sense of perceiving a complete action. (When part of an action is perceived, an *-ing* form is used.)

e.g. *Didn't you hear me shout?* (Compare: *I heard a tap dripping so I got up.*)

I saw him go into the building. (Compare: *I saw him talking to someone.*)

2.3 after *would rather ...*, *had better ...* and *Why not ...?*
e.g. *I'd rather speak to you in private.*

-ing forms

1 -*ing* forms as nouns

-*ing* nouns can be used with an article, with a possessive adjective, and with other determiners that go with uncountable nouns such as *this / that, some / any, much / little, more / less, all* etc.

e.g.   *You'll enjoy the singing*
His handwriting is impossible to read.
Any cheating will be severely punished.
I'm doing less driving now.

When used with an article, an -*ing* noun doesn't normally take a direct object.

Instead of:	* *The signing the treaty ...*
we say:	*The signing **of** the treaty ...*
Instead of:	* *The opening the motorway*
we say:	*The opening **of** the motorway*

* An asterisk indicates an incorrect utterance.

2 Verb + -*ing* form

Certain verbs are followed only by -*ing* forms (or nouns).

e.g.   *You know how he detests going to parties.*
Let me know when you've finished working.

There is a list of verbs which are followed only by *-ing* forms on page 105. A few verbs can take both *-ing* forms and infinitives with little difference in meaning, while there are others which can take both forms but with a difference in meaning (see lists on page 105).

3 Other expressions + *-ing* form

Other expressions which take *-ing* forms, such as *can't stand*, are listed on page 105.

4 Possessive + *-ing* form

An *-ing* form after a verb, preposition or other expression may be interrupted by a possessive pronoun (e.g. *her*) or noun + *'s* to show a change of subject.

e.g.　*We appreciated Helen's offering to help.*
　　　We appreciated her offering to help.
　　　I hope you won't mind my interrupting you.

In informal speech, a noun or personal pronoun may be used instead.

e.g.　*We appreciated Helen offering to help.*
　　　I hope you won't mind me interrupting you.

-ing forms v. infinitive

The following verbs may take either an *-ing* form or an infinitive depending on the meaning.

come

+ *-ing: She came running to meet me.*

If someone comes running, racing, flying and so on, they move in that way.

+ inf: *I came to understand his way of thinking in the end.*

If you *come to do* something, you gradually start doing it.

dread

+ *-ing: I dread telling him that I've lost his book.*

If you *dread doing* something, you are fearful about an action in the future.

+ inf: *I dread to think what your father will say!*

Dread to is only used with the verb *think*.

go on

+ *-ing: He went on writing to her even though she didn't reply.*

If you *go on doing* something, you continue with an action.

+ inf: *After apologising for interrupting, he went on to explain the problem.*

　　　She started as a secretary and went on to become Company Director.

If you *go on to do* something, you begin a new action immediately or at a later stage.

mean

+ *-ing: If she got the job, it would mean moving to London.*

If an action or event *means doing* something, it will involve or inevitably lead to doing it.

+ inf: *I've got a complaint and I mean to see the manager in person.*

If you *mean to do* something you intend to or are determined to do it.

regret

+ *-ing: I've always regretted not learning to play an instrument.*

If you *regret doing* something, you are sorry about an action in the past.

+ inf: *I regret to tell you all the tickets for this performance have been sold.*

Regret to is used with the verbs *say*, *tell*, *inform* and *announce* and refers to a present action.

remember/forget

+ *-ing: I'll never forget arriving in New York the first time. Do you remember meeting them last summer?*

The action you *remember* or *forget* is in the past (before the moment of remembering or forgetting).

+ inf: *Don't forget to write, will you? Did you remember to phone your mother?*

The action is in the present or the future (after the moment of remembering or forgetting).

stop

+ *-ing: Stop making that dreadful noise!*

If you *stop doing* something, you finish an action.

+ inf: *We've only stopped to get some petrol.*

If you *stop to do* something, you interrupt one action in order to do something else.

try

+ *-ing: He tried going to evening classes but his Spanish was still hopeless.*

If you *try doing* something, you make an experiment. The action is possible but it may or may not be successful in helping you to achieve something.

+ inf: *Why don't you try to lose some weight?*

If you *try to do* something, you make an effort. The action is difficult and it may or may not be possible for you to do it.

Inversion after negative introductions

1 The following expressions can be placed first in a clause in order to give more emphasis or a more dramatic effect. The subject and verb are then inverted. If there is no auxiliary verb, *do/does* or *did* are used, as in a question.

Rarely/ seldom ...	*Not only ... but also ...*
Never ...	*Hardly/ scarcely ... when ...*
At no time ...	*No sooner ... than ...*
Under no circumstances ...	
On no account ...	
Nobody ...	
Nowhere (else) ...	
Not (a person/ a soul/ a thing etc.) ...	

e.g.   *Never **have I seen** such an awful sight!*
*Under no circumstances **must you interrupt** the meeting.*
*Not a single word **would he say** on the subject.*
*Not only **does he drop** ash on the carpet, but he also spills his tobacco.*

*Hardly **had I sat down** when the doorbell rang.*
*No sooner **did she hang out** the washing than it began to rain.*

2 The following additional expressions can also be used in this way in certain circumstances.

Only before adverbs of time (*now, later* etc.) or when qualifying an introductory phrase.

e.g.   *Only now **do I understand** why you behaved as you did.*
*Only in Cornwall **can you buy** real Cornish pasties.*

Little, few, so, such when not followed by a noun.

e.g.   *Little **do you know** what's in store for you!*
*So strong **was the wind** that I could hardly control the car.*
*Such **is fate!***

Modal verbs

1 Introduction

Modal verbs are a special kind of auxiliary verb. Like other auxiliary verbs, they are always used with a main verb but modal verbs express an *attitude* to what we say. They can express how certain or uncertain we are about an event, or how willing or unwilling we are to do something, for example. There are three so-called semi-modals: *dare, need* and *used to*. These have some special characteristics which are described later.

The modal verbs in English are:

can	might	shall	would
could	must	should	
may	ought to	will	

2 Special characteristics

2.1 Modal verbs are followed by the base form of the verb or by the base form of *be* (present) or *have* (past) + participle.

e.g.   *I might go.   You could rent a car.   Would you like to sit down?   They might be having dinner. He could have left the country.*

2.2 Modal verbs do not inflect, i.e. they do not take an *-s* in the third person or *-ing* or *-ed*.

2.3 Modal verbs do not take the auxiliary *do*. The negative is formed by adding *not*.

e.g.   *You can't go in there.   It mightn't rain after all.*

2.4 Questions are formed by inverting the subject and the modal. Modal verbs are also used in question tags.

e.g.   *Must you make that noise?   May I come in?
You'd join, wouldn't you?*

2.5 Modal verbs have no infinitive. Other expressions must be used instead.

e.g.   *(can)Will you **be able to** help me?
(must) I'm going to **have to** leave.*

2.6 Modal verbs have no past form, and other expressions must be used instead. (For special uses of *could* and *would*, see notes below.)

e.g.   *(must)I **had to** change the tyre.
(can) **Were** you **able to** find a bank?
Did you **manage** to find a bank?*

3 Detailed Information

3.1 Ability: *can, could*

3.1.1 *Can* is used to talk about present ability and awareness.

e.g.   *Holidays can damage your health.
Can you hear me?*

It can also be used to talk about future ability (but not awareness), often with the idea of personal willingness.

e.g.   *Can we meet tonight?
I can give you a lift tomorrow, if you like.*

3.1.2 As *can* has no infinitive, *be able to* is used with *will, going to, used to* etc.

e.g. *We'll be able to give you an answer soon.*
Will you be able to see the stage?
I used to be able to swim 20 lengths without stopping.

3.1.3 *Could* is only used to talk about general ability in the past. To talk about a specific example of ability, we use *was able to. Couldn't* refers to both general and specific ability.

e.g. *I could drive when I was 15.*
Luckily I was able to find a taxi.
I couldn't drive till I was 25.
I'm afraid, I couldn't find a taxi.

3.1.4 *Could* + perfect infinitive is used to talk about how things might have been different. It can also suggest criticism.

e.g. *He could have been an actor.*
You could have telephoned me to say you'd be late.

3.2 Likelihood: *must, can, could, may, might*

3.2.1 *Could, may* and *might* are used to talk about the possibility of something. Strong possibility is indicated by adding *well*; weak possibility is indicated by adding *possibly*.

e.g. *Don't eat it! It could/may/might be poisonous.*
Prices might well rise.
I might possibly be wrong.

3.2.2 Negative possibility is indicated by *may/might + not. Couldn't* indicates impossibility.

e.g. *He might not have our phone number.*
The news couldn't have been better.

3.2.3 *Must* is used to say that you are confident that something is true or is going to happen while *can't* is used to say that you are confident that something is not true or is not going to happen.

e.g. *It must be 6 o'clock. There's the time signal.*
You can't be serious!

3.2.4 Likelihood in the past is expressed by using a perfect infinitive.

e.g. *You must have been terrified.*
She could have made a mistake.

3.3 Obligation: *must, need, ought to, should*

3.3.1 *Must* and *mustn't* are used to say that it is very important to do, or not to do, something. This can be a personal recommendation, a strong suggestion or an obligation (see also 3.3.2 below).

e.g. *You must try the ice cream. It's delicious.*
We mustn't forget to write and thank them for their hospitality.
You must try and be more punctual.

3.3.2 Obligation in the past is expressed by *had to*. Obligation in the future can be expressed by *must* when the obligation already exists now. If it will only exist in the future, *will have to* is used.

e.g. *He told me that I had to try harder.*
You must telephone first before you arrive next time. If I'm late, I'll have to take a taxi.

3.3.3 *Must* v. *have to*: *must* usually expresses an obligation which comes from the speaker while *have to* generally expresses a more impersonal obligation.

e.g. *You must send me a postcard.* (friend speaking)
You have to have a visa to enter the country (travel agent speaking)

3.3.4 *mustn't* v. *don't have to / don't need to*: *mustn't* expresses negative obligation while the other forms express absence of obligation.

e.g. *You mustn't make too much noise or you'll wake the baby!*
You don't have to / don't need to make an appointment to see him.

3.3.5 *Should* and *ought to* express strong advice or obligation. They are very close in meaning, but note the difference in word order in the examples below. The past is formed with a perfect infinitive.

e.g. *I should really tidy the house up.*
You really ought to tidy the house up.
They should/ought to have been more careful.

3.3.6 *Need* exists both as an ordinary verb and as a modal auxiliary. It is used as a modal auxiliary mainly in questions and negative statements in the present tense, to express lack of necessity, and in the expression *needn't have done* (see 3.3.7 below).

e.g. *Need you ask?*
You needn't shout, I'm not deaf!

3.3.7 *Didn't need to* v. *needn't have done*: *didn't need to* is used when something wasn't necessary so wasn't done, while *needn't have* is used when something was done even though it turned out to be unnecessary.

e.g. *He didn't need to go to court because the case was dismissed.*
I needn't have dressed smartly. When I got there, everyone was in jeans.

3.4 Permission: *can, may, could*

3.4.1 Talking about permission

Can and *may* are used to talk about what is and isn't permitted in the present. *May not* is more formal than *cannot*.

e.g. *You can leave school when you are 16 but you cannot vote.*
Under the law you may make one photocopy for your personal use but you may not make multiple copies.

Could and *was/were allowed to* are used to talk about activities which were generally permitted in the past. Only *was/were allowed to* can be used to refer to permission given on a particular occasion.

e.g.   *At school, we could wear any clothes we wanted,
apart from jeans.
When the World Cup was on TV, I was allowed to stay
up late and watch.*

Will be able to /will be allowed to are used to talk about
future permission.

3.4.2 Asking for and giving permission

When asking for permission to do something, *can* is the
least formal, while *could* and *may* are more polite. The
addition of *possibly* or the use of the form *I wonder if I ...*
makes the request more polite. *Might* is very formal.

e.g.   *Can I borrow your pen for a minute?
Could I (possibly) use your telephone?
May I use your name as a referee?
I wonder if I could interrupt you for a moment?
Might I make a suggestion?*

When replying to a request for permission, only *can* and
may are used.

e.g.   *Yes, (of course) you can / may.
No, (I'm afraid) you can't (cannot)/ may not.*

4 Semi-modals: *need, dare, used to*

These verbs exist both as ordinary verbs and as modal
auxiliary verbs. As modals, they have certain special
characteristics and the main points of these are
described below.

4.1 *Dare* and *need*

These verbs are mainly used as modal auxiliaries in
questions and negative sentences in the present tense.
The meaning is the same as when they are used as
ordinary verbs.

e.g.   *I daren't walk through the park at night.
How dare you speak to me like that?
We needn't hurry. The film doesn't start till 8.*

4.2 *Dare*

In the present simple, *dare* sometimes takes an *-s* in the
third person singular, while the past simple is usually
formed with *-d. Dare* can also be used with the auxiliary
do and *didn't*, and with the modals *will, would* and
should.

e.g.   *She's the only one who dares challenge him.
Don't you dare do that again.
Nobody dared leave before the end.
We didn't dare tell him what really happened.
Would you dare go there alone?*

4.3 *Used to*

Used to only refers to the past; it's base form is *used to*
(not *use to*). In general, its use as a modal auxiliary (*Used
you to ...? He used not to ...*) is more formal and less
common than its use as an ordinary verb with *did*. In the
negative, *never used to* is often used instead of *didn't
used to.*

e.g.   *Didn't you used to play in the school orchestra?
He never used (didn't used to) be so mean.*

Passive

1 Form

1.1 The passive puts emphasis on the person or thing
affected by an action rather than on the agent (whoever
does the action). To change a sentence from active to
passive, the object must become the subject of the new
sentence and be followed by a passive form.

e.g.   **Active**:   *Someone has scratched my car.*
       Passive: *My car has been scratched*

1.2 The passive is formed with the appropriate tense of the
verb *to be* + past participle.

Present simple	*am/is/are* + p. participle *He is called 'Lofty'.*
Present continuous	*am/is/are being* + p. participle *I'm being followed.*
Present perfect	*has/have been* + p. participle *The door has been locked.*
Past simple	*was/were* + p. participle *It was made of silver.*
Past continuous	*was/were being* + p. participle *the cat was being chased.*
Past perfect	*had been* + p. participle *The cup had been broken.*

Future simple	*will be* + p. participle *They'll be criticised.*
going to	*going to be* + p. participle *You're going to be tested.*
Modals (present)	modal + *be* + p. participle *The car might be stolen.*
Modals (past)	modal + *have been* + p. participle *He could have been hurt.*
Infinitive	*to* + *be* + past participle *He's hoping to be invited.*

2 Use

The passive is used:

2.1 when the agent is not known or not important, or when
the agent is obvious from the context.

e.g.   *The roof's been repaired at last.
I'm hoping to be promoted next year.*

2.2 when the agent is people in general (to avoid using *you*
or *one*).

e.g.   *Tickets can be reserved by calling the Box Office.
The centre of town should be avoided during
rush hour.*

2.3 when the action or event is more important than the agent, as in describing processes or scientific experiments.

e.g. *The birds are first cleaned with mild detergent to remove the oil ...   Sulphuric acid is then added to the mixture in the test tube.*

2.4 in order to make a statement more formal and impersonal, often with an *it* structure.

e.g. *It was agreed that membership fees should be raised.*
Your application has not been successful.

Past tenses

1 Past simple

Form:

Regular verbs:

base form + -(e)d	e.g. *They walked towards us.*

Irregular verbs: See list on page 107.
Negative: *didn't* + base form.
Question: *did* + subject + base form?

Use

1.1 The past simple is used to refer to completed actions or events which took place at a particular time or over a period of time in the past.

e.g. *We met last summer. Do you remember?*
I stayed with my uncle until I found a flat of my own.

1.2 The past simple can also refer to repeated actions in the past.

e.g. *He went for a walk every day before lunch.*

Note: It is also possible to use *used to* or *would* + base form with this meaning.

e.g. *He used to go for a walk ...*
He would go for a walk ...

1.3 When two actions happen quickly, one after the other, we usually use the past simple in each case.

e.g. *When the oil warning light came on, I switched off the engine.*

1.4 When we report two actions which happened at the same time, and it is the result that is important, we can also use the past simple in each case.

e.g. *As it grew darker, we found it more difficult to follow the path.*

2 Past continuous

Form

was/were + *-ing*	e.g. *It was raining.*

Negative: *wasn't/ weren't* + *-ing.*
Question: *was/were* + subject + base form ?

Note: Some verbs do not usually occur in continuous tenses. See the list on page 106.

Use

2.1 The past continuous refers to actions or situations which were unfinished at a particular time in the past. It also emphasises how long an action continued.

e.g. *You were living in Brighton then, weren't you?*
I was getting colder and colder all the time.

2.2 It is often used to refer to an action which was going on when a second shorter action interrupted it.

e.g. *I was driving home when I heard the news on the car radio.*

2.3 The past continuous is often used to describe the background to events in a story.

e.g *It was a beautiful day. The sun was shining and the birds were singing.*

2.4 The past continuous can be used to describe two actions which happened at the same time when we are more interested in the fact that they happened together than in the result.

e.g. *While I was waiting for him to ring, he was out having a good time.*

2.5 The past continuous can be used with *always* or *forever* to emphasise the frequency of an action. In this case, the speaker is often expressing criticism or annoyance.

e.g. *They were always having loud parties which went on till the early hours.*

2.6 The past continuous is used in the expressions *I was wondering if / whether* and *I was hoping (that)...* as a way of making an invitation, a request etc. more polite.

e.g. *I was wondering if you would like to join us?*

3 Past perfect

Form

Simple:	*had* + past participle
	e.g. *He had already left.*

Negative: *hadn't* + past participle
Question: *had* + subject + past participle?

Continuous:	*had been* + *-ing*
	e.g. *I'd been waiting for an hour.*

Negative: *hadn't been* + *-ing*

Question: *had* + subject + *been* + *-ing*?

Note: Some verbs do not usually occur in continuous tenses. See list on page 106

Use

3.1 The past perfect refers to actions which happened or situations which existed before another action at a particular time in the past.

e.g. *The shop had closed by the time I got there.*
When I reached the front door, I realised I had lost my key.

3.2 The past perfect is used to make the order of events clear. It's not necessary to use it when the two actions happen quickly, one after the other, or when the order of events is clear anyway.

e.g. *I recognised him as soon as I saw him.*
After he left the office he went to collect his car from the garage.

3.3 The past perfect continuous is used when the first action continued for some time or was unfinished.

e.g. *The fire had been burning for some time before the fire brigade arrived.*
I'd been hoping to meet her for ages when I bumped into her by chance.

4 Past tenses used to talk about hypothetical situations

Past tenses can be used after certain expressions to talk about situations which do not exist or events which did not happen but which we are able to imagine.

4.1 Present or future reference

I wish	would rather	Suppose/supposing	if
if only	as if/as though	It's (high / about) time	

e.g. *I wish I had a car.* (I haven't)
I'd rather you didn't smoke. (You are smoking or may do in future)
He behaves as if he owned the place. (He doesn't)
Suppose you didn't get the job, what would you do?
It's high time we left. (We haven't left yet and it's late)

4.2 Past reference

I wish	would rather	Suppose/supposing
if only	as if / as though	if

e.g. *If only he had telephoned before he came.* (He didn't)
I'd rather you hadn't told me. (You did tell me.)
He speaks as if he had done all the work himself. (He didn't)
Supposing you had had an accident! (You didn't)
I would have been terrified if it had happened to me. (It didn't)

The present perfect

1 Form

Simple:

has/have + past participle
e.g. *He's sold his car.*

Negative: *has/have not* + past participle
Question: *has/have* + subject + past participle ?

Continuous:

has/have been + present participle
e.g. *I've been playing tennis.*

Negative: *has/have been* + *-ing*
Question: *has/have* + subject + *been-ing*?

Note: Certain verbs are not usually used in continuous tenses. See list on page 106.

2 General use

2.1 Both the present perfect simple and the present perfect continuous are used to refer to actions or states which began in the past and have continued up till now. *Since* is used to express the starting point, and *for* is used to express its duration.

The following time expressions are often used:

lately, recently, so far,. up till now.

e.g. *I've had a cold for a week.*
He hasn't been practising on the piano so much lately.
How long have you lived in this flat now?

I've been going to Scotland every summer since I was a child.

2.2 The present perfect simple is used to refer to an action or state which was completed in the past but where the time is unknown or unimportant. The present result is generally more important than when or how the action or event occurred.

The following expressions are often used:

just, already, before, ever, never, yet still.

e.g. *Your father's just come in.* (= He's here)
I've seen that film already. (= I don't want to see it again)
The TV's been repaired. (= It is now working)
Have you ever been to Nepal? (= Can you tell me about it?)

3 Simple v. continuous

3.1 In some cases there is little difference between the two forms.

e.g. *I've lived here all my life.*
I've been living here all my life.

3.2 The present perfect continuous tends to emphasise how long an action has continued.

e.g. *It's been raining all day.*
I've been waiting for hours.

3.3 The present perfect continuous may suggest that an action is temporary rather than long-term or permanent.

e.g. *He's been staying with his sister till he finds somewhere to live.*

3.4 The present perfect simple suggests that an action is complete while the present perfect continuous suggests that it is still incomplete.

e.g. *I've painted the kitchen.* (The job is finished)
I've been painting the kitchen. (The job is probably unfinished)

3.5 The present perfect simple must be used when the quantity of actions or finished products is mentioned.

e.g. *I've done three exercises.*
He's telephoned a number of times.

Present Tenses

1 Present simple

Form | base form + (e)s | e.g. *She plays the violin.*

Negative: *doesn't / don't* + base form
Question: *do / does* + subject + base form?

Use

1.1 The present simple refers to situations which are long-term or permanent and to general truths such as scientific facts.

e.g. *They live in Brighton.*
She works for the Foreign Office.
I love classical music.
Nine planets travel round the sun.

1.2 It can also refer to regular or repeated actions.

e.g. *He swims during his lunch break every day.*
I always spend Christmas with my family.

1.3 It is used with certain verbs to express thoughts, feelings, impressions and immediate reactions.

e.g. *I think you're wonderful!   This tea tastes strange.*
Do you want to try the jacket on?

1.4 The present simple also has certain special uses in reviews, sports commentaries, dramatic narrative and when reporting what you have heard or been told (with say/tell/hear).

e.g. *Dustin Hoffman, who plays the hero, gives a fine performance.*
Black passes the ball to White but he misses ...
There I am, all alone in the house, and the doorbell rings!
I hear you've decided to move.

1.5 The present simple can be used to talk about future plans with reference to timetables and itineraries (see Grammar File page 94), and is also used in time clauses introduced by *when, as soon as, after, if* etc.

e.g. *The train leaves at midday.*
I'll let you know if a fax arrives.

2 Present continuous

Form | *is / are* + *-ing* | e.g. *He's washing his hair.*

Negative: *am / is / are not* + *-ing*
Question: *is / are* + subject + *-ing?*
Note: Certain verbs do not usually occur in continuous tenses (see page 106).

Use

2.1 The present continuous is used to talk about actions which are happening at the moment of speaking or which are changing or developing at the present time.

e.g. *Don't disturb him, he's working.*
My typing's improving.

2.2 It can also refer to actions or situations which are temporary.

e.g. *I'm helping out in the kitchen until they find a new chef.*

2.3 The present continuous can be used with *always* or *forever* to describe a habit which the speaker finds annoying.

e.g. *Why are you forever criticising me?*

2.4 The present continuous is also quite often used to express pre-arranged future actions (see Grammar File page 94).

e.g. *Nigel's coming round to see us tonight.*

Relative clauses

1 Defining relative clauses

A defining relative clause makes it clear who or what we're talking about and is essential to the meaning of the sentence.

e.g. *I'm afraid I've lost the book that you lent me.*

Special points

a *That* often replaces *who* or *which.*

b The relative pronoun can be omitted when it is the object of the clause.

e.g. *The typewriter that you sold me has gone wrong.*
OR   *The typewriter you sold me has gone wrong.*

c Commas are not used before the relative pronoun.

	subject	object	possessive
People	who/that	who/whom/that	whose
Things	which/that	which/that	
Place		where	
Time		when	
Reason		why	

Notes

a *Whom* is very formal and mainly used in written English, e.g. *The man to whom I spoke.* Less formally, we would say: *The man (who) I spoke to.*

b *Whose* can refer to both people and things e.g. *The woman whose dog ran away; A house whose roof collapsed.*

c *That* normally follows superlatives and words like *something/anything/nothing/all/none/many* and *few.*

2 Non-defining relative clauses

A non-defining relative clause gives extra information about a person or thing and is not essential to the meaning of the sentence.

e.g. *We went on an excursion to a wild life park, which was interesting.*

Special points

a *Who* and *which* cannot be replaced by *that.*
b The relative pronoun cannot be omitted.
c A comma is normally used before the relative pronoun.

Reported Speech

1 Reporting statements

To report what someone said, we use a reporting verb followed by a *that*-clause. In informal speech and writing, *that* may be omitted.

e.g. *She said she had been to an interview.*
   I told you I'd be late.

There is a list of reporting verbs which can be used with *that*-clauses on page 106.

2 Reporting questions

Note: Reported questions use normal word order and do not have question marks.

2.1 Yes/no questions

To report a yes/no question, we normally use *ask* followed by an *if*-clause or a *whether*-clause.

e.g. *They asked if we had any children.*
   I asked whether you wanted tea or coffee.

There is a list of other verbs which can be used with *if* and *whether*-clauses on page 106.

2.2 'wh'- questions

To report a 'wh'-question, we use the 'wh' word followed by the reported clause.

e.g. *She asked why she had to pay a deposit.*
   He wanted to know where the bank was.

There is a list of verbs which can be used in this structure on page 106.

3 Reporting orders, requests, suggestions etc.

3.1 To report an order, request etc. which has been made to someone, we can use a *to*-infinitive clause.

e.g. *He told me to wait in the queue.*
   I asked her to switch off the central heating.
   Her doctor advised her to stop smoking.

Other reporting verbs which can be used with this structure include *invite, order* and *warn.* There is a fuller list of such verbs on page 106.

3.2 To report a suggestion, we can use a *that*-clause. This clause often contains the verb *should* but may also contain an infinitive.

e.g. *The Manager suggested that we should put our complaint in writing.*
The Manager suggested we put our complaint in writing.

Other reporting verbs which can be used with this structure include *demand, insist* and *recommend.* There is a fuller list of such verbs on page 106.

Note: The verbs *advise, propose, recommend* and *suggest* can also be followed by an *-ing* form of the verb.

e.g. *He suggested breaking the journey in Chester.*

4 Reporting intentions and hopes

To report a stated intention or hope, we can use either a *that*-clause or a *to*-infinitive clause after certain verbs.

e.g. *I promised to be back before midnight*
I promised that I would be back before midnight.

Other reporting verbs which can used in this way include *hope, propose* and *threaten.* There is a fuller list of such verbs on page 106.

5 Time reference

When reporting speech, the tenses are normally changed as follows:

Direct speech	Reported Speech
Present simple	Past simple
Present continuous	Past continuous
Present perfect	Past perfect
Past simple	Past perfect
Past perfect	Past perfect
shall / will	should / would
can / may	could / might
must	must / had to
now	then
today	that day
tomorrow	the next/ following day
yesterday	the day before / the previous day
this	that
here	there
ago	before

Notes

a It is not necessary to change the tense when the reporting verb is in the present tense or when the original words are still true.

e.g. *He says his car has broken down and he's waiting for a mechanic.*
Professor Cooper explained that family tensions often erupt when the family is thrust together incessantly.

b Certain modal verbs (*could, would, should, ought to, might*) don't change in reported speech.

e.g. *I might be back late.*   *I said I might be back late.*

Spelling: capital letters

Capital letters are used:

1 at the *beginning of a sentence.*

2 in *headings* and *sub-headings* for reports, articles and so on. Also in the *titles of books, plays, films, particular works of art, scientific laws,* etc. In this case, the main words have capitals while the articles and smaller prepositions usually do not.

e.g. *Introduction*   *Focus on Advanced English*   *Hamlet*
Back to the Future   *Mona Lisa*   *Boyle's Law*

3 with *names of people* (also animals and other things which have individual names), *manufacturers, shops, hotels, government departments,* etc.

e.g. *Mr Martin Hall*   *Ford*   *Quicksave*
The Rome Hilton   *Department of Education*

4 with names of *countries, cities, town, regions, areas, streets,* etc., and with *adjectives* and *nouns* describing *nationality* or *place of origin* but not with east, west etc. on their own.

e.g. *France*   *Athens*   *the Middle East*   *Soho*
Fifth Avenue   *French*   *a Dutchman*   *Bavarian*

5 with *names of rivers, mountains* and other *geographical features.* Also with *planets* but not the sun, earth or moon.

e.g. *The Nile*   *Mount Everest*   *The Sahara Desert*
Mars   *The Black Forest*

6 with *days, months, festivals* and *historical periods* but not seasons.

e.g. *Tuesday*   *March*   *Easter*   *the Middle Ages*
(but *summer, winter* etc.)

7 with the names of certain *professions* or *positions* when used as titles for particular people but not when used generally.

e.g. *Let me introduce you to the Principal.* (but: *I'd like to become the principal of a college one day.*)

Spelling: forming participles

1 Doubling consonants

The final consonant is doubled in verbs:

1 which have only one syllable and which have one vowel followed by one consonant.

   e.g. *stop - stopping*
   run, trap, swim, fit, clap

   Exceptions: Final -*w*, -*x* and -*y* are never doubled.

2 which have more than one syllable but where the final syllable is stressed and has one vowel followed by one consonant.

   e.g *regret - regretting*
   begin, admit, refer, occur, forget

   Exceptions: There are a few verbs where the final consonant is doubled even though the stress is on the first syllable:

   worship, kidnap, handicap

3 which end in -*l* after one vowel.

   travel*, cancel*, control, signal*, fulfil

   e.g. *quarrel - quarrelling*

   Note that in American English there are some verbs where the final -*l* is not doubled. Examples are shown with a *.

   The final consonant is therefore not doubled in verbs:

a where there are two vowels followed by a consonant e.g. *sweep - sweeping* (Rule 1.1)

b where there are two final consonants e.g. *warn - warning* (Rule 1.1)

c where the stress is on the first of two syllables e.g. *limit - limiting* (Rule 1.2)

d where final -*l* follows two vowels e.g. *steal - stealing* (Rule 1.3)

2 Other points

1 Verbs which end in a consonant + -*e* normally drop the *e* before the ending -*ing*. e.g. *sneeze - sneezing*
   Main exceptions: *age - ageing, dye - dyeing*

2 Final -*y* after a consonant changes to -*i* before -*ed*. e.g. *try - tried*.

3 Final -*y* after a vowel does not normally change in this way. e.g. *enjoy - enjoyed, play - played*
   Exceptions: *pay - paid, lay - laid, say - said*

4 The ending -*ie* changes to -*y* before -*ing*. e.g. *lie - lying, die - dying*

5 Verbs which end with -*c* usually add -*k* before -*ed* or -*ing*. e.g. *panic - panicked, picnic - picnicking*

Reference Lists

-*ing* forms and infinitive

1 Verbs followed by -*ing* forms

admit	detest	involve	resent
adore	dislike	keep	resist
appreciate	dread	lie	risk
avoid	endure	loathe	sit
celebrate	enjoy	mention	stand
commence	face	mind	suggest
consider	fancy	miss	
contemplate	finish	postpone	
delay	go	practise	
deny	imagine	report	

2 Other expressions followed by -*ing* forms

can't bear	go (e.g. *camping*)	no good
can't help	spend time/money (on)	no use
can't stand		not worth

3 Verbs followed by a *to*-infinitive

afford	ask	consent	expect
agree	attempt	dare	fail
aim	beg	decide	fight
appear	care	demand	happen
arrange	choose	deserve	help
hesitate	mean	promise	threaten
hope	neglect	prove	volunteer
intend	offer	refuse	vow
learn	plan	seem	wait
long	prepare	swear	want
manage	pretend	tend	wish

4 Verbs which take an object followed by a *to*-infinitive

advise	forbid	invite	recommend
allow	force	leave	remind
ask	get	order	tell
encourage	help	persuade	want
expect	intend	prefer	warn

5 Verbs followed by -*ing* forms or a *to*-infinitive

a With little difference in meaning

attempt	cease	fear	love
begin	continue	hate	prefer
bother	deserve	like	start

b With a difference in meaning (For details, see Grammar File page 96.)

come	go on	remember
dread	mean	stop
forget	regret	try

Reporting verbs

1 Verbs followed by *that*-clauses

add	decide*	mention	state
admit	deny	observe	suggest
agree	doubt	persuade	suppose
announce	estimate	promise*	swear*
answer	expect*	propose	tell
argue	explain	remark	think
boast	fear	remember	threaten*
claim	feel	repeat	understand
comment	find	reply	warn
complain	guarantee*	report	
confirm	hope*	reveal	
consider	insist	say	

* These verbs can also be followed by *to*-infinitive clauses.

2 Verbs followed by *if* and *whether*-clauses

ask	remember	see
know	say	

3 Verbs followed by clauses beginning with 'wh' words

decide	guess	remember	teach
describe	imagine	reveal	tell
discover	know	say	think
discuss	learn	see	understand
explain	realise	suggest	wonder
forget			

4 Verbs followed by object + *to*-infinitive clause

advise	command	invite	warn
ask	forbid	teach	
beg	instruct	tell	

5 Verbs followed by a *that*-clause containing *should*

advise	insist	recommend
beg	prefer	request
demand	propose	suggest

Verbs not usually used in continuous tenses

admire	detest	impress	mean	seem
adore	dislike	include	owe	sound
astonish	doubt	involve	own	stop
be	envy	keep	please	suppose
believe	exist	know	possess	surprise
belong	fit	lack	prefer	survive
concern	forget	last	reach	suspect
consist	hate	like	realise	understand
contain	hear	love	remember	want
deserve	imagine	matter	satisfy	wish

Verbs not used in continuous tenses with specific meanings

appear	(= look/seem)
expect	(= feel confident that)
feel	(= have an opinion)
have	(= possess)
hold	(= have a certain capacity)
look	(= have an appearance)
measure	(= have a certain length)
see	(= use your eyes)
smell	(= have a certain smell)
think	(= have an opinion)
taste	(= have a certain taste)
weigh	(= have a certain weight)

Phonetic Symbols for English

Vowel sounds

ɑ:	heart, start, calm
æ	act, mass, lap
aɪ	dive, cry, mind
aɪə	fire, tyre, buyer
aʊ	out, down loud
aʊə	flour, tower, sour
ɛ	met, lend, pen
eɪ	say, main, weight
ɛə	fair, care, wear
ɪ	fit, win, list
i:	feed, me, beat
ɪə	near, beard, clear
ɒ	lot, lost, spot
əʊ	note, phone, coat
ɔ:	more, cord, claw
ɔɪ	boy, coin, joint
ʊ	could, stood, hood
u:	you, use, choose
ʊə	sure, poor, cure
ɜ:	turn, third, word
ʌ	but, fund, must
ə	the weak vowel in butter, about, forgotten

Consonant sounds

b	bed	t	talk
d	done	v	van
f	fit	w	win
g	good	x	loch
h	hat	z	zoo
j	yellow	ʃ	ship
k	king	ʒ	measure
l	lip	ŋ	sing
m	mat	tʃ	cheap
n	nine	θ	thin
p	pay	ð	then
r	run	dʒ	joy
s	soon		

Vowel letters: a e i o u

Consonant letters: b c d f g h j k l m n p q r s t v w x y z

Irregular Verbs

Base form	Past form	Past participle	Base form	Past form	Past participle	Base form	Past form	Past participle
arise	arose	arisen	get	got	got	shut	shut	shut
awake	awoke	awoken	give	gave	given	sing	sang	sung
bear	bore	borne	go	went	gone	sink	sank	sunk
beat	beat	beaten	grind	ground	ground	sit	sat	sat
become	became	become	grow	grew	grown	slay	slew	slain
begin	began	begun	hear	heard	heard	sleep	slept	slept
bend	bent	bent	hide	hid	hidden	slide	slid	slid
bet	bet	bet	hit	hit	hit	sling	slung	slung
bind	bound	bound	hold	held	held	sow	sowed	sown
bite	bit	bitten	hurt	hurt	hurt	speak	spoke	spoken
bleed	bled	bled	keep	kept	kept	spend	spent	spent
blow	blew	blown	know	knew	known	spin	spun	spun
break	broke	broken	lay	laid	laid	spread	spread	spread
breed	bred	bred	lead	led	led	spring	sprang	sprung
bring	brought	brought	leave	left	left	stand	stood	stood
build	built	built	lend	lent	lent	steal	stole	stolen
burst	burst	burst	let	let	let	stick	stuck	stuck
buy	bought	bought	lose	lost	lost	sting	stung	stung
cast	cast	cast	make	made	made	stink	stank	stunk
catch	caught	caught	mean	meant	meant	stride	strode	stridden
choose	chose	chosen	meet	met	met	strike	struck	struck
cling	clung	clung	pay	paid	paid	string	strung	strung
come	came	come	put	put	put	strive	strove	striven
cost	cost	cost	quit	quit	quit	swear	swore	sworn
creep	crept	crept	read	read	read	sweep	swept	swept
cut	cut	cut	ride	rode	ridden	swim	swam	swum
deal	dealt	dealt	ring	rang	rung	swing	swung	swung
dig	dug	dug	rise	rose	risen	take	took	taken
draw	drew	drawn	run	ran	run	teach	taught	taught
drink	drank	drunk	saw	sawed	sawn	tear	tore	torn
drive	drove	driven	say	said	said	tell	told	told
eat	ate	eaten	see	saw	seen	think	thought	thought
fall	fell	fallen	seek	sought	sought	throw	threw	thrown
feed	fed	fed	sell	sold	sold	thrust	thrust	thrust
feel	felt	felt	send	sent	sent	tread	trod	trodden
fight	fought	fought	set	set	set	understand	understood	understood
find	found	found	sew	sewed	sewn	wear	wore	worn
flee	fled	fled	shake	shook	shaken	weep	wept	wept
fling	flung	flung	shed	shed	shed	win	won	won
fly	flew	flown	shine	shone	shone	wind	wound	wound
forbid	forbade	forbidden	shoe	shod	shod	wring	wrung	wrung
forget	forgot	forgotten	shoot	shot	shot	write	wrote	written
forgive	forgave	forgiven	show	showed	shown			
freeze	froze	frozen	shrink	shrank	shrunk			

Writing File

1 Task Types

2 Linking and Logical Devices   **123**

A   Informal Letters

A1 Layout

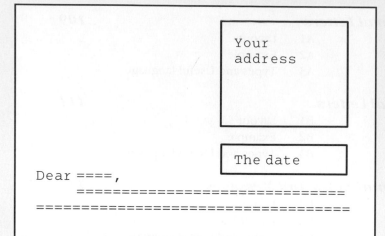

Write your address in the top right hand corner.

Write the date directly below.

Write the first line next to the left hand margin.

Begin the next line under the name.

A2   Example

Never put your name before your address.

Write the house number first, followed by the street, town (and post code, if you know it).

Never begin with *Dear Friend*. Always use a name.

Begin the first sentence with a capital.

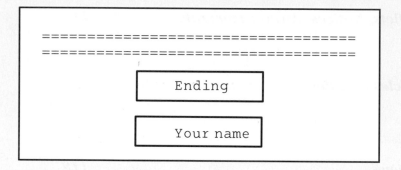

22 York Street
Bridewell
BR8 4SO

24th Nov. 19—

Dear Ken,
　　Many thanks for your letter and for the photographs — they brought back very happy memories of our holiday.
　　I'm glad to hear that your new job is going so well. It must be

　　Do let me know when you're coming to England. It would be lovely to see you and you're most welcome to stay here — there's plenty of room!
　　Hope to hear from you soon.
　　　Best wishes
　　　　Sue.

With closer friends, you could just put *Write soon*.

Best wishes, and *Yours* are useful general endings. For close friends, you can end with *Love*.

A3 Types of Letters

A3.1 Beginnings

In an informal letter to a friend, it may be appropriate to begin by mentioning a letter which you have recently received or by making general friendly comments.

Useful language:

> **Many thanks for your letter ...**
> **It was very nice to hear from you recently ...**
> **I was glad to hear that** *you had a good holiday*
> **I hope** *you and the family are well.*

A3.2 Invitation

Say what the event is and explain the details of date, time and place clearly. You may need to add other details such as who else is coming, what you would like your friend to bring (if anything), whether they can bring a partner or friend, when you need a reply by, and how to get there. Use separate paragraphs for each main piece of information.

Useful language:

> **I'm having a birthday party on** *Saturday the 22nd* **and I hope you'll be able to come.**
> **I was wondering if you'd like to come to see** *'Wild Lives' at the Theatre Royal with me?*
> **Would you like to/ Why don't you** *come and stay for the weekend?*
> **Could you (possibly) let me know if** *you can come by ...*

A3.3 Request

Describe the situation or problem and explain exactly what needs to be done. Make it clear how grateful you would be for the help you ask for and give an opportunity for the recipient to agree or refuse, if appropriate.

Useful language:

> **I'm writing to/ I wonder if I could ask you a favour.**
> **I wonder if/ I was wondering if you could help me?**
> **I'd be terribly grateful . . .**
> **Please don't hesitate to say no if you can't manage it . . .**

A3.4 Apology

Explain why you are apologising, give reasons for your behaviour, express regret for any damage, inconvenience, offence which was caused, and offer to put things right if possible.

Useful language:

> **I'm writing to apologise about ...**
>   **for the fact that**
>   (+ clause)
>   **for (not) (+ ing)**
> **I'm terribly sorry that ...**
> **I do hope that ...**
> **Please let me know** *where you bought it/ how much it cost/ what the bill is* **and I'll gladly** *replace it/ pay for it.*

A3.5 Information/News

Useful language:

> **I thought you'd like to know/ hear about ...**
> **This is just to let you know that ...**

A3.6 Thank you/Congratulations/Good Luck

Useful language:

> **I'm writing to thank you/ Thank you so much for** (+ noun/-ing)
> **It was very kind of you to ...**
> **I'm writing to congratulate you/ Congratulations on** (+ noun)
> **I'm writing to wish you (the very best of) luck in/ with** (+ noun)

A3.7 Endings

It is usual to end letters which expect a reply with a sentence on a separate line. This could be:

> **Looking forward to hearing from you/ seeing you.**
> **Hope to hear from you soon/ see you soon.**
> **Write soon/ See you soon.**

B Formal Letters

B1 Layout

Write your address in the top right hand corner.

Write the date directly below.

Write the recipient's name and address on the left hand side below the date.

Only use *Dear Sir* or *Dear Madam* if you don't know the person's name.

```
┌─────────────────────────────────────────────┐
│                              ┌─────────────┐  │
│                              │ Your        │  │
│                              │ address     │  │
│                              │             │  │
│                              └─────────────┘  │
│                              ┌─────────────┐  │
│   ┌─────────────┐            │ The date    │  │
│   │Other person's│           └─────────────┘  │
│   │name and      │                            │
│   │address       │                            │
│   └─────────────┘                             │
│                                               │
│  Dear Sir/Madam, /Dear Mr Brandon/Mrs White, │
│  ==========================================   │
│  ==========================================   │
└─────────────────────────────────────────────┘
```

```
┌─────────────────────────────────────────────┐
│  ==========================================   │
│  ============                                 │
│  Yours faithfully, / Yours sincerely          │
│         ┌────────────────────┐                │
│         │ Your signature     │                │
│         └────────────────────┘                │
│         ┌────────────────────┐                │
│         │ Your name -printed │                │
│         └────────────────────┘                │
└─────────────────────────────────────────────┘
```

If you begin *Dear Sir* or *Dear Madam*, end with *Yours faithfully*. If you begin with a name, end with *Yours sincerely*.

B2 Example

Write the name and/or title of the person you're writing to. Do not indent their address.

Write the first line next to the left hand margin.

Begin the next line under the name.

Write *Yours* with a capital 'Y' and *faithfully* or *sincerely* with a small 'f' or 's'. These endings are followed by a comma.

Never put your name before your address. Write the house number first, followed by the street, town (and post code, if you know it).

Give your reason for writing at the beginning. If you are replying to an advert, say where you saw it and when. If you are replying to a letter, give the date of the letter.

Print your name clearly after your signature.

> 22 York Street
> Bridewell
> BR8 4SO
>
> 24th Nov. 19-
>
> The Principal
> Clifton College
> Clifton
> CL5 2RE
>
> Dear Sir,
>   I am interested in applying for a place on a computing course in your college and I would be grateful if you could send me full details of the courses you offer and the fees, together with an application form.
>
>   I look forward to hearing from you.
>
>   Yours faithfully,
>   S.M. Gilchrist
>
>   S.M. GILCHRIST (MISS)

B3 Types of Letters

B3.1 Enquiry

Explain clearly what information you would like and why you need it. If there are different points you need to explain or to ask about, use a different paragraph for each.

Useful language:

> ***I am writing to enquire about ...***
> ***I was interested in your advertisement in*** *'The Daily Times'* ***and I would like to have further information about ...***
> ***I should be grateful if you would send me (full) details of ...***

B3.2 Application

Explain clearly which post/job you are applying for and, if you are responding to an advertisement, say where you saw it and when. Give all the necessary information about yourself, including age, qualifications, past employment, relevant experience and any special hobbies or interests, and explain why you are particularly interested in this post. Use a new paragraph for each main topic. It's also helpful to say when you would be available to attend an interview.

Useful language:

> ***I am interested in applying for the post of ... which was advertised in*** *'The Weekend Times'* ***on*** *22nd September.*
> ***My reason for applying is that*** *I would like to broaden my experience and also to make greater use of my knowledge of languages than I do in my present position.*
> ***I would be able to attend an interview at*** *any time which is convenient to you.*

B3.3 Apology

Explain why you are apologising, give reasons for your behaviour, express regret for the damage/inconvenience/ offence which has been caused and promise not to let it happen again or to make up for what you've done, as appropriate.

Useful language:

> ***I am writing to apologise about ...***
> ***for the fact that*** (+ clause)
> ***for (not)*** (+ ing)

> ***The reason I*** *couldn't telephone you was ...*
> ***I'm really sorry*** *to have wasted your time.*
> ***I assure you that*** *this will never happen again.*
> ***If you let me know*** *where you bought it,* ***I'll gladly*** *replace it*

B3.4 Complaint

In the *first paragraph*, explain the reason for writing and in the *next*, explain exactly what the problem is. Give all the necessary details about where and when it happened and who was involved. Give other relevant information in *further paragraphs* if necessary. In the *final paragraph*, explain what action you want to be taken.

Useful language:

> ***I am writing to complain about ...***
> ***I am writing to express my concern about the fact that ...***
> ***I must insist that you ...***
> ***I must urge you to ...***

B3.5 Opinion

If you're replying or reacting to something such as a letter or an article, give the necessary details. Explain your opinion and the reasons for it clearly, using separate paragraphs for each main point. Sum up your argument in the final paragraph.

Useful language:

> ***In reply to your letter of*** *12th September,* ***I would like to say ...***
> ***I would like to respond to the article called*** *'.....'* ***which appeared in*** *Monday's* ***edition of your newspaper.***
> ***In my opinion, ...***
> ***It seems (clear) to me that ...***

B3.6 Endings

It is usual to end letters which expect a reply with a sentence on a separate line. The most common ending is:

> ***I look forward to hearing from you.***

C *Personal Notes and Messages*

C1 Layout

Notes and messages are even more informal than informal letters and are written to friends and people you know well. They usually contain a brief message about one or two main subjects so they are generally shorter than a page. They may or may not be placed in envelopes and are often delivered by hand rather than posted. There are no fixed rules about their layout.

C2 Examples

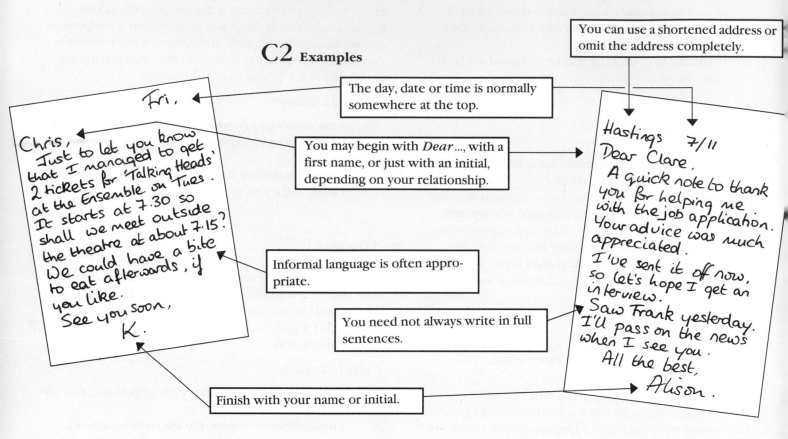

The day, date or time is normally somewhere at the top.

You can use a shortened address or omit the address completely.

You may begin with *Dear ...*, with a first name, or just with an initial, depending on your relationship.

Informal language is often appropriate.

You need not always write in full sentences.

Finish with your name or initial.

Handwritten note 1:
Fri,

Chris,
Just to let you know that I managed to get 2 tickets for 'Talking Heads' at the Ensemble on Tues. It starts at 7.30 so shall we meet outside the theatre at about 7.15? We could have a bite to eat afterwards, if you like.
See you soon,
K.

Handwritten note 2:
Hastings 7/11
Dear Clare,
A quick note to thank you for helping me with the job application. Your advice was much appreciated.
I've sent it off now, so let's hope I get an interview.
Saw Frank yesterday. I'll pass on the news when I see you.
All the best,
Alison.

C3 Types of Notes and Messages

C3.1 Beginnings

Useful language

No special introductory phrases are necessary but notes often begin with expressions like:

Just (a note) to	*let you know/tell you/check (that) ...*
A quick note to	*ask/see if ...*
	thank you for/apologise (for/about) ...

C3.2 Queries

Useful language:

Could you let me know	*what happened about ...*
	what you ('ve) decided about ...
Can you tell me	*what you think about ...*
	if you're interested in ...
	if you'd like to ...

C3.3 Information/News

Useful language:

Just to let you know (that) ...
(I) Thought you might like to know (that) ...

C3.4 Request

Useful language

Could you | let me have ...
| tell me ...
| look into ...
| find out about ...

C3.5 Apology

Useful language

(I'm) Sorry I *couldn't/ wasn't able to/ didn't/ forgot to ..*

C3.6 Thank you/Congratulations/Good Luck

Useful language

Many thanks for ...
Just to thank you for ... *(*+ noun/-*ing)*
Congratulations on ...
Best of luck in/ with ... *(*+ noun*)*

C3.7 Endings

Useful language

No special final phrases are needed but notes and messages may end with expressions like:

See you soon
Speak to you soon
All the best

D Leaflets, Notices, Announcements

D1 Notes

Leaflets, notices and announcements are generally intended to *inform, advise, persuade* or *warn*. The two main aims are therefore to catch the reader's attention and to present the message as clearly as possible.

To do this, layout and organisation need to be as effective as possible. Short paragraphs with clear headings are much easier to read and absorb than long blocks of text, for example. The best approach is to imagine yourself as the reader and to ask what *you* would want to know, and in what order you would find it easiest to absorb the information. Consider these points:

Main heading:

Is this as direct and eye-catching as possible?
Does it give the reader a clear idea of what the subject is?
Does it make the reader want to read on?

Sub-headings:

Are these short and clear? Asking a question in your heading may be more interesting than stating a fact. (See Example 4.)

Text:

Is the information broken up into short easy-to-read sections?
Is the order logical?

Visual help:

Can you help the reader, for example:

by indenting small sub-sections so that they stand out as small blocks which are clearly separate from the main text? or

- by putting important points on separate lines? or

6. by numbering your points? or

● by putting 'blobs' in front of main points? or

by using different *STYLES* and sizes of *writing?* or

by underlining, or using a contrasting colour, or

by putting boxes round important words, or

by drawing arrows to show a progression? or

by adding illustrations? Even if you're no artist, rough sketches or symbols can make a big difference! You won't be marked on your artwork, of course, but you may make a good impression on the examiner!

D2 Examples

D2.1 Notices, Announcements

WARNING

There have been a number of thefts of personal property in this building recently.

You are advised to keep your belongings with you at all times and not to leave bags unattended.

If you see anyone behaving suspiciously, please contact the Security Staff on Extension 250.

Watch out —
there's a thief about!

Have you seen....

A dark brown leather wallet Dropped in the Students Union on Monday afternoon? Contains photographs and other items of sentimental value.
Please contact S.Jones 299710

REWARD

FOR SALE

portable Colour TV. Excellent picture

 manual typewriter Good working condition

Automatic camera. Old but works well.

English language books. As new condition!

The above items are available at <u>BARGAIN</u> prices as I am returning to my country at the end of term.
Please phone Sam on 462235 after 6pm.
but <u>HURRY</u>, <u>HURRY</u>

D2.2 Leaflets

Look after your **HEART!**

A SIMPLE GUIDE

TO FEELING FITTER,

LOOKING BETTER

AND LIVING LONGER

Why do I need to look after my heart?

By looking after your heart, you can feel fitter and look better – and you'll be protecting yourself against heart disease, too.

England is one of the worst countries in the world for heart disease. It causes one in three of all deaths among 55-64 year olds.

What causes heart disease?

Your heart needs a supply of oxygen that comes from the blood in its arteries. Over a number of years, these arteries can get clogged up and the supply of blood to the heart can stop. This causes a heart attack.

I'm fit and healthy. Why should I worry?

Heart attacks usually happen to people in middle age, but the damage to your arteries can start long before that, without you realising it. It can even start to develop in childhood. So it's important to look after your heart now, whatever your age.

Isn't a heart attack a quick way to go?

Not always. Heart disease can cause years of pain, discomfort and worry.

How can I avoid getting heart disease?

No-one can guarantee a way of avoiding it, but the best advice to reduce your risk of getting heart disease is:

**Don't smoke
Eat healthily
Take regular exercise
Go easy on alcohol
Avoid stress if you can**

If you have heart disease in your family, you may have a greater risk of getting it yourself, so it's especially important to follow this advice.

2

3

E   Articles and Reports

E1 Notes

An *article* is a piece of writing on a particular subject which is written for publication in a newspaper or magazine.

The term *report* can also refer to an account of something in a newspaper (e.g. *Did you read the report on homelessness in The Daily News yesterday?*), but more usually it means a formal document which is prepared by one person or a group of people who have been studying a particular subject (e.g. *The committee published its final report, recommending legislation against racism*).

Articles and *reports* may deal with the same subject matter but the treatment will be different. An *article* is designed to make a topic interesting for the general reader while a *report* is usually written for a more informed reader who already knows something about the subject. *Reports* are generally longer and more detailed than *articles*.

E1.1 Articles

Approach:

A wide range of approaches is possible, depending on the subject matter. A light-hearted or humorous topic might be given a fairly personal treatment, for example, while a more serious topic would be treated much more impersonally and analytically. Notice how in the 'Lucky kids' article in E2.1, specific examples are given and quotations are included in order to make the dry facts of the survey more interesting.

Layout and Organisation:

Articles should have a heading which makes the subject matter clear but which also catches the reader's eye and makes him or her want to read. Newspapers and magazines often use dramatic statements, or wordplay in headings for this reason, and sometimes add a sub-heading which gives more information. (See E3.1 for examples.)

As with any other kind of composition, it's important to have an interesting introduction and a suitable conclusion, and to organise the information into paragraphs which help the reader to follow the argument or understand the different aspects of the subject.

E1.2 Reports

Approach:

Reports are the most impersonal kind of writing and this is reflected in the language used (see E3.2). It is usually best to avoid expressing personal opinions or feelings except, perhaps, in a conclusion.

Layout and Organisation:

Reports should have a clear, factual heading and may also have subheadings which divide the writing into shorter sections. Again, a clear introduction and conclusion, and logical organisation of the information into paragraphs or sections are essential.

E2 Examples

E2.1 Articles

Lucky kids: $7 a week and no chores

By KAREN McGUINNESS

While the average Sydney child gets $7.63 a week for doing practically nothing, seven-year-old Nicholas Falkinder is happy with his $1 pocket-money. His sister Anna, 5, gets 50 cents.

Their mother, Ms Christine Krain, says: "Naturally we expect them both to set the table at night and keep their rooms tidy.

"But that's not to earn the money. The money is for them to spend or save. It's to help them get to know the value of money and how it accumulates."

The children, who go to Leichhardt Primary School, both saved their money to buy books.

Only half the Sydney children who receive pocket money are expected to do domestic chores for it, according to the findings of a pocket money survey which are to be released today.

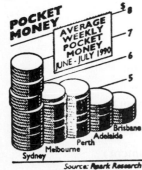

POCKET MONEY

AVERAGE WEEKLY POCKET MONEY JUNE - JULY 1990

Sydney Melbourne Perth Adelaide Brisbane

Source: Roark Research

The study, commissioned by Streets, the ice-cream company, found that only 48 per cent of parents surveyed in Sydney expected their children to earn their pocket-money. In Brisbane, eight in 10 parents made their children work for the money.

Carmelina, 7, whose parents emigrated from Italy more than 20 years ago, gets $10 a week. She uses it to buy lunch at school, but is not asked by her parents to work for it.

Carmelina's 15-year-old sister, Antonella, also gets $10 a week, but helps her mother with the cooking and washing the dishes.

Her mother, who prefers not to be identified, said the money was for Antonella to save to buy a car.

"When I was a child in Italy I didn't have any money," said mother. "I don't want my daughters to miss out. But I will always make sure my daughters spend their money sensibly or save it."

Fishy tales for cheque refunds

AMERICAN Express can relate some strange stories from people requesting refunds for lost and stolen cheques.

Like the couple who presented half eaten cheques to the Lisbon office after the documents had been devoured by mice in a tent in the Amazon.

But the oddest story comes from the United States, where a woman said her handbag had fallen into the water on a boating trip and was swallowed by a shark.

A few days later the woman went fishing and caught a shark.

Inside they found the undigested, undamaged travellers cheques.

Leisure Facilities in Anytown

Introduction

The aim of this report is to describe and assess the leisure facilities available in Anytown. It is based on information made available by the Anytown Tourist Office, and on views expressed by local people who were interviewed.

Sport

Anytown has a wide range of sports facilities, both public and private. There is a large modern leisure centre in the High Street and facilities include a swimming pool, a sports hall for judo, fencing and other activities, and tennis courts. The centre runs courses in all these sports and these tend to be very popular. Membership costs £100 a year, which was felt to be rather expensive, but a special temporary membership is available to visitors. The public swimming pool on the outskirts of town at Downmarket is older, less attractive and often overcrowded, but entry is only 50p.

Theatres

There are two theatres in town, the Kings Theatre in Bee Street which offers mainly 'serious' drama and has a good reputation for its productions of Shakespeare plays, and the Little Theatre in Sea Street which specialises in lighter entertainment and the occasional pop concert. In general, it seems that the Kings Theatre is more popular with the older members of the community while the Little appeals more to people in their teens, twenties and early thirties.

Museums and Art Galleries

The City Museum has an extensive collection of maps, pottery and other articles connected with Anytown's history. The attendants are said to be very friendly and helpful, and there is also a small cafe with reasonably priced home-made snacks. Interestingly, few of the local Anytowners interviewed had ever been to the museum but it was recommended highly by several tourists.

Shopping

Conclusion

Anytown is well-provided with leisure facilities for a town of its size and these are well-used by the townspeople, on the whole. Sport seems to be the most popular leisure activity (after shopping) while cultural activities like visiting the museum or art gallery appeared to be the least popular amongst the Anytowners who were interviewed. Perhaps the City Council should consider launching a publicity campaign to show how much these facilities have to offer.

E3 Useful language

E3.1 Articles

Writers can use a variety of devices to make their headings eye-catching.
Examples from texts in this book:

TODAY IS CANCELLED!	(dramatic statement)
Your Mind: Do you make the best use of it? }	(challenging question)
You are caught in a fire – then what? }	
Lucky kids: $7 a week and no chores	(interesting comment)
Give us a break - from holidays	(paradox)
Fishy tales for cheque funds	(wordplay: *fishy* = 1. connected with fish; 2. suspicious)

For examples of different styles and approaches to writing articles, look through the texts in this book.

E3.2 Reports

Introduction:	*The aim of this report is to ...*	*It is based on ...*
	This report is intended to ...	*It draws on ...*
	This report looks at / describes ...	*It uses ...*
Reporting an observation:	*It seems/ appears that ...*	*It was found that ...*
	... tend (s) to (do)	*It was felt that ...*
	A/ The majority/ minority of ...	*... were in the majority/ minority*
Quoting:	*According to ...* *As X said, ...*	*In the words of ...*
Speculating:	*It may/ could/ might (well) be that ...*	
	... may/ could/ might + (do/ have done)	
Generalising:	*In general* *On the whole* *In the main*	
Commenting:	*Interestingly Curiously Oddly Strangely Surprisingly Predictably*	
	As might be (have been) expected *It is interesting that .... (etc.)*	
Making a recommendation:	*It is recommended that ...*	
	(Perhaps) It is/ would be advisable for X to (do)	
	(Perhaps) X might/ should consider + ing	
Summing up:	*To sum up/ To summarise* *On balance* *In short*	

F   Reviews

F1 Notes

A *review* is an article in a newspaper or magazine in which someone gives their views on a book, play, film, TV programme, etc. The purpose of a review is firstly to give factual *information* about the subject, and secondly to give an *opinion* about it which will help the reader to decide whether to buy the book, see the play or visit the exhibition.

Reviews normally contain the three main ingredients listed below. A review may not always fall into three neat sections, however. The writer may decide to describe one aspect of the subject and comment immediately on strengths and weaknesses, for example, before going on to describe another aspect of the subject.

F1.1 Overview - a description of the subject

Book - non-fiction:
What is it about? Who is it for? How technical is it? How is it organised? What topics are covered? What special features are there? How much does it cost? etc.

Book - fiction:
What kind of book is it (thriller/historical novel/science fiction etc.)? Is it different in any way from other books of this type? What's the story? etc. (You can give an outline but don't give the ending away!)

Play/Film/Programme:
What is it about? Is there anything special/unusual about the production? **Play/film:** Where is it on? Are there any well-known actors? Who is the director? **TV Programme:** Which channel? Is it part of a series? Who is the producer?

F1.2 Pros and cons - detailed comments on the successful and unsuccessful features of the subject

Your comments will probably include both *objective* views (based on fact) - the photographs were poor quality or the costumes didn't fit the actors properly, for example - and *subjective* views (based on personal feelings) - the story wasn't interesting or the film was too violent. Make sure, however, that you give reasons for your comments.

You may have strong positive or negative feelings about the subject of the review and this is no bad thing. A strong opinion, clearly argued, is often more interesting to read than a carefully balanced assessment. Even so, try not to be completely one-sided.

F2 Examples

F2.1 Book - non-fiction

> **The Joy of Sandwiches** - A Munch and Y Knott, The Take Away Press, Neasden, £35.
>
> Despite its rather unpromising title, this is actually a fascinating and comprehensive study of a long neglected aspect of the cook's art.
>
> The first part of the book deals with the background to the subject. There is a detailed history of the sandwich from its invention by the Earl of Sandwich in the 18th century to the latest creations of the present day. There are chapters on 'The Sandwich in Art' and 'The Sandwich in Literature', and this section ends with a survey of the place of the sandwich in the cultures of various countries around the world.
>
> The second part of the book is devoted to 'recipes', some traditional, some new, and each sandwich is beautifully illustrated with a full page colour photograph. The 'recipes' are clear enough even for a child to follow (although it must be said that child might have difficulty lifting the book since it weighs nearly 2Kg!). There are helpful line drawings showing some of the preparation techniques including the correct way to slice bread. All in all this is a superb book which should provide inspiration for all sandwich makers whether they are beginners or 'old hands'. Only the rather steep price of £35 may prevent it from becoming the best seller which it deserves to be.

F2.2 Book - fiction

> **Yes, Mr President** - Ivan Oscar, Blockbuster Press, £12.50.
>
> This is the unlikely story of a second rate actor who becomes President of the United States. Young Donald Beagan seems set for a mediocre career in Hollywood in the 1940's until he ventures into politics and wins a nomination for Governor of California. Ten years and one marriage later, he runs for the White House and ends up the most powerful man in the world.
>
> Ivan Oscar, the author, is well-known for such best-selling thrillers as 'Live Now, Die Later' and this book is certainly packed with action and exotic settings but somehow the formula doesn't work. The hero, Beagan, never really comes to life and his wife, Mandy, (an ex-actress - what else?) is such a cardboard figure that it's hard to feel interested in their relationship. In the end, the story is just too improbable to hold the reader's attention. A very forgettable book.

F1.3 Verdict - summing-up and recommendation

The last paragraph should sum up your feelings and make it clear to the reader whether you recommend the subject without any reservations, recommend it with one or two reservations, or don't recommend it at all. In real life, readers often look at the last paragraph of a review first to see what the general verdict is. Make sure your review gives a clear verdict.

F2.3 Film/Play/TV programme

> **Crazy Plumber**: Plaza Cinema
>
> If you have seen the advance publicity, you might imagine that this was a funny film. Wrong. It's a film which tries very hard to be funny and fails consistently. The story concerns a plumber who isn't very good at his job. When his customers desert, and he can't pay the bills, he decides to turn to crime. He tries a little shoplifting (he's not very good at it, of course) but then he gets involved in bigger things.
>
> Wayne Gibson, who plays the hero, has one or two good lines but most of the time he's struggling with a terrible script. There are a few good moments - the car chase sequence is memorable - but the story line is very slight and the director, seems to have run out of ideas very quickly. As the film progresses, the level of violence increases. Despite the publicity, this is not a film for young children.
>
> A great deal of money went into the making of Crazy Plumber but in the end, spectacular effects are no substitute for real humour.

> **The Secret Life of the Termite**, 9.30 Tuesday, BBC 1.
>
> This was the first in a new series of wild life documentary programmes presented by the well-known naturalist, David Buttonborough. Each programme will focus on one creature and looks at its habitat and life cycle in depth.
>
> This week's subject was the termite and we learnt, among other things, about the amazingly complex architecture of the termite hill. Termites are not particularly attractive looking creatures but the photography was so superb, and Mr Buttonborough's commentary so informative, that it was difficult not to become totally absorbed. I, for one, have certainly learnt a new respect for these industrious little insects.
>
> In the weeks to come, we can look forward to programmes on the earthworm and the sea slug. If they can maintain the standard set in this first programme, this will be a very successful series.

F3 Useful Language

F3.1 Overview

The	book film programme	concerns deals with shows describes tells the story of contains includes

a	study survey history	of
a	chapter section	on

Each	chapter programme	focuses on is devoted to

The	book/ script film/ programme programme part costumes/ set	is/ was	written produced presented played designed	by

The story is based on

Books	Films	Plays	Programmes
chapter	plot/ storyline	scene	episode
plot	script	act	series
characterisation	soundtrack	scenery	commentary
illustrations	set	costumes	photography
design	special effects	cast	studio
contents	stunt	stage	broadcast

F3.2 Pros and cons

really absolutely	extraordinary fascinating amazing beautiful stunning superb brilliant original

quite fairly	interesting amusing entertaining exciting informative attractive successful unusual

really completely	boring unimaginative humourless hopeless awful amateurish over the top predictable

Despite/ in spite of + noun	... while ...
Although + clause	... whereas ...
.... although/ but + clause	... except that ...
On the one hand ..., on the other hand ...	... even if ...

F3.3 Verdict

All in all, In the end	In the last analysis, On balance,	In conclusion To sum up,

G Instructions/Directions

G1 Notes

Instructions and directions give step by step information for other people to follow. They may be written for one person that you know well - directions for reaching your house, for example - or for a number of people you don't know at all - a set of Fire Instructions, for example.

The style may be more or less informal according to the topic and audience but the key thing for all instructions is that they are crystal clear. For this reason they must contain all the necessary information in the most logical order and laid out in the clearest possible way.

★ **All the information**
When you are speaking to someone, you can say *'Do it like this'* or *'Put it over there'* and the meaning will be clear because of your demonstration or gesture. In writing, this information needs to be expressed in words. Make sure all the necessary details are there. For example, *'write your name in the corner'* or *'cut the meat into pieces'* may not be enough - which corner? how big should the pieces be? More complete instructions would say *'the top right-hand corner'* and *'bite-sized pieces'* or *'3cm cubes'*.

When you know how to do something very well yourself, it may be difficult to imagine the problems someone might have when they do it for the first time. Try imagining you're writing for a child or for someone who isn't very intelligent!

★ **The most logical order**
Most instructions and directions involve a sequence of steps. When we are speaking, we may say things like: *'Oh, I forgot to mention, you have to soak the beans overnight first'*. Obviously, this would not be very satisfactory in writing, so it's vital to make notes of all the main points beforehand.

★ **Clear layout**
If you are giving fairly brief, informal instructions in a letter to a friend, for example, it may be appropriate to write them in one or two ordinary paragraphs. In this case, you will probably need to make use of sequence markers like *First, next, then, after that,* and so on.

When the instructions are more detailed or for more formal use, it will be much easier for the reader if you number each point and write it on a separate line. In this case, sequence markers are less important. If you are preparing a notice, don't forget to give it a clear heading.

G2 Examples

Instructions - informal version

Here's that recipe for spicy rice which you asked for:
First melt about 3 tablespoons of butter in a small pan. Next add about an ⅛th of a teaspoon of curry powder and blend well. Combine the butter mixture with 3 cups of cooked rice and then season to taste with salt. After that, add a ⅓ of a cup of chopped parsley and a ¼ of a cup of finely chopped peanuts. Finally, put the mixture in a casserole and heat at 175°C for 20-25 minutes.

Instructions - formal version

Spicy rice
Ingredients
3 Tsp butter
½ tsp curry powder
3 cups cooked rice
¼ cup chopped parsley
1 tsp salt
¼ cup finely chopped peanuts

Method
1. *Melt the butter in a small pan.*
2. *Add the curry powder and blend well.*
3. *Combine the butter mixture and the rice.*
4. *Season to taste with salt and add the parsley and peanuts.*
5. *Place in a casserole and heat at 175° for 20 - 25 minutes.*

Directions - informal version

It looks a long way on the map but you'll be surprised how straightforward the journey is.

Go north over the harbour bridge. When you've crossed the bridge, the road forks. Don't go right. Follow the Pacific Highway which bears left and continue for about 15 km until you get to Pymble. Turn off there and follow the signs to Mona Vale. You'll see the Ku-ring-gai National Park on your left. After about 20 km, you'll come to Mona Vale. Turn right into the main street and take the first turning on the left. We're the house with the white fence in front, half way down on the right!

Look forward to seeing you on Friday!

Directions - formal version

Instructions for using the Photocopier

1. Switch on using the red button located on the left-hand side of the machine.

2. Allow 2 - 3 minutes for the machine to warm up. When it is ready to operate the indicator on top will change from red to green.

3. Raise the cover and place the document to be copied face down between the lines shown.

4. Press the number keys to select the number of copies you require (1 - 999). This number will be displayed in the small window next to the keys. If you have made a mistake, press the CANCEL button and start again.

5. When you are ready to begin copying, press the COPY button.

G3 Useful Language

G3.1 Instructions/Directions (informal)

You	take ...	or	Take ...		**Extra**		You'll	notice ...
	put ...		Put ...		**Information**			see ...
	mix etc. ...		Mix etc. ...					pass etc.

Don't ...
Be careful (not) to ...
Remember to ...
Don't forget to ...

G3.2 Instructions/Directions (formal)

These tend to begin with a verb in the imperative and to use slightly formal vocabulary, e.g. *place* instead of 'put', *select* instead of 'choose' (see examples 3 and 4).

G3.3 Sequence Markers

First(ly)		When	you have (done that)
Second(ly) etc.		Once	
Next/ Then/ After that		After	
Last(ly)		As soon as	
Finally			

	While	you (do)
	Before	(doing)
	After	

G3.4 Directions

Turn left/ right		*Bear* *Branch*	*left/ right (at the fork)*

Take the	*first* *second* etc.		*turning on the left/ right*

Go straight ahead/ on *Keep going* *Carry on*	*until you*	*get to* *come to* *reach*

Follow the signs to ...
It's (the first/ second etc. house) on the left/ right

Linking and Logical Devices

Addition	**Cause and result**
in addition to ... *as well as ...* + N *besides ...* *both ... and ...* + N *not only ... but also ...* + N/clause *Furthermore ...* *Moreover ...* + clause *... also ...* *... too/ as well*	*Because ...* *as ...* + clause *since ...* *in case ...* *due to ...* *owing to ...* + N *as a result of ...* *so* (that) ... *so* + ADJ/ADV + *that ...* + clause *such* + N + *that ...* *therefore* + clause *consequently*
Concession	**Contrast**
although ... *though ...* *even though/ even if ...* + clause *but ...* *yet ...* *despite ...* + N *in spite of ...* *however* *nevertheless*	*while ...* *whereas ...* + clause *but ...*
	Purpose
	in order that ... + clause *so that ...* *in order to/ so as to ...* + V *to ...*
Similarity and comparison	**Time**
as ... *like ...* + N *as* + ADJ/ADV + *as ...* *as ...* *the same* + N + *as/ that* + clause *as* + ADJ/ADV + *as ...* *not as/ so* + ADJ/ADV + *as* + N/clause *not such* + ADJ/ADV + *as* + N/clause *as if/ though ...* + clause	*before ...* *after* + N/clause *till/ until* *as/ as soon as/ when/* *once/ immediately* + clause *while* *then/ next/ after that* *later/ finally* *no sooner ... than ...* + clause *hardly ... when ...*

Exam Focus 1

The Certificate in Advanced English: overview

The examination consists of five papers and each of the papers has equal weighting (i.e. 20%).

Paper 1 Reading (1 hour)

There are four texts and approximately 50 questions which test a wide range of reading skills. Texts may include all the main forms met in everyday life, especially newspapers and magazines. Questions include various types of multiple choice, gap-filling and matching.

Paper 2 Writing (2 hours)

There are two sections, and one task of approximately 250 words is set in each. In *Section A*, the task is compulsory and candidates have to read and respond to written information by producing one or more pieces of writing. In *Section B*, candidates have to write one piece from a choice of four topics.

Paper 3 English in Use (1 hour 30 minutes)

There are three sections and approximately 75 questions which test candidates' ability to apply knowledge of features of the language system. *Section A* concentrates on the correct choice of vocabulary and grammar. *Section B* tests the ability to recognise and correct mistakes and also to adapt a text in a particular style. *Section C* tests the ability to organise written English in an appropriate way.

Paper 4 Listening (45 minutes)

There are four sections, consisting of four texts and approximately 40 - 50 questions, which test a wide range of listening skills. The questions include various kinds of matching, completion and multiple choice items. In *Section B*, the recording is heard once only. In the other sections, the recording is heard twice.

Paper 5 Speaking (15 minutes)

Candidates are examined in pairs by two examiners and there are four phases designed to test general social language, transactional language, and negotiation and collaboration skills. Pictures and other visual or verbal prompts are used in various information-gap and problem-solving tasks.

There is more detailed information on the questions and marking criteria for each of the five papers in each of the Exam Focus sections in Part 2 of this book. Advice on how to tackle specific questions is given in the Exam Strategy boxes in each unit.

Paper 1 Reading

Introduction

In this paper you will have one hour in which to read four texts (about 3,000 words in total) and answer about 50 questions. This is quite a challenging task

but it is intended to reflect real life experiences where information needs to be processed quickly for a particular purpose.

In order to do well in this paper, you will need to read both efficiently and effectively. That means using the right reading skills at the right time and for the particular type of task. Don't waste time by trying to read each text slowly and carefully from beginning to end. If you do, you won't finish the paper in time.

1 Match the reading skill on the left to the description on the right.

Skimming   reading very carefully to be sure you understand *exactly* what the writer means

Scanning   reading the text fairly quickly in order to understand the topic and the main points

Reading   looking through the text to find specific information that you need to
intensively answer a question

2 Which skill should you use when you:

a read the instructions and questions?

b read the text for the first time?

c need particular facts or figures from the text?

d are choosing the right answer to a multiple choice question?

Questions

There are three main kinds of questions.

1 Multiple choice

You are given an unfinished statement or a question and you have to select the best answer from four choices. This is a very common kind of exam question. (There's an example on page 144.)

Multiple choice questions test your understanding of the text *and* the questions so make sure you study the exact words in the question before making a choice. Be careful not to choose answers because they look right if there's no evidence for them in the text. And beware of answers which say *more* than is true. These answers often contain words like *always* or *everybody*, for example, when the truth is *sometimes* or *some people*.

Multiple choice procedure

- Always *skim* read the text before you look at the questions.
- Don't worry about words you don't know at this stage.
- Look through the questions to see which parts of the text you need to read carefully.
- *Scan* to find those parts and then read *intensively*.
- Try to work out the meanings of any words you don't know from the context.
- Check the questions again to be sure you've *really* understood them.

2 Multiple matching

You are given a list of questions (e.g. 1 - 6) and a list of possible answers (e.g. A - H) to choose from. You may have to give more than one answer to a question and you may have to use an answer more than once. (There are some examples of multiple matching questions on page 129 and 131.)

These questions are usually fairly straightforward because the answers are stated in the text - but as the text may be long and the time is short, it's a test of how quickly you can find the answers. For this reason, it's important to scan effectively for the information you need and not to spend time on other parts of the text.

3 Gap-fill

The text has a number of gaps in it where anything from a sentence to a short paragraph is missing. At the end there is a list of possible 'fillers' and you have to choose one for each gap. (There is an example of a gap-fill text on pages 174 /175.)

To answer these questions, you need to be very clear about the development of the writer's argument or, if it's a narrative, about the sequence of events. So read the text carefully and, before you look at the possible 'fillers', think about what kind of information might be missing in each gap. When you are choosing an answer, look for grammatical and logical clues like those below to help you.

Reference:
The first time someone or something is mentioned, there is usually a full description, whereas later there may be only a brief reference. If the indefinite article is used first, the definite article will be used later.

e.g. *Mr Anthony Laughton, Chairman of the BBC*, becomes *Mr Laughton, Laughton* or just *He . . .*

An experiment to classify snowflakes becomes *the/this experiment...*

Logic:
Certain expressions give an indication of what went before.

e.g. *These and other ..., Another..., a different..., a similar...* will give further examples of something already described.

Moreover, however, on the other hand, will add to or contrast with a previous argument.

Marking

For Paper 1, answers have to filled in on a special *mark sheet* and this is checked by computer. You can write your answers on the exam paper first if you like, but be sure to leave time to transfer them to the mark sheet.

Paradise Lost?

Lead-in

1 What are they?

- They are home to half the world's wild creatures
- They are a major source of modern medicines
- They have an important effect on the world's weather
- The world's industries depend on their products
- They may well disappear in our lifetime.

Discuss this question with another student. Then look quickly through the quiz below to find the answer. Were you right?

2 Quiz

How much do you know about the world's trees? Work with another student to discuss the following questions and choose the most likely answer. (Some questions may have more than one correct answer.)

1 Coniferous forests grow in the colder parts of the world.
  True or false?

2 Tropical rainforest soil makes good farming land.
  True or false?

3 An area of tropical rainforest the size of a football pitch is destroyed every
  a week   b day   c second

4 How much of the world's original tropical rainforests have already disappeared?
  a 10%   b 25%   c 40%

5 At the present rate, all the tropical forests will have disappeared in
  a 10 years   b 40 years   c 100 years

6 Most of the world's wood is used
  a as fuel   b for construction   c to make paper

7 Poor countries use far more wood for construction than rich countries.
  True or false?

8 Every year US citizens throw away paper and packaging worth a forest the size of
  a the island of Manhattan   b the city of Chicago   c the state of Delaware

9 Which of the following exports from the Third World is the most profitable?
  a rubber   b cocoa   c timber

10 Destroying forests causes
  a flooding   b drought   c earthquakes

Now find the answers in Text 1.

TREES - THE FACTS

Different kinds of trees

- In the colder parts of the world are soft-wood coniferous forests: pine, spruce, aspens, alders and larches. Often planted commercially for paper pulp, they harbour few plants and wildlife being dark with infertile needle-carpet floors. They produce acidic soil which makes poor farming land.

- Temperate forests are a mixture of conifers and hardwood deciduous trees like oaks, maples and hickories. They are lighter and more diverse than coniferous forests, supporting plants and wildlife. The rotting vegetation produces many nutrients and these generally stay in the soil, which makes good farming land.

- Tropical forests are diverse and include hardwood trees like teak and mahogany. Sometimes 180 million years old, they can shelter up to 100 species of animals and plants in less than two and a half acres. Tropical forest soil is fragile because it is so old and because most nutrients are absorbed by the plant life. It makes poor farming land.

CONIFEROUS

TEMPERATE

TROPICAL

Tree death toll

- An area of tropical forest the size of Britain is deforested every year. That is equivalent to an area the size of a football pitch every second.

- In 1950, 30% of the earth was covered by tropical forest. By 1975, only 12% was left.

- Today more than 40% of the world's original tropical forests have gone. Latin America has lost 37% of its original tropical forests, Asia 42% and Africa 52%.

- The world is now losing its tropical forest at the rate of 7% a year and if this continues, it will have all gone in just 40 years' time.

World wood consumption

- Altogether the world consumes enough wood to cover Manhattan to the height of a 10-storey building (3 billion cubic metres of wood a year). Of this, 55 per cent comes from hardwoods and 45% from softwoods.

- Tropical timber is one of the leading exports of the Third World. It earns as much as cotton, twice as much as rubber and three times as much as cocoa.

- The average citizen of the West consumes more than 150 kilogrammes of paper a year compared to the Third World citizen who uses just five kilogrammes.

Rich and poor countries consume the world's trees in roughly equal proportions. But poor countries use wood to satisfy basic needs while we use it for luxuries.

- Half the world's wood is used as fuel – 80% of it by poor countries.

- 40% is used for construction – 75% of it by rich countries.

- 10% is used as paper – 87.5% of it by rich countries.

Death of the earth

Trees bind the earth with their roots, protecting the soil from erosion and reducing the evaporation of water. When they are cut down the earth is left naked, to be flushed away by rain or desiccated by the sun and attacked by wind. Deforestation is a major factor in the increase of floods. Although it is debatable as to whether or not trees themselves actually produce rain, droughts have increased dramatically in areas of the world where deforestation is most severe.

Waste

- Each US citizen throws away the equivalent of three conifer trees a year. The US is annually discarding paper, packaging and other rubbish made from wood worth a forest the size of Delaware. It is also wasting four times as much paper as is used by all the countries of the Third World put together.

Text 2

Exam Practice - multiple matching

The following questions are in CAE exam style, but remember that in the real exam you will have to write your answers on a special answer sheet.

The four groups of questions illustrate the different types of questions and instructions you may meet. In the real exam, you are unlikely to find more than three groups of questions on any one text.

Questions 1 - 5

These questions ask you to choose the correct title for the article and for each of the four main sections. The box below contains seven possible titles (A - G). Answer each question by choosing a title from the list.

Note: There is only one answer to each question.

What is the best title?

1 The article as a whole
2 Section 1
3 Section 2
4 Section 3
5 Section 4

> *Possible Titles*
> A Industrial Products from the Rainforest
> B The Exploration of the Rainforest
> C The Destruction of the Rainforest
> D Food from the Rainforest
> E Benefits to Man from the Rainforest
> F The People of the Rainforest
> G Medical Advances from the Rainforest

Questions 6 - 9

These questions ask you to say which illness or disease may be helped, now or in the future, by drugs from rainforest sources. A - E list the various illnesses or diseases. Answer each question by choosing from the list A - E.

Note: There is only one answer to each question.

Which illness or disease may be helped by drugs produced from the following sources?

6 Quinine
7 Snakeroot plant
8 Rosy periwinkle
9 Armadillo

> *Illness or Disease*
> A Leprosy
> B Cancer
> C Malaria
> D Hypertension
> E Leukaemia

PARADISE LOST?

Four children out of every five in 1960 who got leukemia died. Now four out of every five survive. The secret of this miraculous increase in remission from one of the world's most feared diseases lies in a pretty but insignificant-looking forest plant called the rosy periwinkle. For generations tribal healers had used it as a medicine, little more than 25 years ago modern scientists took their claims seriously enough to investigate it themselves. 5 10

1 The United States National Cancer Institute has identified more than 2,000 tropical rainforest plants with the potential to fight cancer. And yet, as the forests come down, such plants – and the hopes they embody – are destroyed. 15

Already about 40 per cent of all drugs prescribed in the United States owe all, or much, of their potency to chemicals from wildlife – largely from the rainforest. 20

Quinine, which acts against malaria, comes from the bark of a South American tree. The armadillo is helping us find a cure for leprosy. Sufferers from hypertension and high blood pressure gain relief from the snakeroot plant from Indian forests. And the yam has given us the contraceptive pill. 25

At the present time, drugs from such wild products are worth about $40 billion a year. And plants that could be used to develop new ones worth five times as much may face extinction. 30

2 Nor is this the full extent of the true El Dorado. For the tropical forests contain a cornucopia of new foods. The winged bean, long cherished by forest dwellers in New Guinea, is now grown in some 50 countries. Rich in protein and vitamins, it is sometimes called 'a supermarket on a stalk', for its leaves, flowers, seedpods, seeds and tubers are all edible, and delicious 35 40

Japanese scientists are excited about a plant from Paraguay which, they say, produces a calorie-free, harmless substance 300 times sweeter than sugar. American experts commend the mangosteen, said to be the world's most appetising fruit. And a coffee entirely free of caffeine has been found in the tiny remnants of forest left in the Comoros Islands. 45 50

The forests are also reservoirs of genes that can improve, and rescue, existing

THE ROSY PERIWINKLE lives in drier tropical forests. It supplies vital materials for drugs effective against Hodgkin's disease, leukemia and several other cancers, with commercial sales worth about $100m worldwide each year

crops. A wild relative of corn, recently found in a small patch of Mexican forest, could enable commercial crops to spring up every year like daffodils, abolishing the costly chore of ploughing and seeding. It could also offer resistance to several important diseases. The discovery may well be worth billions of dollars a year. 55 60

3 Every day we use products from the rainforest. We owe rubber to South American Indians who used it to make toys for their children. Chewing gum originated from a Central American tree. Golf ball covers come from rainforest plants. The flowers of the *ylang-ylang* tree give a *je ne sais quoi* to expensive French perfumes. Oils from the forest are already replacing petrol in the synthetics industry, and – in Brazil – to fuel cars. 65 70 75

Spices from the forests earn $144 million a year in world trade. Wickerwork furniture and other rattan products are worth $4 billion a year. Palm oil is used in a hundred products from ice-cream to tinplate, lipstick to jet engines. But hardly any of the 28,000 species of palm have been examined by scientists. 80

4 Less than one per cent of the plant species that make up the rainforests of the world have been intensively examined for their potential. Only a few hundred of their some three million animal species have been investigated. Cures for cancer, unknown miracle foods and products await discovery. But as they wait they are being destroyed. As we fell the forests we are burning a vast library of irreplaceable knowledge – before we have done more than dip into a few of its volumes. 85 90 95

The destruction of the custodians of that library, the forest peoples, is the most shortsighted act of all. For they alone know where the medicines, foods and wealth of the forests are to be found. In north-western Amazonia alone the Indians use over 1,300 plant species as medicines. 100

Much of the destruction is carried out for just one forest product – wood. Tropical hardwoods, exotically coloured and grained, have long had a special value. 105

The South American Indians see it differently. One of their legends says that the trees hold up the sky – and if they are cut down there will be catastrophe. They may well be right. 110

Questions 10 - 17

These questions ask you to say which country or area of the world a particular plant, animal or product comes from, according to the article. A - I list the various countries or areas. Answer the questions by choosing from the list.

Note: There is only one answer to each question but you may use the same letter in more than one answer.

Where do they come from?

10 A new kind of coffee
11 A new sweetener
12 A relation of corn
13 Quinine
14 The winged bean
15 Chewing gum
16 The snakeroot plant
17 Rubber

Country or Area
A South America
B India
C New Guinea
D Paraguay
E Brazil
F Central America
G Mexico
H United States
I Comoros Islands

Questions 18 - 23

These questions ask you about rainforest plants and products mentioned in the text. The various plants and products are listed A - J. Answer the questions by choosing from the list A - J.

Note: Some questions may have more than one answer. The number of answers required is given after each question.

18 Which rainforest plant is used in perfume-making? (1 answer)
19 Which rainforest plant may provide future foods? (1 answer)
20 Which rainforest plants are already used to cure certain illnesses and diseases? (3 answers)
21 Which rainforest product is mainly responsible for the destruction of the forests? (1 answer)
22 Which rainforest product is used in both the cosmetics and aeronautics industries? (1 answer)
23 Which rainforest products are mentioned as multi-million pound industries? (2 answers)

Plants and Products
A wood
B wickerwork
C ylang-ylang plant
D palm oil
E rubber
F rosy periwinkle
G spices
H bark of a certain tree
I winged bean
J snakeroot plant

Exam Strategy: Paper 1

Multiple matching questions are designed mainly to test your ability to scan a text effectively. In the exam there won't be time to read the whole text slowly and carefully, so ...

Don't	• waste time by trying to understand every word.
	• spend time on parts of the text that aren't important.
Do	• read through the questions first to see what kind of information you need to look for.

Focus on Grammar: Relative clauses

1 Relative clauses, which come after the noun they refer to in a sentence, give extra information about a person or thing in the sentence.

Underline the relative clause in the sentence above.

2 Look at these sentences and then answer the questions below.

1 Quinine, which acts against malaria, comes from the bark of a South American tree.
2 Plants that could be used to develop new drugs now face extinction.
3 We owe rubber to South American Indians, who used it to make toys for their children.
4 Less than 1% of the plants which make up the rainforests of the world have been intensively examined for their potential.

a In two of the sentences, the relative clauses make it clear who or what is being talked about. They are essential to the meaning of the sentence and are called defining relative clauses. Which sentences are they? (**1 2 3 4**)
b In two of the sentences, the relative clauses give extra information which is not essential to the meaning of the sentence. These are non-defining relative clauses. Which sentences are they? (**1 2 3 4**)
c In one of the sentences, *which* could be replaced by *that*. Which sentence is it? (**1 4**)
d Commas are normally used with one kind of relative clause. Which is it?
e *Who, which* and *that* can sometimes be omitted from defining relative clauses (*The plants (that) the Indians use could cure Western diseases*), but this is not possible in the examples above. Why not?

Check your answers by turning to the Grammar File, page 103.

3 Make eight complete sentences by matching the beginnings of sentences in Column A with suitable endings in Column B. Use relative pronouns where necessary.

Column A	Column B
a He looks fierce but he's a dog	1 you'll never find.
b She's the best friend	2 can't stand heights.
c Don't make a promise	3 I was hoping to bump into.
d It's not a job for anyone	4 is in charge here.
e The book's by a writer	5 name begins with 'W'.
f You're just the person	6 anyone could have.
g I've hidden it in a place	7 it's impossible to keep
h I demand to speak to the person	8 wouldn't hurt a fly.

4 Complete the following sentences with a suitable relative clause, adding commas where necessary. The first is done for you as an example.

a The person *who runs the fastest* will be the winner. (Def)
b The hotel has no lift so it may be unsuitable for people . . . .
. . . .
c The kangaroo . . . . comes from Australia.
d Anybody . . . . will receive a reward.
e Concorde . . . . was built by an Anglo-French consortium.
f One of the best forms of exercise is swimming . . . .
. . . .
g Drivers . . . . will be prosecuted.
h The longest railway track in the world is the Trans-Siberian line
. . . .

Check: Phrasal verbs 4

Six phrasal verbs are used in Text 2. To see if you remember them, complete the sentences below. Use a verb and particle from the following lists in each sentence.

Verbs	Particles	Verbs	Particles
spring	*down*	*carry*	*up*
make	*into*	*hold*	*out*
dip	*up*	*cut*	*up*

1 South American Indians believe that the trees . . . . the sky.
2 They also believe that if the trees are . . . . there will be a catastrophe.
3 Less than one percent of the plant species that . . . . the rainforest have been studied.
4 A vast library is being destroyed before we have done more than . . . . a few of its volumes.
5 A Mexican plant could enable commercial crops to . . . . each year like daffodils.
6 Much of the destruction is . . . . for just one forest product - wood.

Check with the correct verbs in the Phrasal Verbs Reminder on page 139.

Focus on Listening: Exam practice

Part 1: Multiple Choice

You are going to hear an interview in which Dr Jeremy Knight talks about an organisation called The Rainforest Foundation. *Before you listen*, read through the instructions and Questions 1 - 5 carefully.

Choose the answer, A, B, C or D, which you think fits best in each case.

1 Sting decided to found the Rainforest Foundation when
  A he visited the Amazon area
  B he was giving a concert in Brazil
  C he formed the pop group, 'Police'
  D he discovered the music of the Indian people

2 Dr Knight says the Amazon is important because it
  A provides most of the oxygen we breathe
  B produces half the world's rainfall
  C has the longest river in the world
  D is the largest remaining rainforest on earth

3 Dr Knight thinks it's very sad that rainforest timber
  A is essential for so many purposes
  B is only used to make disposable products
  C is used unnecessarily
  D is so cheap

4 When rainforest is destroyed, the soil
  A cannot be used at all
  B can be used for many years if fertilizers are added
  C can only be used for a few years
  D can only be used to raise cattle

5 The best way to help stop the destruction, according to Dr Knight, is to
  A take a degree in environmental studies
  B stop buying any products made from timber
  C make people understand the role of rainforests
  D refuse to supply rainforest timber

Exam Strategy: Paper 4

Multiple choice questions involve careful reading as well as careful listening. This can be very demanding, so it's especially important to read the questions through in advance, if possible.

When you do this, consider how likely or unlikely each option is and try to guess what the right answer is going to be. This will make the listening task easier.

Part 2

1 The pictures below illustrate the eight points which Dr Knight makes in a short talk about the rainforests. Before you listen the first time, look carefully at the pictures and think about what each one shows.

For Questions 1 - 8, you must number the pictures 1 - 8 in the order in which Dr Knight mentions the points. The first one has been done as an example.

2 As you listen the second time, you must complete the notes below on Dr Knight's talk. Before you listen, look through the notes and think about possible answers.

For Questions 9 - 16 answer with a number or one or two words, as you hear them. For the last question, Question 17, use your own word(s) to describe Dr Knight's opinion.

Rainforests cover	9		%	of the earth's surface.
They contain between	10		%	of all plant and animal species.
They provide food,	11			and culture for indigenous people.
Tea, coffee and	12			are some of the staple food items from the rainforest.
Rainforests are a gene	13			containing wild plants which are resistant to disease.
There are over	14			rainforest plants with anti-cancer properties.
Rainforests regulate	15			by absorbing rain water.
They check and	16			the greenhouse effect.
Dr Knight thinks it's	17			to be cutting down the rainforest.

STUDY BOX ►

1: each/every, either/neither etc.

Each US citizen throws away the equivalent of three conifer trees a year.

Singular	Plural
each -one of a group of two or more **every** - one of a group of three or more **either / neither** - one of two **none** - one of several **all** (uncountable nouns)	**both** - two **all** (countable nouns)

Notes:

each, either, neither, both and **all** can be used with a noun and also as pronouns.

every can only be used with a noun.

none is always a pronoun; **none of** is used with a noun.

Focus on Writing 1 (Section A)

Connect and protect

We all have a part to play in saving trees, and working together makes us more effective. Below are some things you can do.

1 Stop eating hamburgers and explain the reason to your friends.

2 Ask where wood like mahogany and teak comes from. Don't buy tropical hardwoods unless you are sure they have been harvested in a sustainable way – as teak is on some plantations in Thailand and Java. Look for the good-wood seal of approval produced by Friends of the Earth.

3 Use fewer trees by recycling paper and other waste.

4 Plant trees and persuade others to do the same.

5 Share your knowledge on the importance of trees with others.

6 Look for people already involved in saving tropical forests and join their work.

7 Write to the agencies and development banks that provide loans to tropical countries, and explain your views on saving tropical forests. Instruct them to oppose development projects that are socially and environmentally ruinous.

8 Encourage governments to take positive steps like putting a price on tropical forests and exchanging debt for forest conservation.

You are concerned about the future of the rainforests of the world and would like to play your part in saving trees. The extract below, which comes from a magazine feature on the subject, has given you some ideas.

In a magazine called *Beautiful Homes*, you notice two items. The first is a DIY article on building a staircase, and the second is an advertisement for furniture. In both cases, the tropical hardwood mahogany comes from rainforests. When you read the *article* further, you are reassured about the use of mahogany, but the *advertisement* remains very worrying.

Write two short letters, one to the editor of *Beautiful Homes*, and one to the company which is advertising the furniture. In the first, explain how pleased you are that the magazine is showing a responsible attitude on the subject of tropical wood and express your concern about the advertisement. In the second, ask about the source of the mahogany in the furniture and explain the reason for your concern.

Use information below - from the extract 'Connect and Protect', the DIY article, and the advertisement - to help you construct your letters. You may invent extra details to complete your answer (e.g. why you read the magazine or how you first became interested in tropical rainforests) provided that you do not change any of the information given.

Write approximately 250 words in total.

Work Bench: building a staircase

Renovating a staircase probably isn't the sort of job you'd jump at attempting yourself. But it really isn't as difficult as you might think. Beautiful Homes got together with expert, Richard Burbidge, to provide an easy step-by-step guide.

If you live in an older house, you may be able to use the original spindles (the upright posts). If not, you will have to start from scratch. For our staircase, we chose beautiful mahogany * spindles from a range produced by Fleetwood.

* When using mahogany from Brazil, Fleetwood purchases from companies operating ecologically sound forestry policies, including replanting schemes. This policy has been welcomed by Friends of the Earth, so you can have a beautiful staircase and a clear conscience.

Write to us!
Let us know what you think about the articles and products featured in Beautiful Homes. That way, we'll know what you want to see in the magazine in future.
Write to:
The Editor, Beautiful Homes, 22 - 24 Corn Street, London.

MAHOGANY

The Hardwood range of reproduction antique furniture features a wide range of elegant designs, taken from all periods of history.

The desk pictured here is just one of hundreds of items in our comprehensive collection - all pieces made in one of 5 wood finishes. Each wood has its own strength and beautiful characteristics.

Mahogany has a wonderful rich colour and texture, and we create each piece of furniture using traditional patterns to bring out the full character of the wood.

Please send for our full colour Mahogany brochure enclosing £2.00 + postage and packing to:
Hardwood, Forest Lane, Littlehampton, TW2 9HJ, England.

STUDY BOX ▶

2: hardly/scarcely

Hardly any of the 28,000 species of plant have been examined by scientists.

Hardly, and less commonly, *scarcely* mean 'almost not', and are often used:

a before *any, anyone, anywhere, anything* and *ever.*
  There was scarcely anyone there.
  We hardly ever hear from him.

b after *can* and *could* and before main verbs.
  I can hardly read your handwriting.
  We scarcely know each other.

c before adjectives, adverbs and nouns.
  He's scarcely likely to apologise.
  It's hardly something to boast about.

Focus on Writing 2 (Section B)

Read the instructions for the task below. Follow them exactly and write approximately 250 words.

A local English-language newspaper is starting a TV, film and book review section, and readers have been invited to send in suitable reviews to be considered for publication. The theme of the first review section is to be The Natural World. Write a review of a TV programme, film or book (which may have been in any language) on any aspect of this subject to send to the newspaper. Include a clear description of the content, comments on its successful and unsuccessful aspects, and suggestions about why people might find it interesting or enjoyable.

Communication Activity

1 *Work in pair*s. **In this activity Student A will have a photograph to look at and Student B will have a drawing to look at. The two are related in some way. You will each have one minute to describe your pictures (without showing them to each other). After that you must discuss and try to agree on what the relationship between the two is.**

Student A **should turn to the photograph on page 215.**
Student B **should turn to the drawing on page 217.**

Note: This activity is included in the second part of the CAE interview but in the exam, only one candidate describes their picture before the discussion takes place.

2 **Look at each other's pictures and discuss in more detail what the photographer and cartoonist were trying to suggest in each case. What is different about the two messages? Can you think of any similar examples in your own experience?**

English in Use 1: Cloze 1

Read the article below and circle the letter next to the word which best fits each space. The first answer has been given as an example.

Simply . . . Three Ways to Help Save the Planet

1. Discourage Packaging

Next time you are out shopping test this theory; the less (1) . . . a product is, the more packaging it will have. (2) . . ., for example, a box of chocolates with eight (3) . . . of wrapping, to a bag of rice with only one. Overpackaging (4) . . . about ten per cent to our weekly shopping bill. It (5) . . . no real purpose and (6) . . . we have to pay for it to be taken away. It also uses up (7) . . . resources; most plastic is made from oil and does not biodegrade. As a first (8) . . ., you might refuse the plastic bags which are thrust upon you at the supermarket check-out and use boxes to carry home the food.

2. Avoid Poisons

Every day there is another (9) . . . about some product damaging our health. Weedkillers and pesticides (10) . . . their way up the food chain from plants through insects and birds into your family. Bleaches are (11) . . . the most polluting of household cleaners. As well as being a health risk, they (12) . . . killing organisms in rivers long after they leave your home, so it is best to minimize the quantities used.

3. Research Raw Materials

It is important to find out what raw (13) . . . a product uses. Did the table and chair in your living room involve rainforest destruction? If they are made of mahogany, the answer is 'yes'. We should only buy woods that come from (14) . . . which can be maintained long term, without causing damage to the environment. Aluminium cans are made from bauxite, a kind of clay, which is often (15) . . . up in tropical forests. The recycling of these cans is well-established in Australia, Canada and the US, all of (16) . . . re-use more than 50 per cent of the aluminium.

Adapted from an article in the New Internationalist

1	A valuable	B serious	Ⓒ essential	D major
2	A Check	B Contrast	C Match	D Compare
3	A stages	B layers	C levels	D sheets
4	A attaches	B increases	C raises	D adds
5	A serves	B makes	C does	D causes
6	A at last	B at the end	C eventually	D lastly
7	A scarce	B rare	C slight	D short
8	A point	B step	C place	D thing
9	A scare	B news	C danger	D terror
10	A work	B take	C go	D put
11	A in	B of	C among	D with
12	A carry out	B carry off	C carry over	D carry on
13	A ingredients	B materials	C parts	D elements
14	A roots	B situations	C stores	D sources
15	A mined	B dug	C worked	D pushed
16	A them	B these	C which	D whose

English in Use 2: Editing

There is one word missing from most lines in the following text. Read the text and mark the place where each word is missing with a line (/). Write the missing word in the space provided at the end of the line. Some lines are correct. Indicate these lines with a tick (✓) against the line number. The first two lines have been corrected as examples.

Join the birdwatching ritual

Each month across Australia, hundreds / men and women go out   1 of

into the rainforests, parks and even their own backyards -   2 ✓

and count the birds. They're participating a mammoth project   3 _____

called the Australian Bird Count, first official census of   4 _____

birds in the country.

The count, is organised by the Royal Australian Ornithologists   5 _____

Union, aims to establish definitively birds exist, where they   6 _____

are, and roughly how many there are. According to Dr Stephen   7 _____

Ambrose, the five-year census provide invaluable information   8 _____

about the environment generally and the impact of land   9 _____

management practices and climatic changes.

In the 200 years Europeans settled in Australia, seven types   10 _____

of birds have become extinct. Eight others now on the brink   11 _____

of extinction, with another 44 some danger. Overall, out of   12 _____

a total of about 650 bird species in Australia, almost one   13 _____

in ten threatened. The Australian Bird Count will be helpful to   14 _____

conservationists who are trying save rare birds, particularly   15 _____

by revealing changes bird numbers brought about by development 16 _____

projects, land clearing and effects of droughts and floods.   17 _____

Adapted from an article in the Sydney Sunday Telegraph

Phrasal Verbs Reminder

carry out   perform an action or a duty

cut down   cut through the trunk of a tree so that it falls down.
             Compare: cut up (below)

cut up   cut into several pieces

dip into   look quickly at a book without reading it or studying it seriously

hold up   support

make up   join together to form a whole

spring up appear or come into existence quickly

10 Fire

Lead-in: Topic vocabulary

What do you call ...

a a device which makes a noise to warn people when there is a fire? (N)

b an organisation which has the job of putting out fires? (N)

c the specially equipped vehicle used in putting out fires? (N)

d an outside staircase which allows people to leave a burning building safely? (N)

e a metal cylinder containing chemicals for putting out a fire? (N)

f a person whose job is to put out fires? (N)

g a length of pipe used to spray water on fires in order to put them out? (N)

h something which cannot be damaged by fire? (Adj)

Text 1

Reading Skills

1 In the following text, the paragraphs are out of order. Skim the four sections to decide what the correct order should be and then answer these questions.

a How many fires were there?

b Where did they each start?

2 Read the four sections more carefully in the correct order (given on page 220) and answer these questions in your own words.

a What made the first fire spread so quickly?

b What problems did the firefighters have when they fought the second fire?

c Why is such a fire less likely nowadays?

Vocabulary Skills

3 Look through the text again and underline any words in the text which are connected with the topic of fire. When you have finished, compare your answers with another student's and discuss the meanings of any words you are not sure of.

4 Choose words from your list to match the following definitions.

a a large fire in which things are damaged or destroyed; used especially in journalistic English. (N Count) ....

b a very large fire which burns over a wide area and destroys property; a formal word. (N Count) ....

c a small, red-hot piece of coal, wood or other material in a fire, or remaining after the main fire has gone out. (N Count) ....

d a tongue of burning gas in a fire. (N Count) ....

e a small flash of fire as, for example, when two pieces of metal strike together. (N Count) ....

The day Chicago died

A The fire spread through the city so fast that the fire crews were overtaken by the flames and had to abandon their machinery. People stampeded in utter terror, trampling others underfoot as huge billows of flame blasted through the streets consuming everything in their path. Within 24 hours, nearly 10 sq km of the city centre were devastated: 250 people had perished and 17,000 buildings had been destroyed. The cost of the damage was estimated at $200 million.

B In 1871 Chicago was a thriving city of 334,000 inhabitants living and working in some 60,000 buildings. On the night of 7 October, a major fire broke out in the city's timber-yards and spread rapidly, thanks to high winds and the many wooden buildings that existed among newer, stone structures. The entire fire-fighting force of the city fought the blaze throughout the night and for most of the following day. Many were injured and, by the time the fire was put out, everyone was exhausted.

C Today, such a large-scale conflagration would seem to be behind us. Cities are constructed of fire-resistant materials, modern fire-fighting is a sophisticated science, and radio communications bring a rapid response to any such emergency. Nevertheless, the terrible prospect of a major urban fire is always with us.

D A few hours later, an old woman was tending her sick cow by the light of a kerosene lamp. The cow kicked the lamp over - and in seconds the barn was ablaze. By the time the weary firemen reached the scene, more than 50 buildings were burning. Vast clouds of sparks and embers carried the fire from house to house. The heat was so intense that whole structures were exploding instantly into flames.

Reproduced by permission of Orbis Pubishing Limited

5 Say what you think the following words mean.

a *tending* (section D)   d *billows* (section A)

b *stampeded* (section A)   e *devastated* (section A)

c *trampling* (section A)

Discuss your ideas with another student and then check the words in a dictionary.

Focus on Grammar 1: The past perfect

1 a Match each of the following sentences with one of the drawings below. One sentence contains an example of the past perfect - which is it?

a When he got to the bus stop, the bus was leaving.

b When he got to the bus stop, the bus had left.

c When he got to the bus stop, the bus left.

b **Find one sentence like example (a) and one sentence like example (b) in Text 1.**

c **Complete the following description of the past perfect tense.**

The past perfect is used to refer to actions which happened .... another action in the past. The past perfect simple is formed with .... + past participle, while the past perfect continuous is formed with .... + -ing form.

Use the notes in the Grammar File, pages 100 and 101, to check your answers.

2 Put the verbs in the following passages in the correct tense. The tenses may be past simple or continuous, past perfect simple or continuous.

A Until the invention of matches, lighting fires (*be*) not easy. Certain tribes in New Guinea (*not know*) how to light fires until recently and they (*keep*) their fires alight night and day. If they ever found that a fire (*go out*), they (*go*) and (*borrow*) glowing embers from a neighbouring tribe.

B The first matches, invented by the Chinese in about 600 AD, (*consist*) simply of pieces of wood which (*be/dip*) in sulphur. These (*burst*) into flame when they (*touch*) smouldering wood. Modern safety matches (*come*) into use in Britain in the early 1900's when earlier friction matches, which people (*use*) for a hundred years, (*become*) illegal.

C In Sao Paulo, Brazil, in 1974, fire (*break*) out in a new 25-storey office block in which 600 people (*work*). It (*spread*) rapidly upwards through the stairwell which, ironically, (*be/design*) to help occupants escape. By the time the fire fighters (*bring*) the fire under control, 200 people (*die*). Although many (*in fact/manage*) to reach the roof, and (*wait*) there for rescue, the intense heat and smoke (*make*) it difficult for helicopters to reach them.

Text 2

1 Work in pairs to discuss the following points.

a How would you know if there was a fire
  - in the building you are in now?
  - at home?
b If you heard a fire alarm (or other warning) *now*, would you leave the building *immediately*? If not, what would you do before leaving?
c Are there any notices giving fire instructions in the building you're in now? If so, have you read them?
d Is there a fire escape in the building you're in now? If so, do you know how to get on to it? If not, how would you leave the building?
e What are the *dos* and *don'ts* in a fire?

2 Survival Game

Read the introduction in paragraph 1 of the text and then work with a partner.

Student A **should close his/her book.** *Student B* **should look at the first part of the diagram (under '4 MINS') and explain the first five choices. Once A has chosen, B should describe the next five choices or the result, until square with a letter is reached. Do not check the meaning yet.**

Exchange roles. When you both have letters, check the result on page 220.

3 Before you read the rest of Text 2, read through the following statements and see if you can guess whether statements a - e are *True* or *False*. Discuss your ideas with another student.

a People are often too quick to imagine that there's a fire.
b Men are less willing to leave a building in a fire than women are.
c People frequently panic when there's a fire.
d If there's a fire in a public building, most people look for a fire escape.
e 999 (Emergency) calls often take longer than necessary.

4 Now read Text 2 to find out:

a Who devised the game and why.

b Which important aspect of a real fire the game misses out.

c Whether your answers to question 3 are correct. Be prepared to say why/why not.

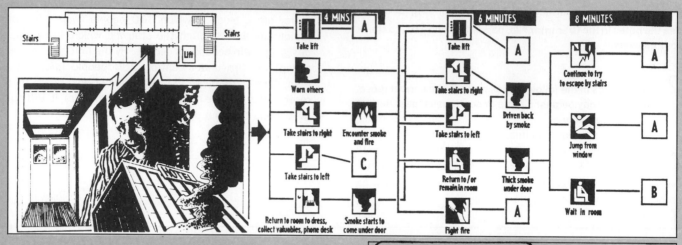

SPECTRUM

The survival game

How would you behave in a fire? The diagram above, based on a real fire, shows some possible courses of action. Trace the path you would take until it ends at a square with a letter. The meanings of the letters are given on page 220

You are caught in a fire then what?

YOU ARE ASLEEP in your bedroom on the fifth floor of a hotel. Suddenly you are woken at 1.30 am by the sound of breaking glass. You get out of bed to investigate, and look out into the corridor. There is nothing to be seen, but there is a smell of smoke. There seems to be a fire. What would your reactions be?

For many people they are never tested until it's too late—they are caught in a real fire. But visitors to the International Fire Safety and Security Exhibition in London this week will have a chance to test their responses, and the consequences, in a specially devised game. A much simplified version is shown above.
Try it for yourself — it is based on a recent hotel fire in Britain.
The game was devised at

Surrey University where a team of scientists led by Dr David Canter is researching human behaviour in fires under contract to the Fire Research Station. Their game cannot reproduce the stresses of a real fire, but it does bring out two very important points: the number of decisions that have to be taken on inadequate information, and the importance of time. A correct decision at the beginning, for example, leads to a trouble-free escape, but there is no way of telling which is the safe route. It is a matter of luck. And a delay closes even that route.

One of the most important discoveries the researchers have made from their hundreds of interviews with people involved in fires is the problems of recognising that there is a fire at all. A fire is such an unusual experience that people will accept almost any other explanation of the early signs of a fire first.

In one hotel fire, for example, guests woken by the sound of breaking glass put it down to someone smashing bottles outside—an event that had occurred on other occasions; in another incident, residents in a block of flats, hearing cracking and popping noises, put it down to vandals at work, made sure their doors were locked, and went back to the television.
Similarly, the research has shown that fire alarms are usually interpreted as drills,

tests or malfunctions—in the vast majority of cases quite correctly. The assumption implicit in all fire regulations—that on hearing the alarm the occupants of a building will evacuate—bears little relation to peoples' behaviour in practice.

In fact, faced with evidence of a possible fire nearly everyone seeks further information. "There is a strong social stigma attached to getting it wrong," says David Canter. So people are reluctant to make fools of themselves by rushing out into the street or calling the fire brigade at what may be a false alarm.

Even when a fire is definitely identified there is no immediate rush for the doors. Smoke is the thing which most frequently persuades people to leave a building, but there are differences in the reaction of various groups. Women are more ready to leave than men, the young than the old, people at home than people at work, and people familiar with their surroundings than people who are not.

Under the stress of a fire many people do things they afterwards see to have been inappropriate. There is a record of one man who twice carried a bucket of water right past a fire extinguisher.

Nevertheless, the Surrey team feel that people "panicking" in fires is something that often happens in Press reports, but seldom in reality. Given

the lack of information normal in fires and the rapidly changing situation when a fire gets a hold, what appears to be senseless may be perfectly reasonable behaviour in the circumstances. In the hotel fire of the game, for example, someone who dashed for the stairs by the lift, found them impassable, dashed to the other stairs to find them impassable too, and then returned to his room would be behaving perfectly rationally. But to somebody else he might appear to be dashing about at random.

The chief lesson to be learned from this research, Canter thinks, is that more emphasis might be laid on the early detection of fires and training people to deal with them before they get out of hand.

Often the fire escape arrangements are not in normal use and are therefore forgotten when they are really needed. Or they may be cut off. Of 85 people involved in fires where there was a fire escape available they were successfully used by only five. The vast majority did not even *try* to use them.

Even the simple 999 call could be streamlined. Analysis of a large number of recordings has shown that it often takes several minutes for the caller to get over the location of a fire. A little training in the best way to elicit the information for the people at the other end could save precious minutes.

© *Times Newspapers Ltd.*

5 Exam Practice: multiple choice

The following questions are in CAE exam style, but remember that in the real exam you will have to write your answers on a special *answer sheet*.

Questions 1 - 6

There are a number of questions or unfinished statements about the text below. You must choose the answer which you think fits best. Give *one answer only* to each question.

1 From the game we can learn
  A how to choose a safe escape route
  B which actions are most dangerous
  C when to leave the building
  D how to fight the fire successfully

2 Residents in the flats ignored the unusual sounds because
  A they guessed there was a party next door
  B they wanted to watch the end of a television programme
  C they thought it was only people mending the road
  D they assumed young people were causing damage nearby

3 When fire alarms go off, people usually
  A telephone the fire brigade
  B pay no attention to them
  C leave the building
  D arrange to have the system tested

4 People are often slow to react when they think there's a fire because
  A they are afraid of making a mistake
  B they don't know the best way to leave the building
  C they can't think what to do
  D they don't want to leave their friends

5 If there was a fire in the 'Wonderpaint' office building, the person most unwilling to leave would probably be
  A Miss White, (30), the Managing Director's secretary
  B Mrs Brown, (40), the office cleaner
  C Mr Green, (60), the new Managing Director
  D Mr Grey, (50), the resident caretaker

6 The research suggests that most people need training in
  A how to prevent fires from starting
  B how to make 999 calls
  C how to recognise the first signs of a fire
  D how to fight a major fire

Exam Strategy: Paper 1

Multiple choice questions check your careful reading of the text and the questions! See Exam Focus 1 for the best procedure for tackling them and remember:

Do	● *skim*-read the text first, then *scan* for the parts which contain the information you need and read those parts more carefully.
	● study the exact words of the questions before making a choice.
Don't	● waste time reading the *whole* text several times.

Check: Phrasal verbs 5

Six phrasal verbs are used in Texts 1 and 2. To see if you remember them, complete the sentences below. Use a verb and particle from the following lists in each sentence.

Verbs	Particles
cut	out
get	out
put	out
put	off
bring	over
break	down

1 On the night of 7th October, a major fire .... in the city's timber yards. (Text 1)

2 Many were injured and, by the time the fire was ...., everyone was exhausted. (Text 1)

3 The game cannot reproduce the stresses of a real fire but it does .... two very important points. (Text 2)

4 In one hotel fire, guests woken by the sound of breaking glass .... it .... to someone smashing bottles outside. (Text 2)

5 Analysis of a large number of recordings has shown that it often takes several minutes for the caller to .... the location of the fire. (Text 2)

6 Often the fire escape arrangements are not in normal use. Or they may be .... (by fire). (Text 2)

Check with the correct verbs in the Phrasal Verbs Reminder on page 147.

Communication Activity 1: Problem solving

Work with a partner to discuss the following questions.

1 Causes of fires

According to statistics for the whole of the United Kingdom, the main causes of fires in buildings are:

- faulty electrical appliances and wiring
- careless handling of smokers' materials (cigarettes, pipes, matches etc.)
- arson (deliberate ignition)
- cooking accidents
- heaters

a One of these is by far the greatest cause of fire in people's homes. Which do you think it is?

b A different factor causes most fires in offices, factories and hotels. Which do you think it is?

You can find out the answers on page 220.

2 What would you save first?

The American writer, Mark Twain, made a joke list of 27 people and things he would rescue from a fire in a boarding house, in order of priority. These included fiancée (at number 1), third cousin (at number 11), landlord (at number 24) and furniture (at number 26).

a You and your partner work for the Fire Services. You have decided to draw up a list of priorities to help fire fighters decide what to rescue from a burning house first, second, third and so on, after all the occupants and any animals have been saved.

Work together to make a list of ten items in order of priority, chosen from the list below. You can add one or two more if you like.

Books	Clothes	Radio/TV/hi-fi
Letters	Study notes/files	Jewellery
Pictures/photographs	Ornaments/souvenirs	. . . .
Records/cassettes/CDs	Furniture	. . . .

b Imagine that you were at home alone and a fire broke out. You have time to rescue three single possessions safely. Which would they be, and why? Explain your choices and reasons to your partner.

Focus on Listening 1: Bush fires

Introduction

bush /bʊʃ/ 2. The bush is the wild, uncultivated area of Australia, New Zealand, Africa and other hot countries.

Fill in the missing prepositions in the text below.

Countries . . . . . Australia, which have large areas of bushland, face the constant threat of

bush and grass fires . . . . . the dry season. These fires can cause devastation . . . . . a very

large scale. . . . . Australia, there are fire-fighting forces . . . . each state whose job it

is to tackle bush fires. They also advise people . . . . how to prevent fires . . . . . . starting

and provide information . . . . . . how to protect themselves and their homes when they do.

You are going to hear Arthur Owens, a member of a Bush Fire Fighting force in New South Wales, Australia, talking about his work. *Before you listen* **to Part 1, read through the questions below and think about the kind of information that is required.**
As you listen, **write the answers in the spaces provided.**

Part 1

When do most bush and grass fires occur?

How many fires are reported each year?

What other kind of disaster does Mr Owens compare a bush fire to?

What *two* frightening features of a bush fire does the speaker mention?

Why is it dangerous when people try and escape from fires by car?

1	_____
2	_____
3	_____
4	_____
5	_____

Part 2

Arthur Owens mentions five ways of protecting a house from the danger of bush fires. The pictures below illustrate the points he makes. *Before you listen,* study the pictures and think about what is going on in them.

As you listen, number them 1 to 5 in the order that the speaker mentions the points. *One* picture is not correct.

Protecting Your Home

a

b

c

d

e

f

Phrasal Verbs Reminder

break out	start suddenly (of fire, disease, war, violence)
bring out	show clearly
cut off	stop, interrupt, isolate (e.g. telephone contact, electricity supply)
get over	communicate information (*get across* also has this meaning)
put (something)	
down to	attribute to/explain as
put out	extinguish (of light, cigarette, fire)

Focus on Listening 2: How to survive a bush fire

1 Consider this question.

You are driving along a lonely road through bushland. You turn a corner and see that a huge bush fire is approaching very fast on one side of the road. What do you do?

Discuss your ideas with another student.

2 In this further excerpt from the interview with Arthur Owens, he explains what to do if you are in your car when you encounter a bush fire. *Before you listen*, study the sentences and try to think what the missing words could be. Discuss your ideas with another student.

As you listen, fill in the missing information for Questions 12 - 21 below with 1 - 3 words.

How to Survive a Bush Fire

12 _____ your car on the 13 _____ of the road from the fire.

14 _____ doors and windows.

Turn on your 15 _____

Place any rugs, towels or clothing 16 _____ as the fire comes through.

Crouch down on 17 _____ with your face and hands

18 _____

As soon as the fire has passed, get out of the car and put out any little 19 _____ on the paintwork.

Never try to 20 _____ a bush fire. The fire will catch up to you and you will have no 21 _____ at all.

Focus on Grammar 2: Conditional 3 and mixed conditionals

1 In the examples below, there are *two* incorrect sentences. Which are they, and why are they incorrect?

a Most people would have been far safer if they had stayed in their homes
b If you hadn't given us a lift, we might have been late.
c If there would have been time, I'd have tried to telephone you.
d I'm sure you would have enjoyed yourself if you were there.
e If he had caught the 6 o'clock train, he would be here by now.

2 Complete the following notes about conditional 3 and mixed conditionals.

a *Type 3 conditionals* are used to talk about something which could . . . . in the past but . . . .
b In a *Type 3 Conditional*, the . . . . tense is used in the *if*-clause, and *would have, should have, could have* or *might have* + ... are used in the main clause.
c A *mixed conditional* is used to talk about the . . . . result of a past condition.

d In a *mixed conditional, would be* or *might be* are used in the .... clause, and the past perfect tense is used in the .... clause.

Use the notes in the Grammar File, page 93, to check your answers.

3 In the following sentences, put the verbs in brackets into the correct tense.

a I can't help feeling that it (*be*) better if we (*never/meet*).

b If I (*not/persuade*) someone to lend me some money, I don't know how I (*get home*).

c What on earth (*you/do*) if you (*be*) in the same situation that night?

d If the motorway (*never/be built*), the city (*not develop*) so fast today.

e If the gorillas in Rwanda (*not/become*) a tourist attraction, they (*possibly/disappear*) by now.

4 The following sentences refer to situations or events in Text 1. Write suitable conditional sentences describing the result if these things had not happened.

a There were high winds which helped the first fire to spread rapidly.

If ....

b An old woman's cow kicked a kerosene lamp over.

If ....

c The fire spread very fast.

If ....

d The firemen were unable to control the fire.

If ....

e Nowadays radio communications have been developed.

If ....

Focus on Writing (Section B)

Read the instructions for the task below. Follow them exactly and write approximately 250 words.

> An English-speaking friend is coming to spend a week in your home while you are away. You have made the basic arrangements so your friend knows how to get to your home, where to find the front door key, and so on. You think it would be a good idea to prepare a set of written instructions about practical matters like how to operate various electrical appliances and where to find essential equipment. Other matters might include dealing with emergencies, keeping the house secure, watering the plants, feeding a pet, taking telephone messages and shopping locally. Write a set of clear instructions, under a number of suitable headings, which you can leave for your friend's information.

Communication Activity 2: Visual prompts

Work in pairs. In this activity you will each have a drawing to look at. The pictures are of the same scene but there are *twelve* differences between them.

1 *Student A* should describe the left-hand side of the drawing in detail. Meanwhile *Student B* should listen carefully and mark or write down any differences he/she notes.

2 *Student B* should then describe the right-hand side of the drawing in detail, while *Student A* makes a note of any differences.

Note: Give your partner a good chance to speak uninterrupted. You may ask one or two questions if necessary, in order to clarify something they have said, but this is not an opportunity for you to interrogate them about their picture!

When you have finished your descriptions, report the differences you have each noted and then compare the two pictures. You can compare your answers with the list on page 220.

Student A should turn to page 215. *Student B* should turn to page 217.

Exam Strategy: Paper 5 (Phase B)

When you're asked to describe a *picture* or *drawing*, it's simply an opportunity for the examiner to hear you speak more or less uninterrupted for about a minute.

Don't
- worry if you don't know the exact word for something.
- stop speaking and wait for encouragement!

Do
- find a way to express something with words you do know e.g. '*a thing you open bottles with*' (if you don't know *corkscrew*)
- keep talking! Once you've given a general description, mention things like the pattern or style of clothes, the shape or exact position of objects, the expression on a person's face.

English in Use 1: Cloze 2

Complete the following text by writing the missing words in the spaces provided. Use only one word in each space.

Radiant heat

Intense fires will radiate (1) _____ much heat that they can

(2)_____ light to outside wooden framework, signs etc., even through closed windows.

Doors of survival

If you're cut (3)_____ by fire, block spaces around doors to stop smoke

(4)_____ in. Most doors will prevent fire (5)_____ spreading for about 20 minutes or more.

The way out

Open or smash a window to (6)_____ attention. Don't panic. Don't jump

(7)_____ the very last moment; you (8)_____ be rescued if you wait. Throw out bedding or cushions to break your fall. Get out (9)_____

your feet first and lower yourself to the full length of your arms (10)_____

dropping to the ground.

Door to disaster

Opening doors will give the fire (11)_____ it needs most - oxygen.

(12)_____ the surface of the door; if it's hot, there's a fire behind,

(13)_____ don't open it. If there's (14)_____ in there, stand

back as they open the door - a tremendous explosion will shoot outwards

(15)_____ air reaches the fire.

Reproduced by permission of Orbis Publishing Limited

English in Use 2: Editing skills

In most of the lines of the following text there is one unnecessary word. It is either grammatically incorrect or does not fit in with the sense of the text.

Read the text, put a line through each unnecessary word and then write the word in the space provided at the end of the line. Some lines are correct. Indicate these lines with a tick (✓) against the line number. The first two lines have been done as examples.

'. . . And we also fight fires'

Being a firefighter in today's Fire Service ~~that~~ is one of the most   1 ~~that~~

varied, satisfying and exciting of careers. Indeed, one of the main   2 ✓

qualities required is in adaptability. Firefighters spend only a   3 _____

small part of their time about fighting fires, in fact. As well as   4 _____

having responsibility for the fire prevention, they deal with just   5 _____

about every other kind major and minor disaster, such as road, rail   6 _____

and air crashes, floods, chemical spills and rescuing people trapped   7 _____
in lifts.

Every year men and women join with the Fire Service from a variety   8 _____

of different backgrounds. Entrants range from those with only a few   9 _____

academic qualifications to those university graduates. The important   10 _____

thing is that all recruits who receive the same basic training and   11 _____

are encouraged to acquire any specialist qualifications as they   12 _____

progress. A firefighter of exceptional ability could not gain   13 _____
promotion to the rank of Station Officer after 5 years.

The Fire Service is a closely-knit organisation, based on teamwork.   14 _____

It offers plenty of opportunities to make up rewarding friendships.   15 _____

In addition to the material benefits, and the Fire Service has   16 _____
excellent sports and social facilities.

A Career in the Fire Service

"We feed the address into the computer and it shows us a map of the area together with the exact location of the fire ."

Exam Focus 2

Paper 2 Writing

Introduction

In this paper, you have two hours to answer two questions by writing about 500 words in all. This may seem quite generous but in fact you will have to organise your time efficiently and both answers will need careful planning, writing and checking in order to gain good marks.

The first thing to consider when planning is the type of writing you are being asked to do, since each type will have particular features of layout, style and language.

1 Match each of the extracts on the left below to a writing task on the right.

a *plenty of food in the fridge but you'll probably need to buy more coffee. See you on Wednesday. June*

b **grey Persian cat by the name of 'Henry', in the Redwood area of the city. Wearing collar and name tag**

c With reference to your letter of 5th November, I should like to confirm my interest in taking up a

d *you get to the main entrance, follow the signs to the Outpatients Department and my office is just next to*

e When she sang the opening words to 'Here We Are' the applause was heart-felt. The show followed the familiar

f Professor David Marshall will be remembered as much for his colourful character as for his pioneering work

g *the weekend? It would be lovely to see you both and we would have a chance to catch up on all the news. Let me*

Formal Letter
Informal Letter
Personal Note/Message
Notice/Announcement
Review
Article/Report
Directions

2 Discuss the following questions about each of the extracts above.

a What features of *language* or *style* helped you to decide what type of writing it was?
b What is the *purpose* of the piece of writing?
c Who is the intended *audience*?
d How would the complete piece of writing be *laid out*?

Questions

There are two sections.

Section A

There is no choice in this section. You will be asked to produce one or more pieces of writing (250 words in all) in response to various kinds of written information. (There is an example of this type of question on page 135.)

You will have to use the information in some way - by selecting and summarising from it, for example, or by responding to it - so the question tests effective *reading* as well as *writing*.

Section B

In this section, you will be asked to write one piece of about 250 words from a choice of four tasks. (There is an example of a writing task for Section B on page 197.)

Each task is described in detail so that you know *why* you are writing, *who* you are writing to, and *what* kind of information to include. Make sure you follow these instructions exactly.

Procedure for Writing Tasks

Reading

● Make sure you read the *instructions* very carefully. Underline or circle the important points. You'll lose marks if you don't do everything the question asks for.

● In Section A, mark the important points in the other pieces of information in the same way so that you can find them easily.

Writing

● Think about the *purpose* and the *audience*.
● Remember any special features of *language*, *style* and *layout* for the type of writing.
● Make a *plan* of the main points.
● Keep to the *word limit(s)*.
● Leave time to check your work carefully afterwards.

Marking

Your work in each section will be marked on the same two scales.

Accuracy and Range of Language

looks at how

- accurate your grammar, spelling and punctuation are.
- precisely you use vocabulary.
- broad your range of grammar and vocabulary is.

Handling the Task

looks at whether

- you do everything the question asks for.
- you use an appropriate style and register.
- your work would achieve the required objective.

There are equal marks for each scale so make sure you consider both aspects of the task carefully.

Personally Speaking

Lead-in: Compliment or criticism?

Work with another student to put the following words into one of the boxes below.

If you think the word has a generally *positive* meaning, put it in Box A. If you think it has a generally *negative* meaning, put it in Box C. If you think the word is *neutral* or could be either positive or negative according to the situation, put it in Box B (but be prepared to explain your reasons).

adaptable   ambitious   balanced   care-free
cautious   critical   disappointed   enthusiastic
generous   hard-working   healthy   imaginative   immature
impatient   inquisitive   insecure   lazy   optimistic
possessive   selfish   sensitive   shy   stubborn
unfeeling   withdrawn

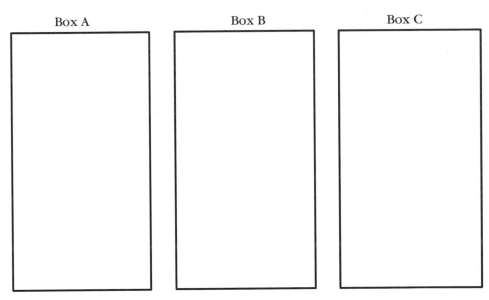

Box A	Box B	Box C

Mini-check: Negative prefixes

Make the following adjectives negative by adding the correct prefix, chosen from those shown.

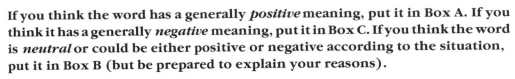

| *in-*   *im-*   *un-* |

a .... balanced	e .... sensitive	i .... practical	m .... ambitious
b .... efficient	f .... selfish	j .... healthy	n .... modest
c .... satisfied	g .... imaginative	k .... critical	o .... stable
d .... moral	h .... considerate	l .... polite	p .... tolerant

Focus on Listening

1 In this first activity, you have to imagine you're going on a walk through a forest. Read the following text or listen as your teacher reads it to you. Be prepared to describe your forest later.

A Walk Through The Forest

You're in a forest. Walking along a path through the forest. Imagine what you can see and how you feel. Is it a thick, dark forest with trees close together, for example? Or is it a light forest with trees spread widely apart?

Now what about the trees? Are the trees clearly separate from one another or are they growing in groups? Are they short or tall? Have they got lots of leaves or fruit or are they bare? Are you attracted to any one tree in particular? If so, describe it.

You continue down the path through the forest and suddenly you come across a bear. Think about this bear. What's it like? What colour is it? Is it large or small? Is it dangerous (perhaps a grizzly bear) or is it friendly? Do you feel afraid? Do you face the bear or do you stay away?

Carrying on along the path, the next thing you see is a piece of pottery on the ground. What is it? A jug or a vase, maybe, or a bowl? Think carefully about the shape and the design. Is it plain or has it got a pattern on it? Is it whole or is it cracked or broken? Do you pick it up and take it with you or do you leave it where it is?

You continue on your way again and the last thing you see is a key on the ground. What's this key like? Is it new and shiny or is it old and rusty? How big is it? Again, do you pick it up or leave it lying there?

2 *Work with a partner.* Describe your forest and the things you saw there to each other. Listen to what your partner says and fill in the first column of the table below. You will be able to complete the second column after you have heard the excerpt from a radio programme which follows.

	Your Partner's Description	*Interpretation*

3 You're going to hear part of a radio programme in which listeners phoned in with their descriptions of the forest and what they had seen. The presenter then tried to interpret their descriptions and say something about their personalities.

When we join the programme, Dave, the presenter is about to speak to the last caller, Chris. As you listen, fill in the information for Questions 1 - 14 in the table below.

	What it represents	*Chris's description*	*Interpretation*
	Your life at the moment	**1** mossy and soft feeling to it **2**	**3** - if things go wrong, he has plans to fall back on.
	7	**4** plenty of low-lying branches, like an English woodland. **5**	**6** - probably has several groups of close friends
	your attitude to aggression and violence	- a grizzly **8**	**9**
	11	**10** ,but broken or misshapen.	- he's been through some hurtful relationships in the past.
	14	**12** -5 -6 inches long and heavyish.	**13** - he's fairly practical.

4 Now look at your partner's description of the forest again and try to interpret what they have written!

Check: Phrasal verbs 6

A number of phrasal verbs were used in the conversation you heard. Look at the examples below and then match each phrasal verb to its definition (A - J).

a If you've just *tuned in*, you will have missed the beginning of the programme . . .

b We asked them to *pick out* particular items and look at certain things.

c . . . I'm trying to *work out* a bit about their personality . . .

d If things are likely to go wrong for you, you've made plans so that you've got things to *fall back on*.

e Just to explain (the different meanings) so that everyone else can *tick off* theirs as well . . .

f If, in your list, you *put down* that you had a lot of trees . . .

g . . . it normally means that it's something that you tend . . . to *steer away from* because you're a bit frightened by it . . .

h . . . they wouldn't tend to walk away, they would tend to face up to the bear and *fight it out*.

i . . . you would tend to keep in your emotion and *eke it out* in little bits.

1 If you *tune in*,	a you accept or deal with it.
2 If you *pick out* one thing from a group,	b you use it when other things have failed.
3 If you *work* something *out*,	c you argue or fight until one of you wins.
4 If you *fall back* on something that you know you can rely on,	d you select it.
5 If you *tick off* items on a list,	e you make it last as long as possible by using it carefully.
6 When you *put down* words or numbers,	f you think about it and manage to understand it.
7 If you *steer away from* a subject or an action,	g you set the controls of a radio or TV so you can listen to a particular station or channel.
8 If you *face up to* a difficult situation,	h you write them down.
9 If you *fight it out* with somebody,	i you avoid talking about it or doing it.
10 If you *eke* something *out*,	j you put a mark next to them to show that you have dealt with them.

Text 1

Study the statements below and consider whether they are *true* or *false*. Discuss your ideas with another student.

1 Green dyes in sweets make people feel ill.

2 Food manufacturers think that colour dyes make their products more appealing.

3 The British like tinned vegetables to be a bright colour.

4 Both Americans and Britons like apples which are bright red.

5 There is no scientific evidence that colours can have an effect on the nervous system.

6 The colour blue can make us feel calm.

7 The colour red is used by fast food chains to encourage customers to stay in their restaurants.

8 People also judge a cleaning product like soap powder by its colour.

Now read the text and say whether the statements are true or false, according to the writer. If you think a statement is false, be prepared to say why.

YOUR TRUE COLOURS

Seeing red can quite literally make you 'see red'. It can also make you eat faster. Colour influences the mind in mysterious ways, and those who wish to influence *you* – to make you buy their products, or work harder – often do so with colour. But you can make this process work to your advantage. Go through the spectrum with Paul Kerton and Deirdre McQuillan; then use our colour test to show you the finer shades of your personality and your temperament.

The marketing world is full of folklore about consumer reactions to colour: how, for example, too much green on a confectionery wrapper is a recipe for disaster. For years the food industry insisted that without its handy 'azo-' dyes the public would find processed produce unappetising. Yet colour preference can often sound like a mix of fad and cultural custom, especially when the French will eat grey tinned peas and beans, while the British will not, and we prefer green apples to the Americans' glossy red. However, there is more to colour than meets the eye.

This, at least, is the view of light researcher John Ott, who has discovered that colour may directly affect our nervous systems.

The idea that colour can affect the nervous system in some way seems strengthened by the fact that experiments have recorded raised blood pressure in red surroundings and lowered blood pressure in blue surroundings. Red evokes subjective reactions of increased energy and hunger; blue evokes tranquillity and relaxation. Whether knowingly or otherwise, the effects of seeing red have been cleverly exploited by fast food chains. As well as making people hungry, red and its close relation, orange, cause time to seem to pass more quickly and influence people to feel in a hurry. By using these colours, places like McDonald's create an atmosphere which increases the appetite but subtly dissuades the customer from hanging around for very long.

Colour has also been used to striking effect in the marketing of consumer products. A group of housewives was once asked to test samples of identical soap powder in three different boxes, one yellow, one blue and one a mix of blue and yellow. Extraordinary results ensued: the powder in the yellow packet was judged to be so powerful that some said it had damaged their clothes, while the blue was said to be so weak that it left stains behind; the powder in the mix of blue and yellow was assessed as just right. Yet the only difference was in the colour of the packet.

© *The Telegraph Sunday Magazine*

STUDY BOX *1: the ... the ... (comparatives)*

Look at these examples from the radio programme in Focus on Listening and Texts 1 and 2.

The small*er* and thinn*er* the pot, *the more* you would keep in your emotion.

The more plain it is, *the more* down to earth you are.

The lat*er* blue appears in the sequence, *the more* unsatisfied you are and *the more* you feel the need to break from the ties that restrict you.

> **This is a convenient and common pattern in English.**
>
> *The* + comparative word ... *the* + comparative word
>   (*more/ less/ -er*)   (*more/ less/ -er*)

Notice that *the* can be followed by both adjectives and adverbs.

The faster he worked (adverb), *the more* mistakes he made (adjective).

The darker it became (adjective), *the more slowly* she drove (adverb).

Text 2

1 **Read the instructions for the Colour Test below and then fill in the boxes with your favourite colours.**

Blue **Brown** **Red** **Black**

Violet **Grey** **Green** **Yellow**

Test your personality

This is a shorter version of the full Lüscher Colour Test, developed over twenty years by Max Lüscher. The colours used were selected for their associations with physical and mental states. To find out what colour says about your personality, briefly study the colours above and then choose the colour which appeals to you most immediately. (Don't choose on the grounds of fashion or whether it does wonders for your hair.) Write this in the first box and then repeat the process with your second favourite colour in the second box, and so on until your least favourite colour is in the eighth box.

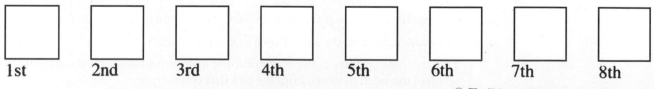

1st   2nd   3rd   4th   5th   6th   7th   8th

© *The Telegraph Sunday Magazine*

2 *Work with another student.* **Exchange your lists of colours and then turn to the main text on the next page. Read out the interpretation for your partner's two top colours and listen while your partner explains what your two favourite colours mean. Discuss how accurate (or not) these interpretations are.**

3 Now read the complete text and then answer Questions 1 - 18 in the Exam Practice which follows.

Test your personality

Red

Red represents passion and energy. Red in the first position means you are impulsive, sexy and have a will to win. You are a good leader. You
5 want to expand your horizons and live life to the full.

Red in the seventh or eighth position means your desire for life and thirst for adventure have become
10 less.

Yellow

Yellow represents happiness and relaxation. Anyone who chooses yellow in second, third or fourth place is a positive, optimistic per-
15 son who always looks to the future - never backwards. You find life easy, and problems simply do not exist for you.

Free from worry, you lead a care-
20 free life; but this does not mean that you are lazy. You can be extremely hard-working, although not consistently. Yellow in first place means that you are ambitious and eager to
25 please. When yellow is in the latter part of the spectrum you have had your hopes and dreams dashed and you feel isolated and disappointed, often becoming defensive and with-
30 drawn.

Green

Green represents firmness and resistance to change. In first place, you are persistent, possessive and quite selfish. You are a high-achie-
35 ver and an accumulator of 'things' - like a penthouse, a BMW, a Rolex, a holiday flat, a compact-disc play-er. You want to be recognised and need to impress but worry about
40 the prospect of failure. If green is a later choice, your ego has been bruised and you have been humbled by the resistance to your progress. Consequently you can be
45 highly critical, sarcastic and stubborn.

Violet

A mixture of red and blue, violet represents a conflict between impulsiveness and calm sensitivity,
50 dominance and submissiveness. The person who prefers violet wants to find a mystical, magical relationship. Both mentally and physically immature, you are
55 stuck in a dream world of wishful thinking and fantasy. Often violet appears in the latter part of the sequence, it indicates that the person choosing it is more mature
60 and has outgrown the 'fantasy' vision of life, confronting harsh reality head-on.

Brown

Brown is the colour of physical well-being and is an indicator of
65 how healthy you think you are. If you put brown in fourth or fifth place you are not very concerned about your health and body. This means that you are probably in
70 good shape. Those worried about illness tend to put brown earlier in their sequence. If you choose brown as your favourite colour, you are restless and insecure. If
75 brown is in eighth place, you don't care enough for your body: you may not be as healthy as you think. Placing brown early also indicates the importance of a secure environ-
80 ment: refugees often pick brown first.

Grey

Grey is a neutral and represents a point between two contrasting and conflicting motivations. Grey in
85 the first position means that you want to shut yourself off from everything and remain uncommitted, so that you can swing with opinion and emotions. You hate
90 joining anything with 'group' connotations and are an observer rather than a doer. Those who choose grey in the eighth position seek to join in with everything,
95 eager and enthusiastic. Such people will try absolutely everything in their efforts to achieve their goals.

Blue

Blue represents calmness and loy-
100 alty. A person who favours blue is sensitive and easily hurt. You never panic and are in total control of your life and content with the way it is going. You desire to lead
105 an uncomplicated and worry-free life and are prepared to sacrifice certain goals in order to achieve this. You need a stable relationship without conflict. Perhaps, as a side-
110 effect of contentment, you tend to put on weight. The later blue appears in the sequence, the more unsatisfied you are and the more you feel the need to break from the
115 ties that restrict you. But you probably aren't unfeeling enough to walk out on a family or job; instead, you will suffer in silence.

Black

Black is the negation of colour and
120 means 'No'. Anyone who chooses it in the first position (which is rare) is in revolt against their fate. Chosen second, it means you are prepared to give up everything else
125 to achieve what you want. It is normally put in seventh or eighth place, representing control of one's destiny and a balanced outlook. If yellow precedes black in the first
130 two positions, then a change is on the way.

4 Exam Practice: multiple matching

Questions 1 - 18

These questions ask you about the colours mentioned in the text. A - H list the colours. Indicate your answer to each question by choosing from the list A - H. Remember that in the exam, you will have to mark your answers on a special *answer sheet*.

Note: When a question asks for more than one answer, you may give the answers in any order.

Red	A	Brown	E
Yellow	B	Grey	F
Violet	C	Blue	G
Green	D	Black	H

Which colour

represents health?   1 ☐

is often popular with teenagers?   2 ☐

Which *two* colours

each represent two contrasting characteristics?   3 ☐ 4 ☐

together suggest that a change is expected?   5 ☐ 6 ☐

Which colour(s) are you likely to have towards the beginning of your list

if you are very energetic and ambitious?   7 ☐ 8 ☐

if you are happy with your life as it is?   9 ☐ 10 ☐

if you need other people's approval and recognition

for what you do?   11 ☐

if you don't like joining in with other people?   12 ☐

Which colour(s) are you likely to have towards the end of your list

if you have a realistic view of life?   13 ☐ 14 ☐

if you are seriously discontented with your life at the moment?   15 ☐

if you have been disappointed in your hopes or ambitions?   16 ☐ 17 ☐

if you are *extremely* keen and ambitious?   18 ☐

STUDY BOX

2: make / cause

Make

Look at these examples from Text 1.

Seeing red can . . . *make* you *eat* faster.
. . . those who wish to *make* you *buy* their products or work harder ...

The pattern is:

make + object + infinitive without '*to*'

Another verb which follows this pattern is *let*:
He *let* me *come* in.

Cause

Look at this example from the text.

Red and orange *cause* time *to seem* to pass more quickly and *influence* people *to feel* in a hurry.

The pattern here is:

cause + object + infinitive with '*to*'

Other verbs which follow this pattern are:

allow	*enable*	*force*	*invite*	*tell*	(= *order*)
ask	*expect*	*influence*	*order*		
convince	*forbid*	*instruct*	*persuade*		

Check: Colourful idioms

Choose one of the colours below to complete each sentence.

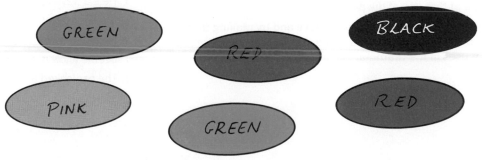

1 When I see people dropping litter in the street, it really makes me see . . . .
2 As long as your account is in the . . . . you don't have to pay any bank charges.
3 His sister lives in a beautiful house and her financial success makes him . . . . with envy.
4 I'm afraid my account is in the . . . . at the moment and I don't think I could afford to take a holiday.
5 Things are going very well for Brenda at the moment. When I saw her she really looked in the . . . .
6 When I started my own business, I was very . . . . and I had to learn some important lessons the hard way.

Focus on Grammar: The passive

Complete the following note on the passive.

The passive puts emphasis on the . . . . or . . . . affected by an action rather than on whoever . . . . the action.

1 Form

Underline the passive forms in the examples below and say:

1 how the passive is formed in general.
2 what tenses (or other forms) are used in the examples.

a Colour has also been used to striking effect in the marketing of consumer products. (Text 1)

b The powder in the yellow packet was judged to be so powerful ... (Text 1)

c Often violet is chosen by adolescents. (Text 2)

d It looked as if the car door had been forced.

e Your ego has been bruised and you have been humbled. (Listening)

f Any complaints should be addressed to the Customer Services Manager.

g We felt as if we were being watched but there was no-one in sight.

h They were hoping to be invited to the party.

i The next committee meeting will be held on April 1st.

2 Use

There are a number of specific reasons for using the passive rather than the active. One is that the agent (whoever did the action) is not known or not important. Sentence (a) above is an example of that use of the passive.

Look through the other examples above and try making them active. Say why the passive was used in each case. (You can find a list of uses in the Grammar File on pages 99 and 100.)

3

Change the following informal information into formal announcements by using a passive construction and more formal vocabulary, if necessary.

e.g. Children have to have an adult with them. (Children . . .)
Children should be accompanied by an adult.

a If you break something, you'll have to pay for it. (All breakages . . .)

b You can't come in if you're wearing jeans. (No-one . . .)

c I would ring the airport before you set off, if I were you. (You . . .)

d They've put off the election till next Thursday. (The election . . .)

e You can't use a dictionary in the exam. (The use . . .)

f It's possible that we'll make some changes to the timetable. (Some changes . . .)

g You can get tickets at the Box Office. (Tickets . . .)

4

Make complete sentences by putting the verbs in brackets into a suitable passive form and adding any other words necessary.

e.g. All entries for the June exam (*receive*) before March 23rd. *All entries for the June exam must be received before March 23rd.*

a There are 4,000 prizes (*win*) in our fabulous competition.

b No entries received after 1st September (*accept*).

c We are unable to give refunds on articles of clothing which (*wear*).

d Faulty goods (*replace*) without question.

e All cheques (*accompany*) by a cheque card.

f He's always (*criticise*) his poor spelling.

g It's not a good idea to pat a strange dog, you (*bite*).

h No baggage (*leave*) unattended anywhere on the station.

i Let me know if you want (*meet*) at the airport.

j The car looked as if it (*not/clean*) for months.

Communication Activity 1: Graphology

1 *Before* reading the text, discuss these questions with another student.

a What is graphology?

b How long ago was a system of graphology developed?

c What features of writing are studied in graphology?

d How accurate is graphology?

2 *Scan* the text fairly quickly to check your answers. Then answer the questions below the text. When you have finished, compare your answers with another student.

According to graphologists, what kind of person are you if

a your writing slopes backwards?

b the dots over the ' i ' are placed to the left?

c you write in lines which slope upwards?

d you make large loops above the line?

e you write in lines which are very close together?

3 Now exchange books with your partner and look at each other's handwriting on page 155. Try to analyse each other's personality using the principles of graphology. How accurate is the analysis?

Focus on Writing (Section A)

You know that an English speaking friend of yours is hoping to get a job in Britain. You notice the Candidate Column in a British newspaper and decide to send your friend the information about how to advertise in it. You are also interested in getting a job in Britain yourself, preferably working for a local TV station, so you decide to send in an advertisement too.

You think some of the advertisements in the column work better than others and you have made some notes on them. You also have an extract from an article about working in broadcasting.

1 Write an informal letter to your friend enclosing the information about the Careers Column. Explain why you think your friend should advertise in the column, give some advice on how to write the advertisement and wish them luck.

2 Write a short advertisement for yourself to send to the newspaper.

Use the information about the Careers Column, the handwritten notes you have made on the ads, and the careers article to help you construct your letter and advertisement. You may include personal information and invent any necessary extra details to complete your answer.

Write approximately 250 words to complete the two tasks.

CANDIDATE COLUMN

CALLING ALL HIGH FLIERS

Have you tried the Candidate Column yet?

It allows you, the reader, to place a free advertisement on this page to sell your skills to potential employers. If you're looking for a first job, a step up the ladder to success or if you want to do something radically different with your career, just fill in the coupon below and send it off.

You have a maximum of 50 words in which to place your qualifications, abilities and ambitions before an audience of over two million educated, professional business readers. Send your ad. today and we'll publish it next Sunday (space permitting). To encourage your creativity, we'll also be offering a prize for the best ad. published every month.

Don't forget to let us know if you succeed through the Candidate Column.

Send to: The Candidate Column, Daily Press Classified, London Bridge House, Kingstown Rd, London SW5 3LL·

© *The Observer*

YOUNG enthusiastic Honours graduate, currently a research technician, requires a challenging post within 40 miles of Chester. I am efficient and I want to work hard! Box 490

— clear and direct

CANADIAN companies help! 29 year old with young family wishes to emigrate to Canada. Experienced journalist, well-travelled and with a sense of humour. Work offers sought. Box 217

HI! I'm Kay. I'm determined, diligent, personable and I'm looking for a career with an international company. I have an Honours degree in languages and I'm successful in my present job. Write to me and find out! Box 220

— nice chatty style (a bit too friendly?)

SPANISH LAW GRADUATE (25) permanently in London, presently assistant in solicitor's office, seeks challenging post using linguistic and academic capabilities. Box 385

— doesn't mention any *personal* qualities

DYNAMIC female, 24, bilingual English/Spanish, with a degree in English, seeks interesting, creative job in the media or publishing. Box 622

LAW graduate, excellent CV, has travelled all over and done lots. Media experience, loves eating pizzas. Wants to boogie in the USA. Darren, Box 760

— too jokey

SALES REP Female mid 20's. exp. publishing/cosmetics, seeks int. well-paid pos. in West Scotland. Box 895

— boring and too many abbreviations

ONCE YOU MEET ME you'll know you need me. I'm intelligent, charming and trustworthy and that's on a bad day. My CV says more. Let me impress you. Box 342

— sounds big-headed! And what kind of work does he want?

EXCELLENT opportunity for company willing to break the no experience no job cycle I'm in. Cheerful, hard-working 18 year-old, keen to start a worthwhile career. Box 980

— positive approach

LAZY LIE-ABED seeks easy job with lots of money. Are you bored with all the cliches and boasts in the other ads? Hire me and you'll get imagination, initiative and intelligence. Honestly! Box 192

— Eye-catching (but a bit dangerous?)

© *The Observer*

Broadcasting

The major requirements in the industry are a capacity to cope with crises and, in television, physical stamina. From your armchair, the people on screen may look peaceful and quiet; in the studio, it will be hot, dirty and almost everyone will be on their feet.

Broadcasters get to the top by having practical ideas for good programmes. 'Everything I do originates in myself,' said a BBC assistant producer. 'I am expected to produce a reasonable quantity and quality of material for the screen but nobody says what it should be. When the idea gets launched, said an ITV producer, 'you eat, sleep and dream the subject'. It may involve long hours and months away from home. 'Workaholics thrive in this business.'

To get on, you need to be pushy and tough. But an openly harsh and aggressive approach will not work: television and radio depend on teamwork and you must be capable of getting on with everybody, including technicians.

© *Times Newspapers Ltd.*

Communication Activity 2: Problem solving

Work in pairs. **Study the three cartoons below and discuss what you think the cartoonist is 'saying' in each one. If you can think of more than one way of interpreting a cartoon try to agree on the interpretation you think works best. Could there be any link between the cartoons?**

Exam Strategy: Paper 2 (Section A)

In this section you will have to read one or more texts in order to complete the writing task.

● Read the instructions very carefully. Underline or circle the key points in the instructions and the text(s). If you miss a point, you'll *lose* marks.

● Use your own words to express the information from the text(s) in the writing task. You'll *gain* marks if you use an appropriate style and register for the type of writing and the intended audience.

English in Use 1: Cloze 1

Read the article below and circle the letter next to the word which best fits each space. The first answer has been given as an example.

Colour Sense

ICI colour consultant Jack Widgery painted one police interview room light green, and another (1)... red Subsequently the police found that suspects (2)... statements more quickly when they were in the red room, again enforcing the idea that too much red (3)... a feeling of being pressurised. The soft green room was for (4)... victims and their families, and there are many (5)... of light colours being used to (6)... feelings and encourage relaxation.

Some institutions in the USA have special pink areas to cool the (7)... of angry prisoners, service recruits and patients. Soft blues, greys, greens and beiges seem to be (8)..., and hospitals, schools and dentists are beginning to take this into (9)... when choosing colour schemes. An airline which (10)... from a yellow and brown interior scheme to one (11)... green and blue reported a forty-five per cent decrease (12)... air-sickness. But the workplace is the biggest challenge: (13)... too much nor too (14)... energy will do . The (15)... fashion for grey with a few details in brighter colours may be a good (16)....

© *The Telegraph Sunday Magazine*

1	A heavy	(B) strong	C lively	D sharp
2	A gave	B said	C admitted	D spoke
3	A makes	B leads	C has	D creates
4	A discussing	B interviewing	C requesting	D explaining
5	A ways	B occasions	C examples	D demonstrations
6	A play up	B play down	C run up	D run down
7	A tempers	B moods	C personalities	D senses
8	A sleepy	B leisurely	C tiring	D restful
9	A view	B mind	C account	D opinion
10	A changed	B turned	C adapted	D altered
11	A by	B for	C from	D of
12	A of	B in	C with	D about
13	A never	B nor	C no	D neither
14	A few	B small	C little	D low
15	A current	B nowadays	C actual	D instant
16	A result	B system	C solution	D way

English in Use 2: Discourse cloze

Choose the best phrase or sentence (given after the text) to fill each of the blanks in the following text. Write one letter (A - H) in each of the numbered spaces. Three of the suggested answers do not fit at all.

How boring can you really get?

Instead of just *thinking* that the person sitting next to you at dinner is the most boring person in the universe you may be able to prove it. (1)_____, for new research says that bores are more intelligent than their fascinating neighbours. (2)_____. Professor Mark Leary, of Wake Forest University in North Carolina, has isolated those boring characteristics which induce chronic narcolepsy (a condition marked by short attacks of extreme drowsiness) and assembled them in a league table:

* Negative egocentrism: droning on about personal problems.
* Banality: talking about superficial things, repeating the same joke over and over again.
* Low affectivity: avoiding eye contact, keeping facial expression to a minimum and speaking monotonously.

* Tediousness: dragging conversations out.
* Passivity: conforming and reluctant to express opinions.
* Self-preoccupation: talking about oneself.
* Seriousness: not smiling, taking everything seriously.
* Ingratiation: trying to win friends, being excessively funny or friendly.
* Distraction: being easily sidetracked, engaging in too much small talk.

(3)_____ on a five-point scale from 'not at all boring' to 'extremely boring'. (4)_____, students who listened to taped 'interesting' and 'boring' conversations, rated participants on their friendliness, competence and strength. (5)_____ . However, they were rated 'significantly more intelligent than interesting targets'.

Reproduced by kind permission of Malcolm Brown

A In another experiment
B Psychologists have just completed a study of what makes people boring
C Researchers who studied behaviour
D Bores were found to be less friendly, less enthusiastic, more impersonal, weaker and less reliable
E The students were trained in research techniques
F But beware
G Leary asked 297 undergraduates to rate behaviour
H To everyone's surprise

Exam Strategy: Paper 5 (Phase C)

This phase of the interview tests your ability to interact successfully with your partner, not to find the right solution to a problem! You will have about three minutes to discuss the problem before trying to reach an agreement. If you can't agree, don't worry, simply agree to disagree!

Do
* decide together how to tackle the task before you begin.
* find out what your partner thinks, and react to what s/he says.
* give reasons for your opinions

Don't
* stick too rigidly to your opinions.
* let one person do all the talking.
* worry if you can't find a solution. It's the discussion that matters.

Mind Your Manners

Lead-in

1 Look quickly at the extracts below and say where you might find them.

With rolls or French bread you should break off one bite-sized piece at a time, butter it and eat it. Slices of bread for breakfast or tea, or with cheese, pate or smoked salmon, should be cut into quarters.

It's 'not done' to handle food which others are going to eat - so don't check peaches for ripeness or pick up hard cheese to cut it.

Don't play 'mother' at other people's dinner tables and 'helpfully' serve other people with food - unless they ask you to.

A soup spoon, unlike a knife, should be held rather like a pen, but with the wrist turned so the spoon faces across the body and is parallel to the table. The soup is then quietly sipped from the side of the spoon as you tilt it towards your mouth. You shouldn't blow on it, or put the spoon in your mouth.

Don't make noises when you eat.

The correct method of drinking tea is to hold the saucer just above the knees and lift the cup to the mouth - head ducking is out.

© *The Observer*

2 Now discuss the following points.

a Are any of these 'rules' the same in your country? Which ones?
b Are any of these rules completely different in your country? Which ones?
c Which of the rules seem sensible? Which seem ridiculous to you?
d Do you think rules like these are completely outdated, or do they serve any purpose?
e Can you think of one or two points of advice about customs in your country (not necessarily only to do with eating) which you could give to a visitor from Britain?

Focus on Listening 1: Section C

You are going to hear a conversation between friends on the subject of manners and etiquette. For Questions 1 to 11, complete the notes with a few words. You will hear the recording twice.

One definition of manners is 'behaviour which is calculated to put other people

[1] _____'.

In Britain, when eating with friends, it's normal to [2] _____
to show you've enjoyed the meal.

In some countries, if you did this, your host would have to keep

[3] _____ until you left some food.

One speaker thinks this is not so much manners as a method [4] _____ .

Another speaker thinks manners would be whether you [5] _____

to food on the table, or whether you wait to be served; whether the host serves his
guests, and whether you share [6] _____ between friends.

One speaker describes etiquette as [7] 'a _____' which tell people
what to do on certain occasions, but she thinks good manners are more to do with

[8] _____ .

Another speaker says her best definition of good manners is 'considering other people', and she gives as an example ⑨ _____ other people when they're speaking.

It's suggested that someone with bad table manners may make other guests feel ⑩ _____ .

This speaker also doesn't think it's a good idea to let someone talk on until they've ⑪ _____ they have to say.

Focus on Listening 2: Section D

You are going to hear five people giving examples of behaviour which they consider to be bad manners. You will hear the recording twice.

Task One lists the places where the examples of bad manners occur. Put them in the order in which you hear them by writing a number from 1 - 5 in each box. Two boxes will remain empty.

TASK ONE

in an office	1	
in somebody's home	2	
in the street	3	
in a restaurant	4	
in a shop	5	
in the street or on public transport	6	
in a shop or on public transport	7	

Task Two lists the things that the five speakers complain about. Put them in the order in which you hear them by writing a number 1 - 5 in each box. Two boxes will remain empty

TASK TWO

somebody not talking at all	8	
somebody speaking too much	9	
somebody speaking rudely	10	
somebody not getting out of the way	11	
somebody allowing noise to go on during a conversation	12	
somebody who can't do their job	13	
somebody interrupting a conversation to talk to another person	14	

Communication Activity 1: Embarrassing situations

1 Work with another student to discuss briefly what you would do if the following things happened.

1 a friend kept mispronouncing a word
2 you fell asleep on a social occasion
3 you had a streaming cold on a night when you'd been invited out
4 people behind you in a cinema kept whispering or rustling paper
5 you accidentally committed a blunder - like jumping a queue or stalling your car and blocking the road - and people were very angry
6 you felt faint or ill in a public place

2 Now look at the six pieces of advice below. Match the advice to the correct situation above.

a *Ring your host, explain the problem, and say you have to cancel. If you're feeling ill, stick to this. If you're pressed to come despite the infection, and feel like going, do so.*

b *Nothing - hardly anyone is glad to be corrected. If you can't resist the dangerous urge to do them good by putting them right, use the word correctly in their hearing some other time.*

c *Don't be embarrassed; it isn't a crime. Say you feel unwell, ask for a chair and sit down until you recover or, if you need it, ask for medical help.*

f *Let them express their fury - trying to stop them will only increase it. Then say, 'You're absolutely right', which is so unexpected that it should silence them!*

d *Apologise, say you were up working the whole of the previous night and press them to finish the interesting story they were telling if they were talking.*

e *If you can't bear it, show increasing disapproval. First glance pointedly, then glare, then ask them politely to stop.*

Reproduced by permission of Century Hutchinson

3 Now discuss what it would be good manners to do in these situations. Write pieces of advice similar to those above.

1 You are sitting in the middle of a row of seats during a concert when you are overcome with coughs.
2 Someone starts to tell you a story they've already told you before.
3 A friend asks you to give your honest opinion of a new item of clothing they've bought. (You think it's awful.)
4 You have been invited to dinner but miscalculate the journey and arrive half an hour early.
5 You have invited friends to dinner but they arrive before you've finished cooking.

When you've finished, compare your advice with what other students have written.

Now compare your answers with the Key on page 220. Do you agree or disagree with the advice which is given?

Focus on Grammar: Modal verbs 2

For general information about modal verbs, and detailed information about the verbs below, see Grammar File pages 97-99.

1 Obligation: *must, need, ought to, should*

You must remember to set the alarm clock.
We needn't hurry, there's plenty of time.
We ought to write and thank them for their hospitality.
You shouldn't blow on your soup.

Complete the following sentences with suitable verb forms expressing obligation or strong advice.

a I'm sorry I'm late. I . . . . . (*make*) an urgent phone call.

b You really . . . . . (*apologise*) to him at the time. It's a bit late now.

c You . . . . . (*shout*). I'm not deaf!

d We . . . . . (*take*) a tent with us because we never had a chance to use it.

e You . . . . . (*tell*) a soul what I've said. Promise!

f Deborah . . . . . (*work*) a lot harder if she wants to do well in her exams.

g Do you think I . . . . . (*complain*) in writing? Or . . . . . I just telephone?

h You . . . . . (*have*) a medical certificate before you can get a work permit.

i We . . . . . (*take*) a taxi because Colin gave us a lift in his car.

j Don't worry, you . . . . . (*be*) especially fit to join the aerobics class.

2 Permission: *can, may, could*

Complete the following sentences with suitable verb forms expressing permission.

a You . . . . a tractor at 16 in the UK but you . . . . a car until you are 17.

b Before 1969, you . . . . in an election until you were 21.

c They wanted to keep him at the police station for questioning but when his solicitor arrived, he . . . . home.

d A: . . . . your pen for a second?
  B: Yes, of course . . . .

e I apologise for interrupting but . . . . a suggestion?

f Do you think we . . . . when we're inside the museum?

Text

1 The following article offers advice to people who do business overseas. The title makes joking use of a rather unusual adjective. Check the meaning in the dictionary entries below.

becoming /biˈkʌmɪŋ/; a formal, fairly old-fashioned use. **1** A piece of clothing, a colour, or a hairstyle that is **becoming** makes the person who is wearing it look attractive. EG *She was dressed in an extremely becoming trouser suit.* ◊ **becomingly**. EG *She was dressed becomingly in black.* **2** Behaviour or language that is **becoming** is appropriate and proper in the circumstances. EG *Is such language becoming?* ◊ **becomingly**. EG *...becomingly modest.*
ADJ QUALIT = fetching
◊ ADV WITH VB = fetchingly
ADJ CLASSIF : USU PRED
◊ ADV + ADJ = suitably

unbecoming /ʌnbiˈkʌmɪŋ/; a rather old-fashioned word, used showing disapproval. **1 Unbecoming** clothes or colours make you look unattractive. EG *...ill-fitting, unbecoming garments... ...that dreadfully unbecoming shade of apricot they wore.* **2** If you say that a person's remarks or behaviour are **unbecoming**, you mean that they are rather shocking and especially unsuitable for that person. EG *Maria, such thoughts are unbecoming to you... ...conduct unbecoming to an officer.*
ADJ QUALIT = unflattering
ADJ CLASSIF : IF + PREP THEN to/in = discreditable

2 Exam Practice: Gapped text

In the following text, some sentences are missing. Choose suitable sentences from the list on the next page to fill the spaces and write the correct letter in each space. Remember that in the exam you will have to mark your answers on a special *answer sheet*.

Conduct Becoming

A breach of etiquette may mean a breach of contract when doing business abroad. By Christopher Stoddard

So, you've finally made it - chief assistant to the assistant chief (overseas division). And now you've the chance to show what you're really made of in your company's drive for overseas sales.

5 The flight went well and now you're in the middle of your first business meeting abroad. (1) _____ . You feel that your hosts like your relaxed, laid-back attitude - quite different from the starchy Brit they were expecting. The atmosphere's easy so you crack a harmless joke. Disaster -

10 the room goes quiet. (2) _____ . Unsigned contracts vanish into briefcases faster than you can say 'credit card'. Without knowing it, your little joke was a major blunder. (3) _____ .

Putting that expensive lesson down to experience you go

15 to see your next prospect. It's now over 30°C in the shade so you take off your jacket and tie. You're keyed up for the kill this time - straight down to business - strictly no jokes! (4) _____ . Sitting in sombre ranks on the other side of the table, your negotiating adversaries are all in dark suits and

20 ties.

You're immediately at a disadvantage. But how were you to know it's expected that all business is conducted in a business suit, however hot it is outside? (5) _____ .

It's not hard to see that a thorough knowledge of how your

25 business counterparts conduct their business is as vital as your own knowledge of your business. Knowing the social conventions is just another part of being a true professional.

Reproduced from Expression Magazine

A You open the door. Another disaster.

B But then, how were you to know that they take their royal family so incredibly seriously?

C In fact, come to that, how is anyone other than a seasoned traveller going to know these vital points of business etiquette before they commit a business blunder that can have far-reaching effects?

D Luckily, you expected to face this problem.

E Everything's going fine.

F In an instant the meeting is over.

3 Reading Skills

There are some words and expressions which you may not know in the text. Look at the possible meanings below and choose the one which fits the context best. You may find that two meanings are possible in one case.

1 *to show what you're really made of* (line 3)

    a to show how fit and healthy you are

    b to show off everything you know

    c to show your qualities and abilities

2 *drive* (line 3)

    a a journey by car, van etc.

    b a special effort made by a group of people for a particular purpose

    c a very strong need or desire in human beings that makes them act in a particular way.

3 *laid-back* (an informal expression) (line 7)

    a calm, relaxed, easy-going

    b leaning back comfortably in a chair

    c keeping yourself to yourself

4 *starchy* (line 8)

    a overweight as a result of overeating

    b strong or powerful

    c very formal, not showing a sense of humour

5 *blunder* (line 12)

   a a slight error of judgement
   b a big mistake, especially one which seems to be the result of carelessness or stupidity
   c a complete waste of time

6 *keyed up* (line 16)

   a very nervous or frightened before a dangerous event
   b very excited or tense before an important event
   c very relaxed before an enjoyable occasion

7 *sombre* (line 18)

   a dark or dull (of colours)
   b sad or serious
   c laughing or joking

8 *adversaries* (line 19)

   a colleagues you work with
   b friends you spend time with
   c people you are competing with

9 *counterparts* (line 25)

   a people who have a similar function or position in another place or organisation
   b people who have a different function or position in the same place or organisation
   c people who have the opposite function or position in another place or organisation

Mini-check 1: Dependent prepositions

The following expressions all come from the text. Fill in the missing prepositions. There is a list below if you need help.

1 Let's get down . . . . business!

2 I feel . . . . a bit of a disadvantage as I haven't read the report.

3 Nine times . . . . ten he's late!

4 I think this matter should take priority . . . . everything else.

5 You don't have to speak . . . . that aggressive manner.

6 When he opened the door, he was confronted . . . . two policemen.

7 She seems to be unaware . . . . the fact that money doesn't grow on trees.

8 Several people complimented her . . . . the speech she made.

9 I thought your birthday card was . . . . rather poor taste, actually.

10 He's the one who's responsible . . . . locking up each night.

    by   of   in   out of   to   for   in   over   at   on

"Whatever happened to good old-fashioned hospitality?"

Sunday **14**

Exam Strategy: Paper 1/Paper 3

With *gapped texts*:

- read the incomplete text very carefully first.

- make sure you understand what the argument or sequence of events is.

- think about what *might* be missing from each gap before you look at the possible answers. You may not be able to guess but this thought process will make it easier to choose the right answer.

- check that your answer fits the space grammatically *and* logically (see Exam Focus 1 (page 126) for clues to look for).

Focus on Writing 1 (Section A)

You recently started working for a company called Wheeler Dealers Ltd and yesterday you went to a reception which your boss, Mr Spencer, held at his home. Unfortunately, you feel you didn't make a very good impression for a number of reasons, and you have decided to write a letter of apology to Mr Spencer.

Use the invitation and the information from an informal letter which you have just written to a friend to help you construct a suitable letter.

You may invent any necessary extra details to complete your answer (e.g. reasons which may excuse your behaviour) provided that you do not change any of the basic information given.

Write approximately 250 words.

The Director, Wheeler Dealers UK Ltd
Mr E F Spencer

requests the pleasure of your company

at a buffet reception to welcome new staff members
on Saturday, April 1st from 6 - 8pm
at 12 Denmark Street, Forest Green, London N5.

RSVP

You asked how I'm getting on in my new job. Well, it's a bit of a sore point, I'm afraid. I started last week and things went quite well. The boss (Mr Spencer) seemed pleased with my work, and the other people in the office were very friendly. Then Mr Spencer invited all the new staff round to his house this weekend for a kind of reception to welcome us to the company. A nice idea, you may think. Unfortunately it didn't turn out very well for me personally. In fact, it was a disaster!

The first problem was that I got there late. I hadn't wanted to be the first to arrive because it's awkward when you have to make small talk to the host for ages while you wait for everyone else to come, so I thought I'd get there about twenty minutes after the start.

Unfortunately, I got lost so I was about three quarters of an hour late and it seems everyone else had got there at the very beginning. Black looks from the boss! Then because it was a Saturday, I thought it would be OK to go in jeans. Wrong! Everyone else was dressed up to the nines! The boss even had a bow tie on! I felt really embarrassed.

After that, things went from bad to worse. Mrs Spencer had gone to great trouble over the food. There was cold roast beef, kebabs, meat balls and a special duck pate. As you know, I'm a vegetarian so I had to say 'no' to everything. I'm sure she thought I didn't like her cooking. Then I started to sneeze because I'm allergic to cats and they had to put their darling 'Tiddles' out in the cold. By then I knew who they would rather be putting outside!

I didn't think anything else could possibly go wrong, but it did. I don't know how it happened but as I was topping someone's glass up, my hand slipped and - you've guessed it - I spilt red wine on their new cream carpet.

I'm going to write a letter of apology now and I only hope Mr Spencer can forgive and forget (and maybe even see the funny side of things) because, if not, I'm going to be out of a job! I'll let you know what happens,

Mini-check 2: Expressions with *make*

So, you've finally *made it* - chief assistant to the assistant chief (overseas division).

The expression *made it* here means 'achieved an ambition'. *Make* is used in a number of other common expressions. Match the meanings on the right with the use of *make* in each sentence.

1 There are six adults and two children.
   That *makes* eight of us altogether.   a attend
2 What do you *make* the total? I *make* it 94.   b tell from your watch.
3 What time do you *make* it? I make it nearly 7.30.   c add up to
4 Do you think I'll *make* the station in five minutes?   d calculate
5 We're having a party on Saturday evening.   e succeed in reaching
   Do you think you'll be able to *make* it?

Communication Activity 2: International etiquette quiz

How successful would you be as an international executive?

Work with another student to choose the correct answer to the following questions.

1 If a Chinese businessman asks if your business is prosperous, it is polite to reply that it is doing

a well
b moderately
c poorly

2 Which of the following gifts would a Chinese friend consider to be in bad taste?

a a clock
b an oil painting
c a cut glass vase

3 Which part of the body should not be exposed in an Asian home?

a the knees
b the soles of the feet
c the ankles

4 When you receive someone's business card in Japan, do you

a study it carefully and put it on the table in front of you?
b thank the person and put it in your pocket quickly?
c look at it quickly just to memorise the name before putting it in your pocket?

5 When you take leave of your Japanese counterparts, do you

a shake hands and thank them warmly for their hospitality?
b make a rapid departure, not knowing what to say?
c bow and thank them for their hospitality?

6 What is the customary way of greeting in the Middle East?

a embracing
b bowing
c shaking hands

7 Which of the following would be likely to offend your Middle Eastern host?

a smoking a cigarette
b refusing a cup of coffee
c leaving some food on your plate

8 In Africa, when you meet someone for the first time, it is considered polite to

a ask about the health of your host's family
b talk about the weather
c compliment your host on his appearance

9 If you are invited to a home or a school in a Buddhist country, you shouldn't

a pat a child's head
b shake a child's hand
c give a child a present

10 Which American habit is likely to be seen as a sign of disrespect in Asian countries?

a taking off one's jacket
b crossing one's legs when sitting
c looking people in the eye

11 If you are invited to British friends' home for dinner, it is usual to arrive

a well before the stated time
b exactly on time
c a few minutes after the stated time

12 In Britain, it is not considered polite to ask your host

a how his wife is
b how much he earns
c how his business is going

Compare your answers with other people's and then check them with the Key on page 220.

Vocabulary: Collocation

Decide which verbs from Column A go with phrases from
Column B in each of the two boxes below. The first one is done
for you in each case.

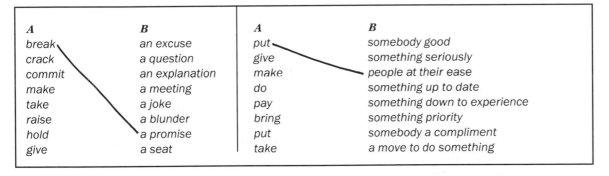

A	B		A	B
break	an excuse		put	somebody good
crack	a question		give	something seriously
commit	an explanation		make	people at their ease
make	a meeting		do	something up to date
take	a joke		pay	something down to experience
raise	a blunder		bring	something priority
hold	a promise		put	somebody a compliment
give	a seat		take	a move to do something

Focus on Writing 2 (Section B)

Follow the instructions below and write a piece of approximately 250 words.

> **You have a friend who is a teacher in an English speaking country. Your friend is helping to organise a short study-visit to your country for teenage pupils at his/her school. The pupils will stay with local families while they are in your country. Your friend has asked you to write a short article about the basic customs in your country, which can be given to the pupils before they leave. Your article should explain any habits to do with greeting, eating, being a good guest and so on, together with any aspects of family or social life which you think would be helpful to the pupils.**

English in Use 1: Cloze 2

Complete the following article by writing the missing words in the space provided. Use *only one word* in each space.

Table Manners

In France, (1)_____ one time, socially selective mothers (2)_____ test prospective sons-in-law (3)_____ serving raw peaches at dinner. (4)_____ who failed to eat one gracefully - and with a knife and fork - was (5)_____ to be acceptable. Such deliberate testing has surely died (6)_____ , but good table manners still (7)_____ a good impression - and the more (8)_____ as they become rarer.

The details vary (9)_____ country to country, but the essential aim is usually to (10)_____ eating in a way which is unpleasant to watch and to look after other people's needs as well as your (11)_____ . Be guided (12)_____ the behaviour of your host and hostess. Do as they do, not as you would do at home - unless their manners are (13)_____ dreadful that you can't go quite that far. It is far better manners to drink cola from a can, when the host is serving it (14)_____ way, (15)_____ to make everyone feel uncomfortable by asking for a glass.

Ⓒ *The Observer*

English in Use 2: Guided writing

You recently spent a weekend with some English-speaking friends at their house in the country. Unfortunately, you didn't have a very good time: the food was awful, the children, Donny and Jane, were badly-behaved and there was nothing to do. All the same, you feel you should write and thank your friends.

You have made some initial notes on which to base your letter. You must use all the words in the same order as the notes. You may add words and change the form of words where necessary. The first point has been expanded for you as an example.

> a Write thank you enjoyable weekend - recently.
>
> b So nice see you all. Children grown - last met?
>
> c Donny - talent football. (Hope window repaired)
>
> d What sense of humour - Jane! If find door keys - hid, send me? (no problem - climb through kitchen window, got home.)
>
> e Lot of trouble cooking. Nice change - plain food, no sauces or spices.
>
> f Thought house lovely, very peaceful no TV/radio.
>
> g Pity - weather. Pleasant walk or sit garden - while there.
>
> h Visit me next time? Spend day - when children school. Take you favourite Italian restaurant - lunch - love it!

Dear Frank and Jennifer,

a *I'm writing to thank you for the enjoyable weekend I spent with you recently.*

b_____

_____

c_____

_____

d_____

_____

e_____

_____

f_____

_____

g_____

_____

h_____

_____

Thanks once again for your hospitality. Hope to hear from you soon.

Love

Exam Strategy: Paper 2 (Section B)

Remember that your answer will be marked on two scales:

A Accuracy and Range of Language

- Don't lose marks! Take time to check your grammar, spelling, punctuation and vocabulary systematically (see Learning Focus 4 on page 68).

B Handling of the Task

- Read the instructions very carefully. You'll lose marks if you don't do everything the question asks for.
- Before you start, plan the layout for the writing task and make notes on the points you want to include and appropriate expressions to use.

Exam Focus 3

Paper 3 English in Use

Introduction

This paper tests your knowledge of different features of the language system such as grammar, register, spelling, punctuation, cohesion and coherence (the way language is used to link different parts of a text or different ideas together). You will have 1 ½ hours to complete the three sections of the paper, so there won't be a lot of time to spare.

The three sections each have a different emphasis:

Section A   concentrates on the correct choice of vocabulary and grammar.

Section B   tests your ability to recognise and correct mistakes, and also to adapt a text in a particular style.

Section C   asks you to organise written English in an appropriate way.

Note: The questions may vary a little from exam to exam, particularly in sections B and C, but they will always test the same skills. Typical questions are described below.

Questions

Section A: You the Student
You will have to complete two passages with 15 gaps each (cloze exercises).

<u>Cloze 1</u>   focuses mainly on *vocabulary*: you choose the best answer in each case from four options. (There is an example of this type of question on page 168.)

Tip: Read through the passage carefully before you look at the possible answers.

<u>Cloze 2</u>   focuses mainly on *grammar* and here there are no multiple choice answers to help you. (There is an example of this type of question on page 181.)

Tip: Think about grammar *and* meaning. Sometimes you need a negative (*not, no, no-one, never*) to make sense.

Section B: You the Editor
You will have to recognise and correct mistakes in a written text (error correction) and also complete a short gapped text in an appropriate style (stylistic cloze).

<u>Error correction</u>   You have to focus on a particular kind of mistake, e.g. spelling, prepositions and make corrections. (There is an example of this type of question on page 210.)

Tip:	Read the passage once for general meaning. Then read again, paying close attention to every word. It's easy to miss small mistakes if you are concentrating on meaning.
Stylistic cloze	You have to transfer information from a text in one register (e.g. formal) to a text in another register (eg informal) by writing one or two words in gaps in the second text. (There is an example of this type of question on page 199.)
Tip:	Make sure you give exactly the same information and that the language fits grammatically *and* stylistically.

Section C: You the Secretary

You will have to complete a text ('discourse' cloze) or expand notes into a fuller form (guided writing).

Discourse Cloze	You have to choose the best phrase or sentence to complete a text. This question is similar to the gapped text in Paper 1. (There is an example of this type of question on page 169.)
Tip:	Read through the passage carefully before you look at the possible answers.
Guided Writing	You will be given information in an abbreviated form - e.g. a set of notes for an article, a small ad, a telex etc. - which has to be expanded into a fuller form. (There is an example of this type of question on page 54.)
Tip:	Notice the register, tone or style of the original information and make sure you retain this in the new version.

Marking

Each section carries approximately equal marks. Before the exam it's a good idea to experiment to find out which questions take you longer to answer. You may find, for example, that you can do a vocabulary cloze exercise or an error correction task quite quickly, while a discourse cloze or guided writing task takes longer. When you take the exam, make sure you plan your time well so that you can give the necessary amount of time to each section.

Guided Writing:	In this question, each sentence is marked on a 0-1-2 scale, with 2 for the correct information and only very minor errors; 1 for the correct information but more serious errors, and 0 for the wrong information and/ or very serious errors.

Lead-in

1 **Look at the following examples. They all refer to measurements of time. Can you interpret the last two?**

60 S in a M = 60 seconds in a minute   *7 D in a W* = ?   *100 Y in a C* = ?

These examples all refer to the human body. With a partner, work out what they mean. The answers are given on page 220.

a 5 T on a F

b 32 T in the M

c 1 N on the F

d 2 L in the C

e 200 B in the S

f 1 B in the H

g 5 L of B in the B

h 4 basic BG

i 40% of the B is M

j The H B 70 times a M

2 **The figures on the left below all refer to facts about the average human body. Those on the right refer to facts about exceptional cases - the biggest, longest etc. examples ever recorded. Work with a partner to see if you can guess what any of them refer to.**

The Average Human Body

a 637

b 150,000

c 30 tons (30,481 kg)

d 226 kg crushing force

e enough to make 7 bars of soap

Exceptional cases

a 111 years 339 days

b 57 cm

c 7.92 m

d 69

e 103.6 miles/hour (167 km/hour)

Now read the text below to find out the correct answers.

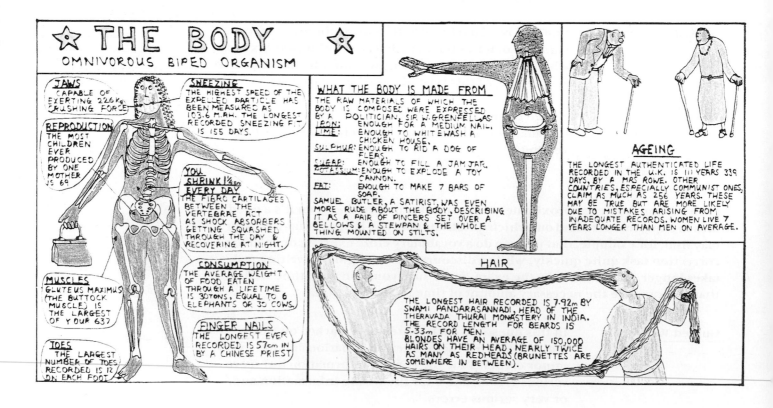

Text 1

1 The text below explains that there may be a connection between the kind of face we have and our particular talents. Read the text to find out more about the theory of 'facedness'.

When you have finished, discuss the ideas in the article with another student and see if you can tell which kind of face you each have.

PHYSIOLOGY: ● Our features may reveal hidden talents, says REBECCA FOWLER

  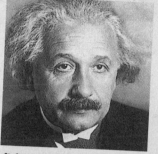 

Famous four: Beethoven and the Princess of Wales are left-faced, while Einstein and Burton fall in the right camp

At first glance, you would be hard put to find any common ground between the angry features of Beethoven and the budgerigar coyness of the Princess of Wales.

Of course, if you were Karl Smith, emeritus professor of psychology at America's Wisconsin-Madison University, and had spent 15 years in research, you would know that both are left-faced.

"Facedness" is the new theory that proposes, just as most of us are either left-handed or right-handed, we have a more dominant facial side. It also claims to reveal the physiognomy of musical genius.

Left-facers, according to Smith's studies, are better able to tune into the right side of the brain, which is associated with musical performance, while right-facers tap into the left hemisphere, which is specialised for cognitive processes — to the layman, thinking.

His surveys show that 85-90% of people are right-faced. "With rare exceptions, all musically talented people are left-faced," he says.

Wagner has one of the most marked left-faces that Smith has looked at, "dominant to the point of deformity". He is joined by Mozart, Beethoven, Brahms, Schubert, Tchaikovsky and Liszt. "I have yet to come across a great musical talent who is not left-faced," says Smith.

His work at New York's Metropolitan Opera shows that 98% of opera singers over a 50-year period have been left-faced. Most contemporary musicians looked at also had a dominant left side, from jazz musicians to pop stars.

"The Beatles were all left-faced," says Smith, whose work suggests that facedness ratios are the same in Europe as in the United States.

Although at first bemused by the discovery that Princess Diana is left-faced, he says he heard through contacts that the royal piano tutor believed Diana would have been a talented musician if training had started early enough. Prince Harry is the only other member of the royal family who may have a career in music as a left-facer.

"Parents should not be wasting their money on right-faced children," says Smith. It is not, contrary to popular belief, hands or ears that will suggest a Mozart in the making, but facial features.

The test for dominance is simple. Researchers measured signals from muscles and recorded resistance changes in jaw and lip movements.

But simply looking in a mirror will reveal a larger, more muscular side that is more flexible in speech and has a deeper dimple when you smile. The eyebrow will be higher and the skin smoother.

But right-facers should not despair. Dexterity in cognitive processes means that most great mathematicians and scientists have been dominant on the right. "The marked right-facedness of Einstein is remarkable," says Smith.

Right-facers also have the edge in speech. Most great orators and all British prime ministers have been right-side dominant, from Walpole to Thatcher. And we have yet to see a pope or monarch cloaking musical genius.

While left-facers have a better control of vowels, right-facers have the hold on consonants. Smith can recall no American newsreader who has been left-faced.

Actors should also be looking for a higher right brow, since most of the greats have been right-faced — such as Richard Burton.

Smith's theory also maintains that right-facers make better dancers and athletes. They depend on a highly articulate understanding of movement and cognition, born out in the relation between a dominant right-face and left brain.

All athletes in the last Olympics were right-faced, he found, and a study of the Chicago and New York ballets showed 99% of dancers were right-faced. The one group of people who did not fall clearly into right or left were painters.

"The evidence has been astoundingly consistent right across the board," says Smith. As a music lover, he is reconciling himself to his own right-facedness.

Unlike handedness, which develops at the age of three or four, facedness is determined before birth. For would-be composers and politicians there is no defying facedness, and parents should take note before signing up hopeful youngsters for music lessons — a glance in the mirror will tell if the expense will be worth it.

© *The Sunday Times*

2 Now read the text again to answer the questions in the Exam Practice sections.

3 Exam Practice 1: Multiple matching

These questions ask you whether various groups of people are more likely to be left-faced or right-faced. A - C list the types of facedness mentioned in the article. Answer each question by choosing from the list A - C.

Note: There is only one answer to each question.

actors	1 . . . . . .
scientists	2 . . . . . .
composers	3 . . . . . .
long-distance runners	4 . . . . . .
artists	5 . . . . . .
pop singers	6 . . . . . .
political leaders	7 . . . . . .
the majority of people	8 . . . . . .
opera singers	9 . . . . . .
speech makers	10 . . . . . .

> *Types of Facedness*
>
> **A Right-faced**
>
> **B Left-faced**
>
> **C Either right- or left-faced**

4 Exam Practice 2: Multiple choice

There are a number of unfinished statements about the text below. You must choose the answer which you think fits best. Choose *one answer only* to each question. Remember, in the exam you will have to mark your answer on a special *answer sheet*.

1 The author suggests that when you first compare the faces of Beethoven and the Princess of Wales

   A they seem to have a lot of similar features
   B they look completely different
   C they're both left-faced
   D they both look common

2 Among left-faced composers, Wagner is said to be

   A an extremely attractive example
   B a faulty example
   C an unusually clear example
   D a typical example

3 When Karl Smith discovered that Princess Diana was left-faced, he was

   A disappointed
   B delighted
   C impressed
   D surprised

4 The side of your face that is dominant will

   A have more wrinkles
   B move more easily
   C be flatter
   D have a thicker eyebrow

5 The advantage of being right-faced is that you will probably

    A be an optimistic kind of person
    B be a successful athlete
    C pronounce different sounds more correctly
    D be able to reason clearly

6 According to Karl Smith, the evidence for his facedness theory

    A is extremely convincing
    B has been confirmed by the whole academic community
    C is generally accepted by music lovers
    D contains a number of interesting exceptions

7 Facedness is said to be different from handedness in that

    A it's of interest to politicians
    B it's easy to detect
    C you are born with it
    D you inherit it from your parents

Focus on Grammar:
Past tenses used to talk about hypothetical situations

One way to talk about a situation which does not exist but which we imagine is to use *if* + conditional clause:

If you were Karl Smith and had spent 15 years in research ... (Text 1)

There are a number of other expressions which can be used in a similar way. These include:

I wish	*as though/as if*	*would rather* + object
If only	*supposing*	*it's time*

When they refer to the present or future, these expressions are followed by a past simple or continuous tense. When referring to the past, they are followed by a past perfect tense. (See Grammar File page 101.)

Wave your hand back and forth in front of you *as if* you *were chasing* a mosquito away . . . (Text 2)

a **Complete the following sentences by adding one of the expressions above and putting the verb in brackets into a suitable past tense.**

  a . . . . I (*can*) help you but I'm afraid I can't.

  b I . . . . you (*not/tell*) me how the book ends, if you don't mind.

  c . . . . you (*not/find*) a spare key, how would you have got in?

  d Don't you think . . . . the children (*go*) to bed?

  e . . . . I (*learn*) to read music at school! I'd love to be able to join a choir.

  f The trouble with Jim is that he treats everything . . . . it (*be*) a joke.

b **Now complete the following sentences.**

  a You shouldn't keep lending him your car. It's time . . . .
  . . . .

  b We rely too much on the car. Supposing . . . .
  . . . .

  c Don't treat me as though I . . . .
  . . . .

  d It was quite a good course but I wish . . . .
  . . . .

  e You shouldn't have spent so much on my present. I'd rather
  . . . .

Focus on Listening 1

You are going to hear a short talk on the benefits and dangers of the sun as far as our skin is concerned. Before you listen, look through the notes below. As you listen, fill in the information for Questions 1 - 9.

SUN FACTS

Benefits

- Stimulates the circulation.
- Good for skin complaints.
- Produces [1 _____] which is vital for health.
- Good psychological effects.
- Try and spend [2 _____] a day in natural daylight during summer.

Dangers

- Sunlight is the cause of [3 _____] % of skin cancers.
- 80% of sun damage occurs before the age of [4 _____]
- The risk of skin cancer doubles every [5 _____] km nearer the equator.
- Ultra Violet light can pass through water, [6 _____] and thin clothing.

Protection

- The skin is naturally protected from [7 _____] % of Ultra Violet light.
- Use a sun screen for increased protection.
- A tan protects the skin [8 _____] more than an untanned skin.
- A tan lasts approximately [9 _____] days.

Text 2

gesture / dʒestʃə / N Count

1.1 A gesture is a movement that you make with a part of your body, especially your hands or your head, to express emotion or information, either instead of speaking or while you are speaking.
e.g. *She made an angry gesture with her fist ...*
He held one hand over his eyes in a gesture of pain.

1 ***Work in pairs*** **to label the parts of the body shown in the drawings below. Which parts of the body can be used to make gestures? What do those gestures mean?**

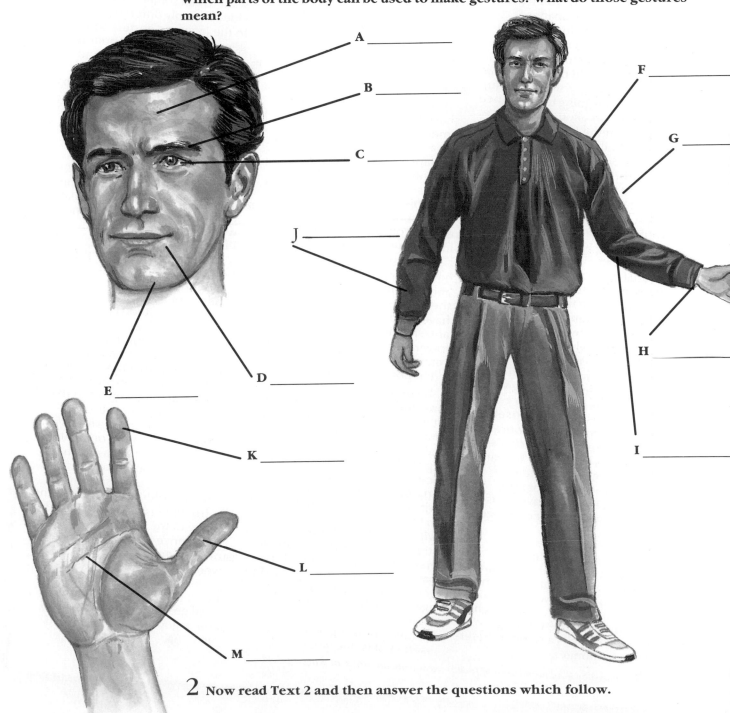

A _____

B _____

C _____

F _____

G _____

J _____

E _____

D _____

K _____

H _____

I _____

L _____

M _____

2 **Now read Text 2 and then answer the questions which follow.**

So, waving the hand means goodbye, right? Wrong, as *Jack Seward* discovers when he looks at ...

Gestures IN JAPAN

Unless you are proficient in the Japanese language, it is certain you will have a communications problem should you visit Japan. Just how serious this problem will be depends on where you go and how long you stay and whether or not you travel in the company of a Japanese-speaking friend. But no matter what you do, you will have this problem, at least to some extent.

So what should be done? Give up your plans to visit Japan? No, that would be going too far, since Japan is a marvellous experience. Try to learn the Japanese language? Well, for the sake of a two or three-week visit, it would not be reasonable to spend months trying to pick up some conversational ability in Japanese, but you might arm yourself with a phrase book and memorize a few handy expressions to help out in a difficult spot

What else can you do? Why, use some gestures!

But wait. Are these gestures universal? Or, more to the point, are they used by the Japanese?

Unfortunately, no. Japanese gestures are a world of their own, just as their language is. They seldom coincide in meaning with the gestures of any other country. You must resign yourself, therefore, to learning entirely new gestures, but be not dismayed. It's a lot easier to learn the gesture than it is to pronounce and remember the phrase you would have to use to convey the meaning of the gesture.

Let's review some basic Japanese gestures first:

Form a circle with the thumb and index finger of your right hand. To us, this would mean everything is O.K., it's all right, but to a Japanese this finger-formed circle is a standard reference to money.

Now quickly memorize one more gesture. Wave your open hand back and forth in front of you, as if you were chasing a mosquito away from your nose. (Your hand can be right up against your nose or it can be held ten or twelve inches away from your face.) This is the sign for No, none, not, negative, I haven't any, I don't want any.

Clench your fist tightly. If you shake that clenched fist at an American, he would know you are angrily threatening him. To the Japanese, however, you are making the sign for someone who is stingy with his money. In fact, this should be easy to remember since we have the expression "tight-fisted" that means the same thing.

Traditionally, the Japanese have regarded the stomach as the abode of the spirit or soul (not the region of the heart), but they have felt that the nose is the entrance leading eventually to the lower abode. Accordingly, when referring to themselves, they will often point to their noses,

If you are talking about someone and crook your index finger at the same time, you are saying that the person has the unfortunate habit of taking objects not rightfully his. The little finger pointing straight up in the air originally meant a baby, but nowadays it is more commonly used to mean girlfriend, or wife. The right thumb held straight up in a similar manner means boyfriend, father, husband, or master. The first two fingers of the hand tapped lightly against the lips is a reference to kissing.

Now this next gesture is very useful but is one you must be careful about. We often signal goodbye by extending our right arm straight to the front and waving the fingers up and down, but the Japanese have a similar gesture which is used when they want to call someone to their side. The only difference is that in the Japanese gesture the fingers are moved while pointing at a slight downward angle and not held straight out.

When a Japanese rapidly crosses his two index fingers, he is telling you there is bad blood between the two people being discussed. The thumb rubbed against the side of the nose means a card game called *hana*, the name deriving from the pictures of flowers on the backs of the playing cards. *Hana* is the word for nose as well as for flower.

Cupping the left hand just below the level of the mouth, with the right hand going through the motions of using chopsticks, is a readily understood reference to food or to eating.

Pointing the forefinger at one's ear or temple and making a circular motion with it has two meanings, depending on the direction of the finger movement. If the forefinger moves anti-clockwise, the gesture refers to a perverse, eccentric, or mentally unstable person. Moving the finger in the opposite direction, or clockwise, equals vanity.

If one holds his stiff right hand in front of his face with the palm facing to the left, he is asking indulgence for crossing the path of another or for passing between two persons. Accompanied with a slight bow of the head, this is a very frequently used gesture and should stand you in good stead in crowded Japan.

Reproduced by kind permission of Jack Seward from an article in Wings of Gold

Questions 1 - 5

These questions ask you to match different Japanese hand gestures to their correct meanings. The pictures A - H show the possible gestures. Answer each question by choosing from the pictures A - H.

Which gestures have the following meanings?

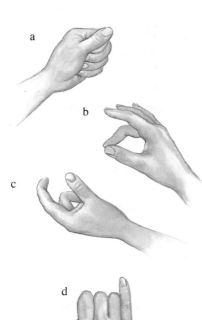

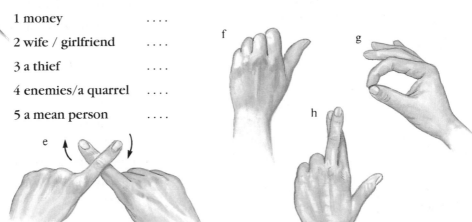

1 money   . . . .

2 wife / girlfriend   . . . .

3 a thief   . . . .

4 enemies/a quarrel . . . .

5 a mean person   . . . .

Questions 6 - 13

These questions ask you to match more Japanese gestures to their correct meanings. A - J list the possible meanings. Answer each question by choosing from the list A - J, and writing the correct letter in the boxes.

Note: Be careful about 'right' and 'left', 'clockwise' and 'anticlockwise'. You should imagine these from the point of view of the person making the gesture.

What do the following gestures mean?

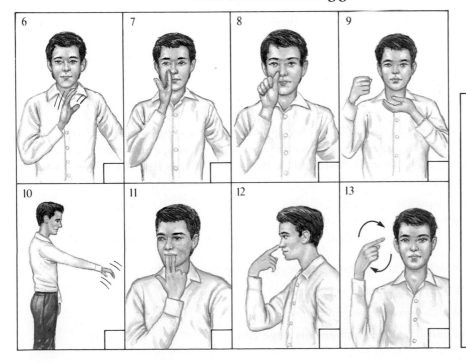

A food

B kissing

C a card game

D me

E Goodbye

F negative

G mad

H a vain person

I Come here!

J I'm sorry/Excuse me

Vocabulary

1 Collocation:

Match the following verbs to parts of the body. The first has been done as an example. The next four (b - e) come from Text 2.

a clap
b clench
c crook
d cup
e bow
f shrug
g cross
h screw up
i twiddle

1 your head
2 your fingers
3 your thumbs
4 your fist
5 your hand
6 your finger
7 your face
8 your hands
9 your shoulders

2 Metaphor

The following nouns can be used metaphorically as part of certain compound adjectives. Complete the sentences below with suitable words from the list. The first one has been done as an example.

heart   finger   head   face   fist   skin

a Although he's quite famous now, he hasn't become big-**headed** ... at all.

b You would have to be very thick-......... to ignore so much criticism.

c Take care of your belongings. There are some light-......... people around.

d I didn't think my father would be hard-........... enough to punish me.

e Don't bother asking him for any money. He's extremely tight-.............. .

f I trusted you! How could you have been so two-............ with me?

3 Idiom

a Complete the following sentences with words from the list.

teeth   neck   foot   eyes   ear   nose

1 I'd like to come but I'm up to my .... in work at the moment.

2 I can't understand why he turned up his .... at such a good job.

3 He lied through his .... to the police.

4 You'll have to put your .... down if he asks to borrow more money.

5 Keep your .... to the ground in case there's any more news.

6 I see no point in risking my .... just to prove how brave I am.

b Complete the following sentences with expressions from the list below.

fingers and thumbs   head and shoulders   eye to eye
hand to mouth   hand over fist   tooth and nail
head over heels

1 He'll fight .... to prove his innocence.

2 They were obviously .... in love.

3 He was making money .... and spending it as quickly.

4 I was so nervous as I opened the letter that I was all ....
....

5 She left the firm because she didn't see ....
with her boss.

6 One particularly good candidate was ....
above the rest.

7 We lived from .... in the early days, never knowing where our next meal would come from.

Focus on Listening 2

1 Stamina is the ability to keep going over a long period of time, and it's essential if you're in a physically demanding job, running for a bus or even taking care of small children all day. Look at this list of activities and discuss the questions below.

Disco dancing	Golf	Tennis	Weight-lifting
Climbing stairs	Digging	Yoga	Football
Judo	Sailing	Rowing	Gymnastics

1 Which *one* is the best for developing stamina?

2 Which *four* are also very good?

3 Which *three* are not much use?

You can find the answers on page 220.

2 You are going to hear a short talk about the amount of time it's advisable to spend on five other types of exercise which are good for stamina. *Before you listen*, look carefully through the table below. *As you listen*, fill in the information for Questions 1 - 12.

Listen carefully as you will hear this piece *only once*.

STAMINA EXERCISE

Activity	Minutes	Days		Minutes	Days
Walking	1	5	plus	2	2
3	15	4	plus	30	2
5	30	5	plus	6	2
Skipping	7	5	plus	8	2
9	20	5			
or	30	10			

Remember: • It's important to choose an activity you [11]

  • You must [12] to these exercise times slowly, over several weeks.

Communication Activity 1: Relax as you fly

1 In this activity, you and your partner will each have a set of pictures illustrating simple exercises you can do during a flight. The pictures are the same but one set has letters and the other has numbers in a different order. Read the instructions below carefully before you turn to the pictures.

Student A should look at the pictures on the next page. Listen as your partner describes each one and write the numbers 1 - 8 by the pictures in the order they are described.

Student B should look at the pictures on page 219. Describe each one to your partner as clearly as possible, starting with picture number 1 and continuing to number 8. Give the number each time.

You can either give *instructions* for each exercise e.g. *Sit up straight, with your arms..., then...* or you can *describe* what the woman in the picture is doing e.g. *She's sitting up straight ... and then...* . If the picture doesn't give enough information to make the exercise clear, don't worry - just describe what you can see.

a

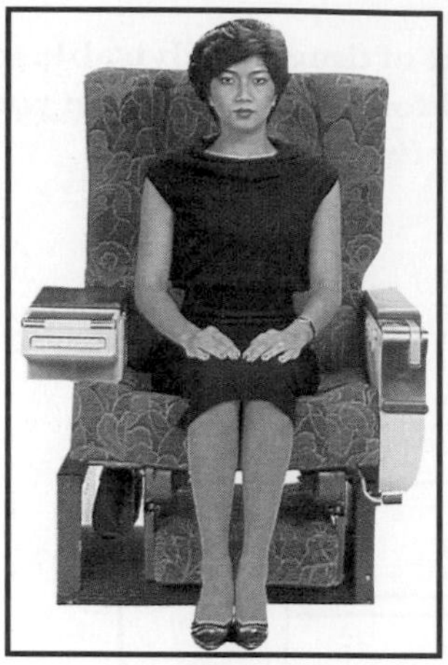

b

Student A

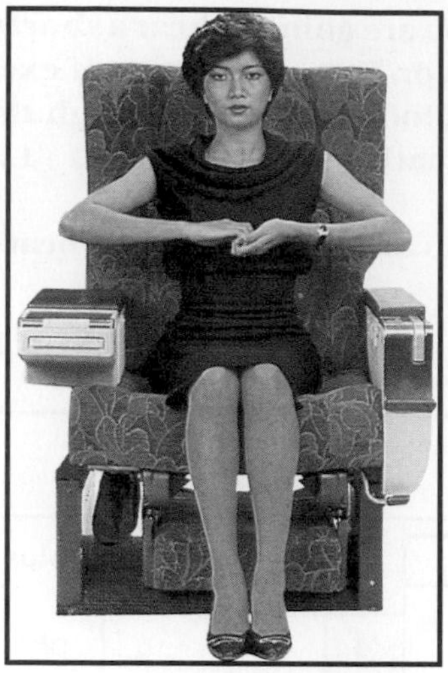

c

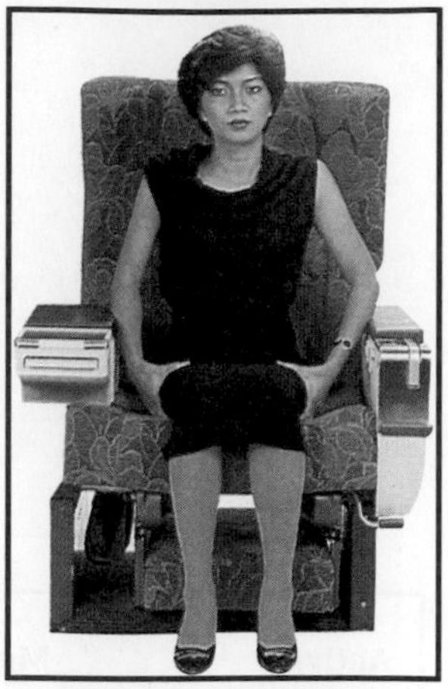

d

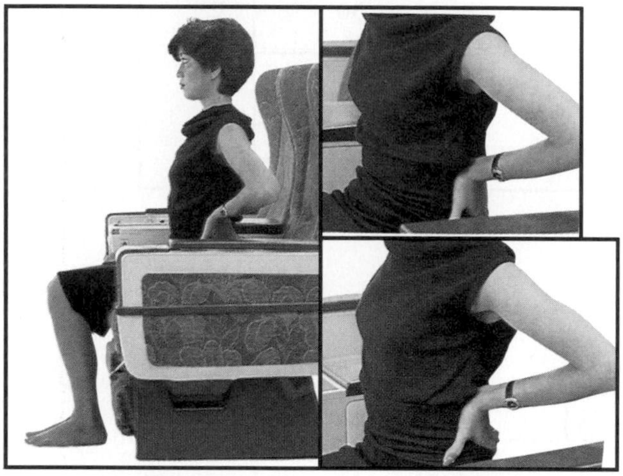

e

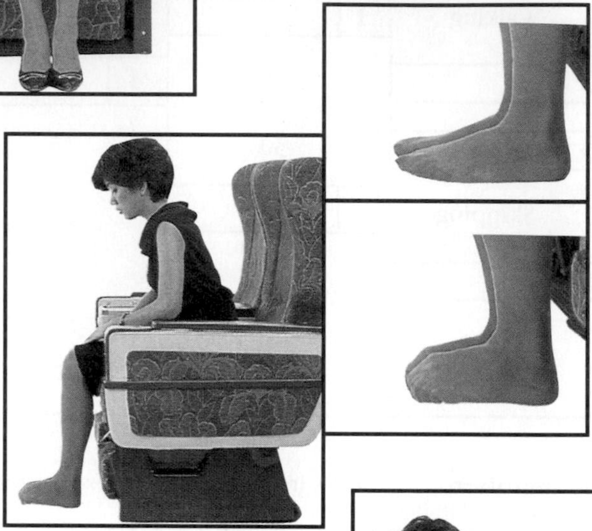

f

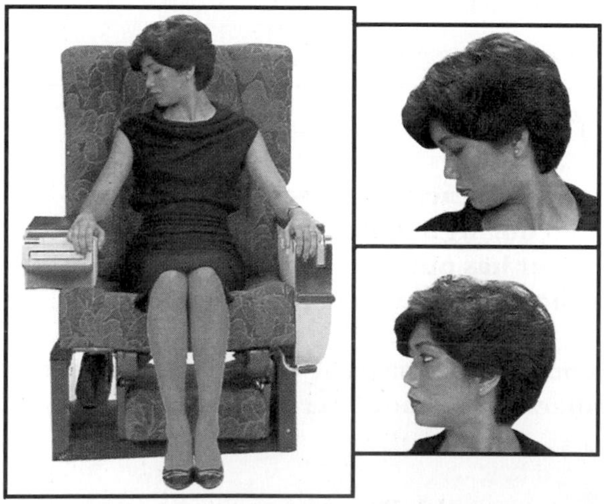

g

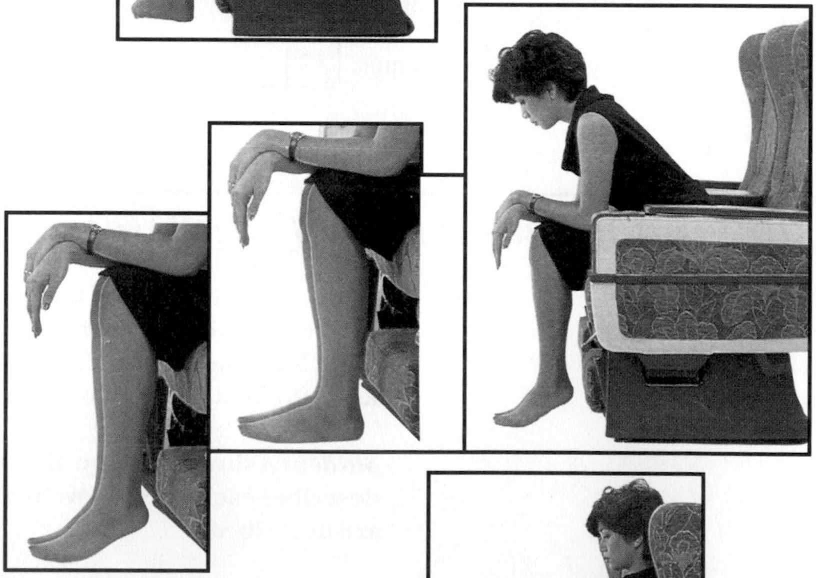

h

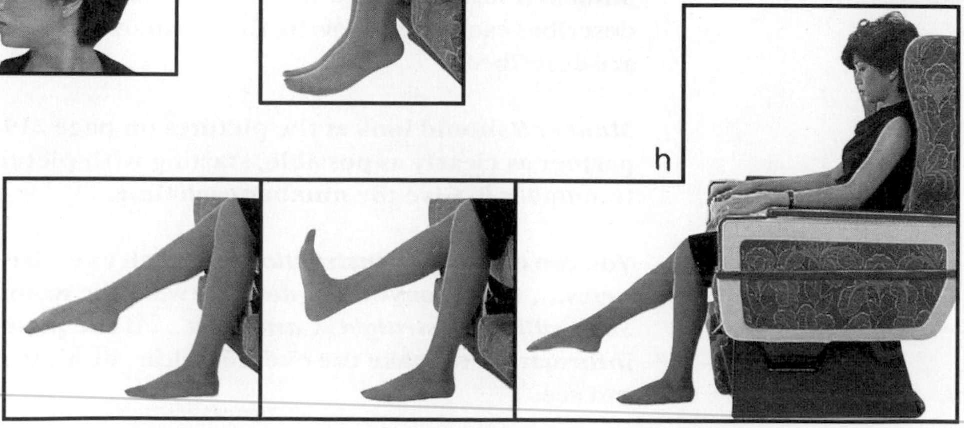

2 **Work with a partner to match each picture with a relaxation exercise and a set of instructions, chosen from those given below. Write the letter of the correct picture in the column on the left and the number of the correct instructions in the column on the right.**

PICTURE	EXERCISE	INSTRUCTIONS
	Back stretching - relieves back stiffness Head turning and nodding - stimulates joints of neck and upper spine Pulling hands apart - for the muscles of the shoulders and back of arms Squeezing the feet - relieves aching and swollen feet Pressing in on thighs - for chest, shoulder and thigh muscles Toe pointing and raising - for muscles of the lower leg Pulling back abdominal muscles Rising on the toes improves blood circulation in the legs	

1 Sit with your elbows on your knees. Bend forward with your whole weight pressed down on your knees. Raise your heels as high as possible. Drop your heels and lift your toes. Repeat 20 times.

2 Place both feet firmly on the floor. Pull your toes suddenly towards your heels so that you arch your feet. Repeat 20 times.

3 With one leg stretched out in front of you, point your toes up and down vigorously. Repeat 20 times with each leg.

4 Place your hands behind your back. Arch your spine forwards and backwards. Repeat 20 times.

5 Sit upright. Inhale fully before drawing your abdominal muscles up and back towards your spine. Hold for 20 seconds. Then breathe out. Repeat 20 times.

6 Turn your head fully to the right. Nod 5 times. Do the same to the left. Repeat 6 times.

7 Sit upright. Bend your arms and interlock your fingers at chest level. Take a deep breat + h and then try to pull your hands apart. Hold for 5 seconds. Repeat 20 times.

8 Sit with your legs comfortably apart and your feet flat on the floor. Place your palms on the sides of your thighs. With your body straight and your head level, take a deep breath and press your thighs inwards with your hands. At the same time try to move your thighs apart. Hold for 5 seconds. Repeat 20 times.

Courtesy of Wings of Gold

Focus on Writing (Section B)

Read the instructions for the writing task below. Follow them exactly and write about 250 words.

> You have been asked to write an article for a leaflet for English-speaking visitors to your district. The article will be in a section about opportunities for exercise and sport in the area. It would be appropriate to cover subjects such as enjoyable walks, health clubs, dance classes, outdoor and indoor sports facilities in general or individual sports in particular, and any special sporting events like marathons. Choose one or more topics from the above list to deal with in your article. You can use your own headings if you prefer, and you can include general comments (e.g. on the advantages or disadvantages of a particular activity) as well as practical information if you wish.

Communication Activity 2: Problem solving

Work in pairs. Look at the two pictures below.
Discuss what they each show and what they have in common. Try to decide where the pictures might have appeared and why. You should try to reach agreement or 'agree to disagree'. Afterwards you should be ready to report your decision to other students or to the teacher.

You can find the solution on page 220.

Exam Strategy: Paper 5 (Phase D)

In the last part of the interview you will probably have to report back to the examiners on the decision you reached in your discussion and you may have to answer questions. Again, the important thing is not whether you reached the right conclusion but how well you express yourself.

Do
- make sure you remember the details of your discussion.
- be ready to talk about your partner's opinion as well as your own.
- explain the reasons for your conclusions.

Don't
- give one word answers to questions.
- worry if you didn't reach a clear conclusion - just explain the problems.

English in Use 1: Cloze 1

Read the text below and circle the letter next to the word in the list on the next page which best fits each space. The first answer has been given as an example.

'Use it or lose it' is the new approach to back pain. In the (1) . . . few years, there has been a radical (2) . . . in the way doctors treat this most common ailment. Weeks or months of rest in bed, - the standard method of treatment for so long - are now thought to be (3) . . . harmful. Muscles become flabby, joints become stiff and what started out as a temporary acute condition quickly (4) . . . a chronic disability. Far better, (5) . . . current thinking, to (6) . . . with a little pain and get moving.

The change has not happened overnight. For years, some specialists have had an instinctive (7) . . . that bed rest was not the answer. But what finally (8) . . . an end to prolonged bed rest was a study, (9) . . . by Doctor Richard Dejo, of more than 200 patients who were treated for back pain in a clinic in Texas. (10) . . . did patients who had two days' bed rest do (11) . . . as well as those given seven days, they required only half as much time altogether off work.

As a result of Doctor Dejo's work, experts now (12) . . . that hardly anyone with acute back pain should spend more than a few days lying down - just long enough to give the body a chance to repair any obvious (13) . . . to muscle tissue. After that should come a programme of gradually increasing exercise, probably (14) . . . some passive therapy such as massage, heat or ultrasound from a physiotherapist.

Because of hospital waiting lists, most people have to wait several weeks before receiving the treatment they need. Unfortunately this wait is often spent in bed or inactive for (15) . . . of doing further damage to the back. It has been (16) . . . that for every day an injured muscle is rested it loses at least one per cent of its strength. Stay in bed for two or three weeks and it will be far harder to rebuild a damaged muscle.

© The Observer

1	(A) last	B recent	C latest	D next
2	A difference	B change	C transfer	D exchange
3	A reliably	B surely	C confidently	D positively
4	A develops	B turns into	C increases	D results
5	A agreeing with	B due to	C according to	D conforming to
6	A put on	B put over	C put out	D put up
7	A thinking	B feeling	C knowledge	D information
8	A gave	B made	C put	D had
9	A carried out	B carried on	C carried over	D carried through
10	A Neither	B At no time	C Not only	D No sooner
11	A just	B equally	C totally	D even
12	A forbid	B prescribe	C consult	D recommend
13	A hurt	B damage	C wound	D pain
14	A attended by	B joined with	C united by	D accompanied by
15	A fear	B anxiety	C care	D worry
16	A tested	B studied	C estimated	D considered

English in Use 2: Stylistic cloze

Read the following information about treating cramp from a First Aid manual. Using the information, complete the more informal advice on the subject in a booklet for young people. Write the missing words in the spaces provided on the right. The first answer has been given as an example.

Use *not more than two words* in each space.

Cramp

Cramp is caused by an involuntary contraction of a muscle which may occur during exercise or as a result of chilling, as in swimming.

Occurrence -   calf of leg   50%
                hand or foot 25%
                thigh   15%

The remedy is to stretch the shortened muscle.

Self-management

In the calf
* Straighten the knee and with your hand draw the foot up towards the shin.

In the foot
* Grasp the bent toes and draw them firmly up towards the shin.

In the thigh
* Raise the leg, using one hand to support the heel. With the other hand, apply pressure to the knee.

Note: Cramp may also occur when there has been excessive loss of salt, as in severe sweating. In this case make good the salt deficiency by giving the patient water containing half a teaspoon of salt to the half-litre to drink.

CRAMP

Cramp is caused by a muscle suddenly (1) . . . up. This can happen while you (2) . . . or when you (3) . . . while swimming, for example. The (4) . . . place to get cramp is in the calf of the leg. (5) . . . cramp, you need to stretch the muscle. If you get cramp in your calf, straighten your knee and (6) . . . the foot towards you. If the cramp is in your foot, take (7) . . . your toes and do the same thing. If the cramp is in a thigh muscle, lift your leg (8) . . . one hand under the heel and (9) . . . the knee with the other hand. (10) . . . who has been sweating heavily and who has (11) . . . a (12) . . . salt may also get cramp. The best way of (13) . . . the salt is to drink half a litre of water with half a teaspoon of salt (14) . . . in it

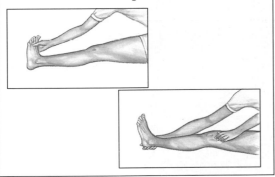

1 tightening
2 _____
3 _____
4 _____
5 _____
6 _____
7 _____
8 _____
9 _____
10 _____
11 _____
12 _____
13 _____
14 _____

Exam strategy: Paper 3 (Section B)

In Question 4, you have to transfer information from one text to another and also to 'translate' the language from one register (e.g. informal) to another (e.g. formal). It's important to remember this translation aspect of the task.

Read carefully!

- The *instructions* will explain what the two registers are.
- Make sure you understand the *first text* fully. Notice any special features of style.
- Skim-read the *second text* and notice the differences in style.

Think before you write!

- What kind of text is it? Who is the audience?
- Are you giving exactly *the same* information as in the first text?
- Does the language fit the new text grammatically and stylistically?

Testing Times

Lead-in / Communication Activity 1

1 *Work with another student.* **Look at the picture below and discuss its connection with the title of this unit. What has the artist tried to illustrate? Be prepared to report your ideas to the class.**

2

a **Tell your partner about the last exam you took. What was the subject? Where did you take it? What was the exam like? How did you feel about it?**

b **How do you prepare for exams? Discuss the following points with your partner: revision, health, nerves.**

c **What alternatives are there to traditional written exams? What are the advantages/disadvantages?**

Text 1

1 Exam Practice 1: Multiple matching

Skim-read Text 1 on page 203 to answer questions 1 - 7 which follow.

Questions 1 - 7 ask you to choose the correct title for each section (1 - 7). A - J list the possible titles. Answer each question by choosing from the list A - J and then write the correct title in each space in the text. Remember that in the exam you will have to mark your answer on a special *answer sheet*.

1	section 1	A	How to annoy the examiner
2	section 2	B	After it's over
3	section 3	C	Be prepared
4	section 4	D	Watch what you eat
5	section 5	E	Coping with difficult questions
6	section 6	F	How to study
7	section 7	G	Look after yourself
		H	Don't panic
		I	Make a revision timetable
		J	Choosing which questions to answer

2 Exam Practice 2: Multiple choice

Read the text more carefully in order to answer Questions 8 - 13 below. You must choose the answer which you think fits best. Choose *one answer only* to each question. Remember, in the exam you will have to mark your answer on a special *answer sheet.*

8 The writer urges us to remember that exams
   A are the key to success in life
   B are not a good test of ability
   C are not the most important thing in life
   D are nothing to be concerned about

9 The writer's advice about difficult questions is
   A not to spend any time on them
   B to leave them till the very end of the exam
   C to tackle them after those you can do easily
   D to guess the answers

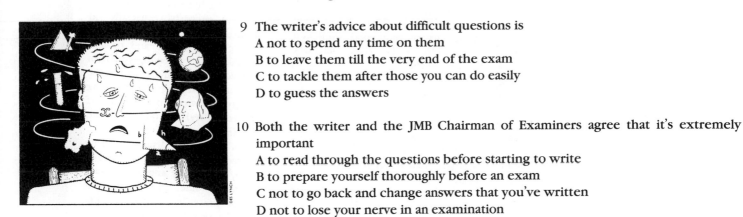

10 Both the writer and the JMB Chairman of Examiners agree that it's extremely important
   A to read through the questions before starting to write
   B to prepare yourself thoroughly before an exam
   C not to go back and change answers that you've written
   D not to lose your nerve in an examination

11 Candidates often imagine that examiners
   A mark exam scripts carelessly
   B enjoy finding mistakes in people's work
   C are easily irritated
   D are gentle, tolerant people

12 One thing which is sure to annoy an examiner is when a candidate
   A gives an answer that they've learnt in class
   B doesn't answer all the questions
   C has very bad handwriting
   D writes very long answers to questions

13 The writer suggests that before an exam it is not helpful to
   A consult a doctor
   B discuss the exam with friends
   C drink any coffee
   D miss a meal

The Big Day

Nothing is more important than staying CALM during an exam. More good candidates have failed because they lost their nerve than
5 for any other reason . . .

1

Yes, exams are important and yes, you do need qualifications, but keep a sense of proportion. Exams are just one way of measuring a
10 particular set of mental traits— they do not test how clever you are, or how original you are. And it is not the End of the World and Civilisation As We Know It if you fail.
15 The best way to prevent panic is to do everything you can to make life easier for yourself . . .

2

Before you go into the exam, make sure you know in advance the date,
20 time and place for each paper and carry the timetable with you.

Keep an exam bag to carry all your writing kit, with two of everything.
25 Also in your exam bag, keep a piece of paper with your candidate number, your examination centre number and telephone number.

3

Spend *at least* 10 minutes reading
30 the paper, working out which questions you can do and planning your answers. If you can't see any questions on the paper you like, try the bargepole* method. Cross off
35 the ones you wouldn't touch with two bargepoles tied together, then cross off the ones where a single bargepole would do, until you arrive at a few you can tackle.

4

40 Never spend ages trying to work out a question. Go through the whole paper at least twice, first doing only the questions you know the answers to immediately.
45 The second time, try to work out what the answer should be and don't guess until you've tried every other way. Never go back and correct answers. Studies have shown
50 that most people change right answers to wrong ones.

5

In the depths of every exam candidate's nightmares lurks the toadlike Examiner, dripping red
55 ink all over the painfully written exam script and laughing fiendishly. But examiners are remarkably tolerant and unembittered people. They all stress that
60 they try to find good work and would far rather pass somebody than fail them.

However, there are certain things which are guaranteed to irritate the
65 most friendly of examiners . . .

Says Bob McDuell, a chief examiner and writer of chemistry revision books for Letts, "Any paper that's roughly presented
70 starts off as a loser. How can we be fair to someone if we can't read what they've written?"

The one thing that most infuriates them all is not answering the
75 questions as set.

"It happens again and again," says JMB Chairman of Examiners, Alan Prosser-Harries. "They pick out one or two words in the written
80 question and they think, 'Ah, I remember those words,' and just pour out what they did in class.

"I think it should be statutory that no exam candidate is allowed
85 to pick up a pen for the first quarter of an hour. They should spend that time just making sure they understand what's wanted and then planning answers."
90 Some pupils pride themselves on their ability to waffle—but there are no prizes for writing a longer script than anybody else, so stick to the point and don't pad. On the other
95 hand, it's better to resort to waffle rather than leave one question out.

6

Exam time is also a time to learn to look after yourself. Your health is particularly important during the
100 revision period as well as the actual exam weeks.

DON'T stay up all night before the exam. Taking an exam when you're half asleep is a good way to fail it.
105 DO make sure you get enough exercise during the exam weeks. Sitting down all day can make it hard to sleep at night.

DON'T panic if you can't sleep the
110 night before the exams start—most people can't. Make sure you have everything you need for the morning, that your alarm clock is set, and have a hot milky drink.
115 DO eat properly, especially on exam mornings. A good breakfast with plenty of fibre and protein will take longer to be digested than a chocolate bar wolfed down on the
120 bus, and won't leave you feeling hungry and weak in the exam. If you really feel too queasy to eat, take fresh fruit with you.

DON'T take *any* drugs. If a drug
125 is strong enough to do you any good, it's strong enough to have unwanted side effects. If your doctor prescribes anything, make sure she knows you have exams.
130 DON'T drink pints of strong coffee. Too much caffeine can make you feel even more twitchy and nervous, and will make you want to go to the loo.

7

135 Try not to get involved in drawn-out post mortems with your friends.

Stretch your legs and get some air in your lungs instead; your brain won't function without oxygen!

* A barge *is a flat-bottomed boat which is used to carry loads on rivers and canals.* A barge pole *is the long pole used to push the barge along. If you say you* wouldn't touch *something* with a barge pole, *it means you don't want to have anything to do with it.*

Reproduced by permission of Express Newspapers plc from an article by Anne de Courcy

Focus on Listening 1

You are going to hear a short talk on Cambridge examinations. As you listen, fill in the information for questions 1 - 12. Listen carefully as you will hear this piece only once.

Examination	Year when introduced	No. of papers	Exam Times	Special Points	Number of candidates in 1990
Certificate of Proficiency in English (CPE)	1 ___	5	June/Dec	Listening and Speaking make up one third of marks	50,000
First Certificate in English (FCE)	2 ___	5	June/Dec	Listening and Speaking make up one third of marks	3 ___
Diploma in English Studies (DES)	1941	4 ___	June	Only people who have achieved 5 ___ in Proficiency can enter	500
Preliminary English Test (PET)	6 ___	7 ___	5 fixed dates	Tests students' 'survival' skills in social and work situations	8 ___
Certificates in Communicative Skills in English	1990	9 ___ at each level	November and 10 ___	In the Writing Paper you can 11 ___	1,000
Certificate in Advanced English (CAE)	1991	5	June/Dec	The emphasis is on 12 ___ tasks	no figures available

Exam Strategy: Paper 4 (Section B)

In this question, you only hear the recording once. The task will probably be quite straightforward but as you only have one chance to get it right, it's especially important to read through the question carefully in advance. Make sure you:

- know what the topic is.

- understand how the table of information is organised.

- notice the order of questions (the numbers may not be exactly in sequence) and think about what's needed in each one.

It's also helpful to make a guess about answers, where possible. This will make the listening process easier.

Text 2

Exam Practice: gapped text

The following text has a number of gaps in it. A - F list the possible sentences to fill the gaps. Answer each question by choosing from the list A - F and writing the correct letter in each of the numbered spaces. Remember that in the exam you will have to mark your answer on a special *answer sheet*. One of the suggested answers does not fit at all.

Book Review: Beating Exam Nerves

It was the psychologists Yerkes and Dodson who first demonstrated that high levels of anxiety cause disorganised behaviour and have a negative affect on performance. (1) _____

Of the seven 'How to Pass Exams' books which we reviewed for this article, six were rejected because apart from rather obvious advice like 'read the questions carefully' or 'eat a good breakfast', they seemed to have little to offer. Only one, 'Maximizing Exam Performance: A Psychological Approach' by Don Davis, a principal lecturer and former examiner for Birmingham University, looked at the question of why performance in exams is not necessarily related to ability and why good students occasionally do badly.

(2) _____ He does not offer a substitute for knowing your subject, only practical suggestions for those who know they react badly to stressful competitive situations.

The outcome of his book is extremely encouraging. (3) _____ A technique proposed by Davis is to learn 'positive self-talk'. He suggests replacing such sentences as 'I never have any luck with the question' and 'I'm hopeless at exams' with 'Now I know how to relax I shall do better' or 'I'm gaining confidence every day'. Every time you hear yourself making one of those negative statements in your mind, he says, replace it with a positive one, until it becomes an automatic response.

Davis also suggests that as uncertainty can cause anxiety, we should keep uncertainty about the event to a minimum. As well as checking the date, time and duration of the exam, check out the location of the exam and become familiar with the place, if possible. (4) _____ Doing your own practice tests, sticking rigidly to actual procedures, particularly time limits, makes exams lose some of their strangeness and therefore their stress.

(5) _____ They may not be a substitute for study but they do offer a more positive approach to overcoming exam nerves than simply watching television. And if this book helps just one of our readers to improve their exam performance, then the money we spent on the six discarded books was well worth it!

A   As far as study is concerned, the more skilled you become at answering exam questions, the less likelihood there is of your performance breaking down on the Big Day.

B   Another book that we looked at recommended taking part in vigorous sporting activities. This is undoubtedly a good way of tackling stress but it may be rather impractical when you're revising intensively for an exam.

C   Before progressing any further, however, it's worth saying that the advice Davis offers is only useful for overcoming anxiety about exams.

D   Some 80 years later, it seems incredible, therefore, that students are still not emotionally prepared for exams.

E   These and other techniques, including simple methods of relaxation, are described in detail in Davis's book. The author promises that after 10 years of using them on his own undergraduates, they do work if practised regularly.

F   As anxiety reactions are learned from past experiences, he says, so they can be unlearned. Ability to perform well under pressure is a skill that can be acquired.

Focus on Listening 2

You are going to hear a teacher giving some advice about exams. For Questions 1 - 11, complete the notes using a few words. You will hear the piece twice.

The most important point is that you [1] the actual day of the exam.

Make sure:
• you have a good night's sleep beforehand.

• you've had [2] beforehand.

• you're not [3] .

People who study too hard the night before an exam may be mentally [4] when they get to the exam.

Anything that relaxes you or [5] , like yoga, is a good idea.

During the exam, the most important thing is [6] .
Look at the questions and [7] accordingly.

If you put all your energy into one question and do another quickly you're   .
giving a [8] .

Even if you [9] a question at the end of your time, you have to go on [10] .

Try to remain relaxed; don't [11] !

Focus on Grammar: *-ing* v. infinitive

The following verbs may be followed either by an *-ing* form or by a *to* infinitive, depending on the meaning.

come	go on	remember
dread	mean	stop
forget	regret	try

. . . try to work out what the correct answer should be. (Text 1)
We've tried pushing the car but it still won't start.

The differences in meaning are explained in the Grammar File on page 96.

1 Put the verbs in brackets into the correct form.

a I haven't told my parents that I've given up my job at the bank and I dread (*think*) what they'll say when they hear.

b He's always regretted (*leave*) school so young.

c Have you tried (*hold*) your breath? That usually cures hiccups.

d I thought he was arrogant at first, but I came (*value*) his advice in time.

e There's a man in Reception who seems very angry and I think he means (*make*) trouble.

f Do you remember (*sign*) the letter?

g Do stop (*complain*) all the time!

h I don't think he's even tried (*give up*) smoking.

i We regret (*inform*) you that your application has been unsuccessful.

j Several people came (*run*) to help when they saw what had happened.

k You can't go on (*work*) this hard.

l Will you remember (*lock*) the door when you leave?

m The place I dread (*go*) more than anywhere else is the dentist's surgery!

n I wouldn't mind changing jobs, but not if it means (*move*) to another city.

o He was in such a hurry that he hardly stopped (*draw*) breath before he was off again.

p After explaining the government's position, the Minister went on (*criticise*) the Opposition.

2 Complete the following sentences using suitable verb forms.

a Your mother phoned again. You won't forget . . . .
. . . . , will you?

b 'I just can't seem to lose any weight.' 'Have you tried . . . .
. . . . ?'

c I think he really regrets . . . . It was so embarrassing!

d She hated me at first but now she's come . . . .
. . . .

e You've ruined my best jacket and I'd like to know what you mean . . . .

f I'll never forget . . . . It was such a surprise!

Focus on Writing (Section A)

You must answer all the parts of the question and your answers should come to approximately 250 words in all.

When you return from holiday, you find a number of letters waiting for you. Read the extracts from the letters below.

Yes, I'd love to come to the International Party at your school on Friday. I'll be coming by car, so do you think you could send me directions for getting to the school from the town centre? Make them pretty clear - you know what I'm like for getting lost! As there isn't much time, would you mind sending the directions by fax? (You've got the fax number of my office.)
Looking forward to seeing you soon,   Sheila

I nearly forgot to mention that I'm taking my driving test again next week, let's hope I'm lucky this time! If only I didn't get so nervous beforehand - I got left and right confused last time, and I also made a complete mess of the questions the examiner asked me on the Highway Code. I don't suppose you've got any tips on how to keep calm or how to revise for the test? If you have, let me know.
Best wishes, Roger

MEMO

From: Brian Dayes, Manager.

As you have kindly offered to write a short report on the recent staff training day for next month's staff magazine, I thought I would remind you of some of the details:

Attendance: 24 out of a total of 25 members of staff
Programme: 9.00 Introductory speech (given by myself)
                  9.30 – 12.30 Customer Care – workshop with role play exercises
                  12.30 – 1.30 Buffet lunch (provided by the company)
                  1.30 – 3.30 Demonstration of new office technology

I think you will agree that the morning session was very useful for all concerned, and that everyone enjoyed the buffet lunch. It was a pity about the problem with the computers in the afternoon session but I think everyone felt they had learnt something all the same. One last thing, I'd be grateful if you could mention that I was responsible for organising the event.

As you're on holiday, I thought I'd send this to your home address.

Now write:

a   a *note* to your friend, Roger, wishing him luck in his driving test and offering a few words of advice (about 75 words).

b   a set of *directions* for Sheila (about 75 words).

c   a short *report* on the recent staff training day (about 100 words).

Communication Activity 2: Describe and draw

Here are two light-hearted activities which will test your ability to give accurate instructions for a drawing.

1 Draw three straight lines

Try to work out these puzzles on your own for a moment first and then work in pairs. One student should turn to the solution and give instructions for drawing the lines, while the other draws the three lines as instructed.

a   The picture below shows six goats which are about to eat the cabbages in a field. Can you fence off the goats from the cabbages by drawing three straight lines?

Student A should turn to the solution on page 218 and give instructions.

b Draw three straight lines to divide the rectangle into six sections, each containing a hat, a pair of gloves and a magician's wand.

Student B should turn to the solution on page 219 and give instructions.

2 Describe the shapes

You must take it in turns to describe six shapes for your partner to draw. You will need a piece of paper to work on.

a *Student A* should turn to page 220 and give instructions for Student B to draw.

b *Student B* should turn to page 221 and give instructions for Student A to draw.

English in Use 1: Cloze 2

Complete the following article by writing the missing words in the spaces provided. Use *only one word* in each space.

The inner secrets of swotting

A very basic point about memory is that it works by association. A table makes you think of a chair, which makes you think of a seat and so on. One thing the mind is good (1) _____ remembering is pictures or images. (2)_____ Roman times, people have used this fact to create mental images to associate (3) _____ facts that they wanted to remember.

The (4) _____ you play about with information when you are revising, the more (5) _____ you are to remember it. Suggestions (6) _____ various ways of becoming involved with your material come from Colin Rose, author of *Accelerated Learning*. The book describes a new system that, its supporters claim, can reduce the time (7) _____ to learn a foreign language (8) _____ up to seven times.

He recommends drawing (9) _____ are called memory maps, which are diagrams of the main points of, say, the causes of the First World War, to give you a summary (10)_____ visual form. He also suggests a degree of play acting - march up and down saying irregular verbs, use funny voices, do quick tests with a friend - anything to (11)_____ the material stand out in your mind.

Dr Peter Morris, a psychology lecturer who specialises (12) _____ learning, agrees that these techniques can be effective but issues a warning. 'People sometimes get the wrong idea about memory aids,' he says. 'They don't mean that you can get (13) _____ with doing less work - in fact to begin (14) _____ you may have to do extra work to get (15) _____ to them. But there is no doubt that they can improve your performance.'

English in Use 2: Editing

In most lines of the following text there is one word which is wrongly spelled.

Read the text, underline each wrongly spelled word, and then write the correct spelling in the space provided at the end of the line. Some lines are correct. Indicate these lines with a tick (✓) against the line number. The first two lines have been done as an example.

Relax!

If your heart starts <u>biting</u> rapidly, your mouth goes dry and   1 <u>beating</u>

you feel unable to cope, don't panic. This thirty second   2 ✓

relaxation exersise will get rid of anxiety and help keep exam   3 _____

nerves under control. First, calm the body. Sit or lie down in   4 _____

a quite place. Remove your shoes and loosen any tight clothing.   5 _____

Tense your muscles like this: clench your firsts; try touching   6 _____

the front of your rists to your shoulders; hunch your shoulders;   7 _____

frown hard; clench your jaws; press the tip of your tounge to   8 _____

the roof of your mouth; take a deep breath; flaten your stomach;   9 _____

stretch your legs and paint your toes; notice the tension and   10 _____

hold the position as you count slowly to five. Now just let go.   11 _____

Flop out like a puppet who's strings have been cut. Feel tension   12 _____

following freely away from your body. Next relax your mind. With   13 _____

your eyes closed, breath slowly and deeply. Imagine being on a   14 _____

tropicale island with a blue sky, warm sun and a golden, sandy   15 _____

beach. See yourself lying there very peacefuly. Hold this image   16 _____

for 20 seconds. Now open your eyes and go calmly about your   17 _____

work.

From an article in Living magazine

Exam Strategy: Paper 3 (Section B)

When you're checking a text for mistakes, you need to read it at least twice.

The first time, **read the text fairly quickly in order to understand the general meaning. This is when you will spot an extra word which doesn't fit in with the sense of the text (look especially for words like *no* or *not*), an important missing word or a major spelling mistake.**

The second time, **read the text word by word concentrating on grammar and spelling. This is when you will notice small mistakes like a missing article, a wrong preposition or an extra letter in a word.**

Exam Focus 4

Paper 4 Listening

Introduction

There are four sections in this paper and they focus on different kinds of spoken English such as monologues and dialogues, formal and informal conversations, public announcements and private messages.

There are normally four listening passages in all, and these are recorded on tape. The voices you hear will be in standard English in terms of grammar and vocabulary; some may reflect a slight accent. Don't worry about this. You have already experienced a range of accents including British, Australian, New Zealand and Canadian English in this book, and you should have no problems in understanding any accents you hear in the exam.

Questions

The questions provide different reasons for listening - listening for specific facts, for gist, to understand the speaker's attitude etc. - and together they require a variety of listening skills to be used.

The tasks you have to do will include answering multiple choice questions, filling in tables, completing notes and putting sentences or pictures in the right order. In the exam, check each question to see exactly what you have to do. Different questions need different approaches. As a general guide:

- It's *always* important to spend time reading through the question in advance.
- It's usually best *not* to try and read through multiple choice questions while you are listening the first time. It's hard to listen *and* read effectively at the same time.
- When you have to fill in a table or complete notes, it is important to follow the text in the question. But don't expect the words in the recording to be exactly the same as on the page.

Note: The instructions for the task will be given on the tape and on the question paper.

Sections A and B

In both these sections you will hear a *monologue* which lasts about 2 minutes. This could be a short talk, a radio announcement or a recorded message, for example. The questions will test your understanding of *specific information* in the recording and you will usually have to fill in missing words or figures in a table, chart or diagram.

Note: The recording is played twice in Section A but only *once* in Section B.

Tip: Make sure you understand how the table or diagram in the question is organised. Look at the headings and the different columns or sections. You won't have time to work this out while you're actually listening.

Section C

A longer recording (about 4 minutes) of a *conversation*, played twice. It could be a formal conversation like a meeting or interview, or an informal conversation between friends.

The questions test your understanding of the recording as a whole, including the gist of what is said, specific information that is given, and also the speakers' attitudes. You will usually have to complete some notes with single words or short phrases, or answer multiple choice questions.

Tip: **Read through any notes carefully in advance and think about what *could* go into the spaces. This will make the listening task easier.**

Section D

A number of short extracts (up to 30 seconds long), played twice. You may be asked to identify the situation or topic - in each case or overall, to say whether each speaker is making an enquiry, complaining, explaining and so on, or to give specific information from the extracts.

Tip: **Read the question carefully - it will probably give you some clues about what you're going to listen to.**

Paper 5 Speaking

Introduction

The interview is in pairs and there are two examiners. One examiner works with you, explaining the tasks, helping with problems and so on, while the other generally sits apart, assessing your English. The interview is in four phases which each test different speaking skills. The examiners may arrange the chairs in different ways at different phases of the interview.

Phases

Phase A

In this phase there will be a relaxed conversation round a table where you and your partner meet the two examiners and answer general questions about yourselves. During this phase, your general social English and your ability to interact with other people in English will be assessed.

Be prepared to:

- introduce yourself and say where you come from.
- introduce your partner (if you know them) and say something about them.
- talk about your family in a general way.
- talk about how long you have been studying English, and why.
- talk about your job or course of study and your future plans.
- talk about your interests and hobbies.

You may also have to ask your partner questions in the same areas.

Tip: **It's not a good idea to prepare too much for this phase. Think about the possible topics but don't try to learn impressive answers by heart. If you do, you will sound unnatural.**

Phase B

In this phase you and your partner sit facing each other and you will each have an opportunity to speak for a minute or so about a visual prompt - a photograph, cartoon, map, or set of pictures, for example.

One candidate describes a visual prompt in detail while the other compares the description with their own visual, which will be similar or related in some way. Then the second candidate responds briefly - by saying what's similar or different about their own visual, for example, or by saying which picture from a set has been described. Afterwards, the second candidate performs a similar task with a different visual.

This phase tests your ability to give information clearly. (There are examples of different Phase B tasks on pages 137 and 194.)

Tip: **This is your main opportunity for the examiners to hear you speak. Make the most of it. Use all the details in the visual and, if you don't know the exact word for something, use words you do know to describe it.**

Phase C

In this phase, you and your partner will have a problem-solving task to discuss for about two minutes. You might have to arrange pictures in a sequence, for example, put points in order of importance, give advice, or write a caption for a cartoon.

This phase tests your ability to negotiate and collaborate with your partner. It does *not* test your ability to find the correct solution. If you can't agree on a solution, it will be perfectly acceptable if you 'agree to disagree'. (There are examples of Phase C tasks on pages 197 and 201.)

Tip: **If your partner is very quiet or less confident in English than you are, help them to play a part in the discussion by asking their opinion and reacting to what they say. If you do all the talking or if you dismiss what your partner says without really listening, you will lose marks.**

Phase D

In this last phase, examiners and candidates sit round the table together again for a short discussion. You will be asked to report and explain the decisions you reached in the Phase C task and may also be asked general questions about your feelings about the exam or about your future plans.

This phase tests your ability to report, explain, summarise and to develop a discussion naturally.

Tip: **Be prepared to talk about your *partner's* opinions and ideas as well as your own.**

Marking

Your speaking skills in Paper 5 as a whole will be marked on five scales.

Fluency	- Do you speak with natural speed and rhythm, and without long hesitations?
Language Accuracy	- Do you use a wide range of structures and vocabulary and make only a few minor mistakes?
Pronunciation	- Are you easy to understand? Do you use English pronunciation features naturally?
Task Achievement	- Do you deal with the tasks effectively and use appropriate language for each one?
Interactive Communication	- Do you contribute fully and effectively to the discussion with your partner and with the examiners?

There are equal marks for each scale.

Keys and Roleplay

Unit 5
Communication Activity (page 52)

Student A

Arrival Hall-Hong Kong International Airport

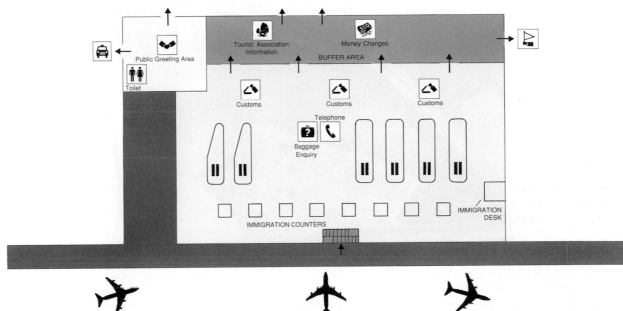

Unit 8
Communication Activity (page 88)

Student A: Dissatisfied Guest

Read through your instructions. Then form a group with other students who have the same role in order to discuss the parts in *italics*.

You booked your 'bargain break' holiday with Cheapotours three months ago and specifically asked for a room with a sea view. In fact, when you arrived a few hours ago, you discovered that your room overlooks a building site *(think of the disadvantages)*, and the balcony seems to get no sun.

In your view, the hotel is generally below the standard you'd expected *(decide in what ways)*. You also had reason to complain once or twice during the journey *(decide why)*.

You've just spotted the courier for your party in the reception area. S/he looks as if s/he would like to avoid you!

Decide what you are going to say.

Unit 9
Communication Activity (page 137)

Student A

Describe the photograph below to your partner, as clearly as possible.

Unit 10
Communication Activity 2 (page 150)

Student A

Unit 8
Communication Activity (page 88)
Student B: Courier

Read through your instructions. Then form a group with other students who have the same role in order to discuss the parts in *italics*.

You work for Cheapotours as a courier and a few hours ago you arrived with a party at the hotel above. It's the first time the company has used this hotel and, from what you have seen, it seems to be a typical 'budget' hotel with simple food and clean but fairly basic accommodation.

The only problem is that a few people in your party (mostly people who booked late) have rooms at the side of the hotel without the view of the sea that they'd expected. (Actually the small print in the Cheapotours brochure states that the company cannot *guarantee* rooms with a sea view.)

There's very little you can do to solve the problem *(decide why this is so)* but it's very important to keep your party happy because you may lose your job if the company gets a lot of complaints.

You've just seen one of your party coming your way. As it's someone who's already complained several times during the journey, you're not looking forward to the conversation! Try to avoid catching their eye!

Think of as many positive things to say about the hotel and the resort as you can. (Feel free to use your imagination!) Decide how to deal with a complaint about the room.

Unit 5
Communication Activity (page 52)
Student B

Arrival Hall-Hong Kong International Airport

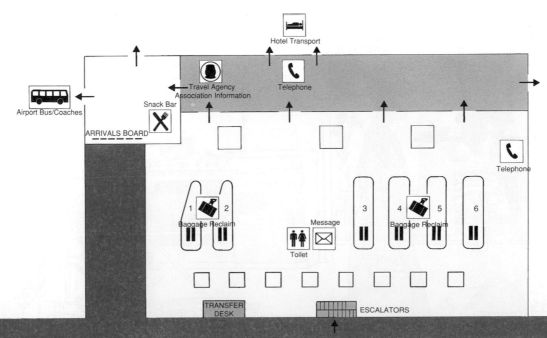

Unit 9
Communication Activity (page 137)

Student B
Describe the cartoon below to your partner, as clearly as possible.

Unit 10
Communication Activity 2 (page 150)

Student B

Unit 14
Communication Activity 2 (page 208): Key

1 Draw three straight lines

a Student A

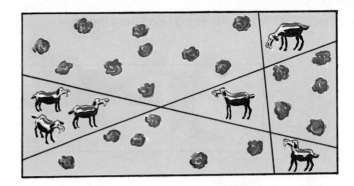

Unit 2
Communication Activity (page 22): Key

1 Mini crossword

¹C	²A	³R	⁴D	⁵S
²A	P	A	R	T
³R	A	T	I	O
⁴D	R	I	E	R
⁵S	T	O	R	E

3 Spot the difference

Picture B has these differences:
1 There is no keyhole.
2 There is only one dart.
3 There is a spider's web on the ceiling.
4 The Paris poster has 'in the the spring'.
5 There is no button on Clueless's shoulder.
6 His shoes have shoelaces tied in a bow.
7 There is no magnifying glass on the floor by the table leg.
8 There is no meat cleaver in the wanted poster.

2 Word square

Deutschmark Dollar Drachma Escudo Franc Peseta Lira Rouble Rupee Schilling

K	L	I	R	A	D	I	R	I	M	D
M	R	G	R	L	R	O	F	A	E	S
R	N	E	N	O	P	R	L	U	C	L
O	I	E	L	I	A	E	T	L	F	L
U	D	P	R	N	L	S	S	L	A	E
B	C	U	C	T	C	L	N	E	E	R
L	L	R	F	H	S	I	I	R	T	L
E	B	B	M	D	R	A	C	H	M	A
L	I	A	U	O	T	P	I	U	C	D
S	R	U	L	O	D	U	C	S	E	S
K	G	F	S	U	R	S	U	F	R	D

9 There are two pieces of paper pinned to the wall under the wanted poster.
10 The poster behind the unwanted poster has fantastic instead of fascinating.
11 The top row of typewriter keys is missing.
12 The date on the calendar is the 9th instead of the 6th.
13 The note on the filing cabinet says fired instead of sacked.
14 This/That is reversed on the filing cabinet drawers.

Unit 7
Communication Activity (page 79): Key
The ideal ages suggested in a recent survey were:

racing driver 30   surgeon 50   gymnast 14
marathon runner 30   judge 65   airline pilot 45
footballer 25

Language Focus 3: Phrasal verbs (page 43): Key

Quiz

1 False. The statement is too general. Some phrasal verbs are informal (e.g. *muck about*) but others are quite appropriate in most spoken and written English. In addition, many single-word synonyms sound very formal in everyday situations (e.g. *admit* for *let in*).

2 False. A few phrasal verbs consist of a verb + particle + preposition (e.g. *get away with, get round to*).

3 48.   4 True.   5 Up.   6 Aback.

Unit 13
Communication Activity 1 (page 194)

Student B

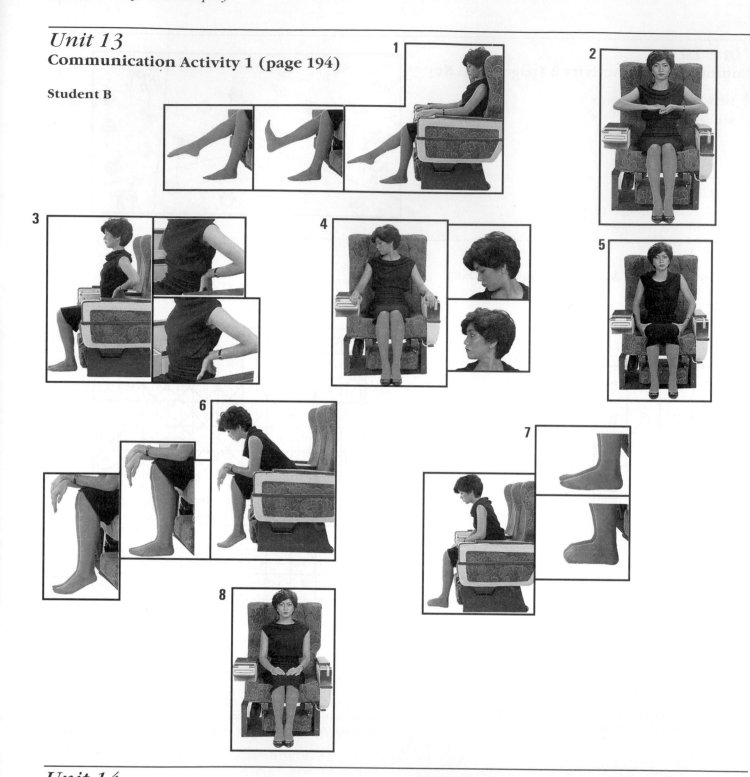

Unit 14
Communication Activity 2 (page 209): Key

1 Draw three straight lines

b Student B

Unit 14
Communication Activity 2 (page 209): Key

2 **Describe the shapes**
a **Student A**

  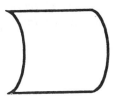 

Unit 10
Text 1 (page 141): Key
The correct order for the sections is B, D, A, C.

Text 2 (page 143): Key
A - You are probably severely injured or dead.
B - You may be slightly injured or suffering from shock.
C - Congratulations! The only course that leads to a trouble-free escape.

In general, avoid lifts, don't waste time collecting valuables; if you are trapped, wait by a window for the fire brigade rather than jump, if you can possibly stay in the room for some time.

Communication Activity 1 (page 145): Key

1

a cooking accidents (40%); electrical appliances and wiring (15%); arson (13%); smokers' materials (10%); heaters (7%).

b arson (28%); electrical appliances and wiring (18%); smokers' materials(9%); cooking accidents (8%).

Communication Activity 2 (page 150): Key
Student A: left-hand side of picture
(Student B differences in brackets)
1 no glass on table. (glass)
2 no lamp flex (or wire) running under mat to wall. (flex running to wall)
3 no cigarette in ashtray. (cigarette in ashtray)
4 rolled newspaper in woman's hand. (heater in woman's hand)
5 girl wearing flowered skirt. (girl wearing striped skirt)
6 train above fire. (boat above fire)

Student B: right-hand side of picture
(Student A differences in brackets)
1 nothing above cooker. (dishcloth above cooker)
2 cupboard door closed. (cupboard open)
3 1 pan on wall. (4 kitchen tools on wall)
4 no child reaching for matches. (child reaching for matches)
5 laundry basket empty. (laundry basket full)
6 no electric fire by ironing board. (electric fire)

Unit 12
Communication Activity 1 (page 173): Key
1 Leave swiftly. One major disturbance is better than numerous coughs.

2 Perfect politeness is to listen carefully and be as appreciative as the first time. Next best is to remember it warmly, e.g. 'Yes, I remember, that's a great story'.

3 Be careful: few people want the honesty they ask for. If the item of clothing is awful, you can't really praise it - but good manners prevent you from telling the truth. 'It's a nice shape, but I'm not sure the colour really suits you' will suggest it's bad news without making the person feel a fool for buying it.

4 Sit in your car, or in the nearest cafe, until the correct time - few social blunders are worse than arriving too soon.

5 Either introduce them, give them drinks and leave them to it or, if it's an informal meal, invite them into the kitchen, or do some preparation in the sitting room. Don't feel a failure. Guests who normally are prepared can feel delightfully superior and those who normally aren't can feel comforted.

Communication Activity 2 (page 179): Key
1 b
2 a Clocks are symbols of death since the Cantonese word for 'clock' can also mean 'to go to a funeral'.
3 b   4 a   5 c   6 c
7 b It would be an offence against hospitality.
8 a
9 a It's a great insult as the spirits are thought to come and go through a person's head.
10 c   11 c   12 b

Unit 13
Lead-in (page 185): Key
a 5 toes on a foot
b 32 teeth in the mouth
c 1 nose on the face / 1 nail on the finger
d 2 lungs in the chest
e 200 bones in the skeleton
f 1 brain in the head
g 5 litres of blood in the body
h 4 basic blood groups
i 40% of the body is muscle
j The heart beats 70 times a minute

Focus on Listening 2 (page 193): Key

Climbing stairs	•••	Disco dancing	•••
Digging	•••	Football	•••
Golf	•	Gymnastics	••
Judo	••	Rowing	••••
Sailing	•	Tennis	••
Weight-lifting	•	Yoga	••
not much benefit	•	good effect	••
very good effect	•••	excellent effect	••••

Communication Activity 2 (page 197): Key
The pictures are based on those used in information about the Advertising Standards Authority, an organisation which keeps a check on advertising and asks advertisers who misrepresent their produce to withdraw their advertisements.

Unit 2
Communication Activity (page 23)

3 Spot the difference

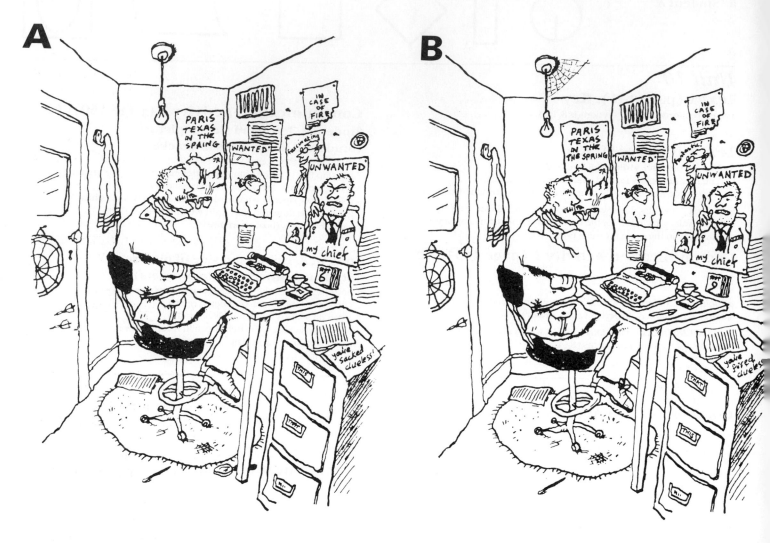

Unit 14
Communication Activity 2 (page 209): Key

2 Describe the shapes
b Student B

Index

Key: FG - Focus on Grammar; SB - Study Box; GF - Grammar File; WF - Writing File; EF - Exam Focus; LF - Language Focus; LeF - Learning Focus; ES - Exam Strategy; MC - Mini-check